THE CRUCIBLE

FORGING
SOUTH AFRICA'S
FUTURE

Dr. Don Beck & Graham Linscott

NEW PARADIGM
PRESS

New Paradigm Press
P.O. Box 787, Denton, Texas, 76202
P.O. Box 143, Honeydew, 2040

First Published October 1991

ISBN No: 0/620/16241/4

Printed by Penrose Press Johannesburg
Colour seperations by Hirt and Carter Repro., Johannesburg
Jacket illustration and graphics by Gavin Johnson

To the memory of Clare W. Graves, pathfinder.

SOUTH AFRICA

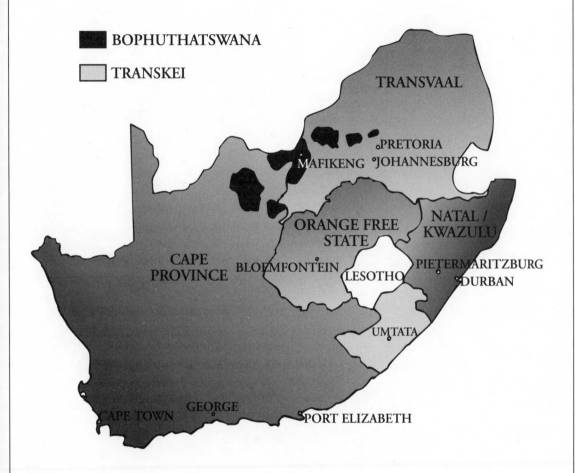

BOPHUTHATSWANA

TRANSKEI

TRANSVAAL

PRETORIA

MAFIKENG °JOHANNESBURG

ORANGE FREE
STATE

NATAL /
KWAZULU

CAPE
PROVINCE   BLOEMFONTEIN

PIETERMARITZBURG

LESOTHO   DURBAN

UMTATA

CAPE TOWN   GEORGE

PORT ELIZABETH

CONTENTS

ACKNOWLEDGEMENTS

This book is inspired by the work of the late Clare W. Graves, Professor of Psychology Emeritus at Union College, New York. The shadow of his influence will lengthen as more learn of his powerful and imaginative thinking regarding the emergence of, and change in, value systems.

The authors express special thanks to Christopher C. Cowan, of the National Values Centre, Denton, Texas, for his substantial contribution to the theoretical description of the Graves technology; to Gavin and Jenny Johnson and Janice Netherton for professional competence in getting the book produced at great speed; and finally to Rodger Farren, of Pietermaritzburg, for making available the solitude and tranquillity of his holiday home in the Natal Midlands, where the book took shape.

Six men are in a dark place with an elephant which none has seen before but which they are called on to describe.
"It's a piece of rope," says the man who has it by the tail.

"No, it's more like a fire hose," says the one who has the trunk.

"That's no fire hose," says his companion who is fingering the tusk. "It's more like a spear."

"Rope? Hose? Spear?" says the fourth man who has his arms round a leg. "What nonsense - it's a tree!"

"No, no," says the sixth, who has it by the ear. "It's a huge leather curtain."

"You're all wrong," the last calls derisively as he feels with arms outstretched along the elephant's side. "It's a great big wall!"
Each is right in his limited way. Each is totally wrong about the complete nature of an elephant. And tugging at the tail of an elephant in the dark is really no place to be. You can very easily get hurt.

South Africa is our elephant. It is a colonial problem. It is a racial problem. It is a problem of political franchise. It is an economic problem. It is an ethnic problem. It is a problem of haves and have-nots. It is a problem of colliding ideologies.
South Africa is all these and more. But none describes the entire elephant.

We have been presumptuous enough to strike a flint. We see a huge, ponderous beast of many attributes, most of them alarming. But that is no reason at all to keep on feeling around in the dark. That is where real danger lies.
In the pages that follow we set out to kindle the flame of our torch so that we can get a better idea of just what this elephant is - and devise a strategy for handling him.

The Global Rubik's Cube

The mere mention of the name "South Africa" evokes emotional response from all quarters. The reason is that South Africa is the global Rubik's Cube.

All the world's collective ills (racism, ideologies, unscrupulous exploitation and oppression) have been twisted and compressed into this southern region of Africa. Apartheid has become the icon by which the world can rage at Hitler's evils, Simon Legree's ravaging of Uncle Tom and all the bigotries which have blemished this planet.

At the same time the international community is wearying of the mess. The sea lanes around the Cape are not as vital as they once were. The Information Age thrives in a world of advanced technology requiring fewer of the Industrial Age metals and resources produced by South Africa. Events in the Middle East, Europe, the Soviet Union and the Far East demand and receive attention. The American and European anti-apartheid struggle industries are moving on to other, non-South African issues which command more media exposure and funding. F.W. de Klerk's stunning speech to parliament on February 2, 1990 disarmed so many critics around the world that it is now less clear just who are on the side of the angels and who not.

Yet something is being created in the turmoil and chaos of the crucible which is South Africa that may rekindle interest in this isolated land south of the Limpopo River. Its society may well be on the brink of a series of innovative breakthroughs which offer promise to the rest of the planet. A solution to the race problem, creative strategies in redressing First and Third World disparities and the models for managing ethnic mosaics may yet emerge from a land torn by three centuries of turbulence and conflict.

While this book is about South Africa and its search for equations and models that can resolve its deep-seated conflicts and earn for itself a position of respect among the nations of the world, it is really a story about all peoples, everywhere. To visit South Africa is like going back to the future. One goes "back" in the sense that all the value systems that have blessed and cursed our planet are still present, in mint condition. The journey is into the "future" in that South Africans are dealing, in that explosive microcosm, with the same issues that confront the entire planet. It is simply a matter of scale.

What is this "new" South Africa that is supposed to be emerging? Who knows what it is likely to be? Different people have different definitions. We set out here a range of definitions and invite readers to ask themselves which fit with what they would want in the future post - apartheid society. They should not be surprised if they identify with more than one. These different perspectives are fundamental to the technology by which we analyse South Africa, as will become apparent very early. For extra clarity we have colour coded them.

- The New South Africa should protect the tribal ways and rituals, honour the traditional festivals and ceremonies, preserve the sacred places, protect the blood line and propitiate the spirits of the ancestors by preserving the ways of the folk. (A Purple view)

- The New South African should liberate the individual who struggles to get what he wants by breaking out of restrictions, limitations, and barriers that stand in the way of or threaten personal power and freedom. (A Red view)

- The New South Africa should permit, protect and preserve the ways, traditions, standards, religions, and cultures of people who do what is right and wish to see their beliefs passed on to their children and grandchildren. (A Blue view)

- The New South Africa should protect individual (rather than group) rights, encourage a sense of free enterprise and achievement and reward those individuals who show initiative, are willing to take risks, and pay the price to succeed. (An Orange view)

- The New South Africa should instil a feeling of community and equality, provide for those less privileged and who have been oppressed and facilitate the full development of each human being. (A Green view)

- In the New South Africa, individuals should learn to manage themselves in a new and constructive fashion by utilising all available resources — natural, human and technological – to live in a responsible and functional manner through a long-term, step-by-step evolutionary process . (A Yellow view)

- The New South Africa should act collectively to protect the fragile environment, be a good global citizen, mandate a respect for healthy systems and be pro-active in resolving planetary problems and concerns.

Outline of the Crucible

This book is organised in five parts, with a natural flow from beginning to end.

•Part I - Chaos, Complexity and Order - describes the emergence of a new paradigm of thinking, flowing out of major global changes in science, politics, economics and social transformations. This new framework will then be used, as a total system, in analysing South Africa today and in forging its future over this final decade of the 20th century.

•Part II - South of the Limpopo - tracks the historical evolution of South Africa since earliest times and provides an up-to-date profile of the country in terms of its social, economic, political and military features.

•Part III - The Psychological Rosetta Stone - meshes Parts I and II, displaying and illustrating South African history as well as current political parties and points of view in terms of the Psychological Map.

•Part IV - World to the Power of Seven - constructs a fresh, comprehensive and practical framework for moving South Africa through essential and inevitable evolutionary stages.

•Part V - Forging the Future - lays down a methodology for managing the South African complexity through the remainder of the 1990s and well into the next millenium. Finally we shift our focus from the South African microcosm to the global macrocosm to illustrate the power of this technology in understanding and dealing with issues in various countries, regions, societies and cultures.

Our analysis integrates almost 40 years of scientific research in the United States with 10 years of practical application in South Africa. We are convinced there are major and profound lessons to be learned for the entire planet. If South Africa is a microcosm, vital global issues might be focused more clearly. It would be ironic indeed if light to guide the rest of the world should emanate from the so - called Dark Continent. We hope to provide at lease enough illumination to show the six men mentioned in the prologue that they are each of them right and each of them wrong about the nature of an elephant.

The South African crucible is approached at some risk of disturbing comfortable assumptions. Personal paradigms could be challenged; readers could experience turbulence. We will address sensitive and controversial issues which many prefer to avoid. We do not intend sketching scenarios, trusting to those in authority making the right choices; we intend getting to the essence of what is happening in the crucible. We do not believe South Africa's future to be cast in concrete. We are neither pessimistic nor optimistic. We are as vulnerable as anybody to subjectivity and bias, but are influenced by no party, group or persuasion.

Spread out and examine the pattern of events and you will find yourself face to face with a new scheme of being, hitherto unimaginable by the human mind.
H.G. Wells

Chaos, Complexity and Order

History is often divided into epochs, eras, movements, phases and stages. Looking back we can more easily identify the key breakpoints that started revolutions, launched cultural waves and established major lines of demarcation which clearly separated what was from what was to be. Many believe we are passing now through such a momentous transformation, a major turning point, a history-making sea change.

Chapter 1 advances the premise that we are indeed going through a mind-shift in virtually every aspect of our lives as individuals and as members of collectives. We will introduce readers to the concepts of "crucible" and "paradigm" and indicate the relationship between the two. We will also define the basic components of a paradigm - the pattern of thinking that engulfs and permeates an entire society or cultural age.

Chapter 2 describes the emergence of a new and powerful paradigm in the last few decades of the 20th century, based on the work of the late Professor Clare W. Graves. This complex technology generates an understanding of how human value systems are formed, producing spectrums of difference in individuals and societies. We believe this New Paradigm has the potential to sort out South Africa's Rubik's Cube of apparently intractable complexities.

Chapter 3 shifts the focus to the processes of transition and transformation in individuals, organisations and entire societies by describing the construction of the evolutionary Spiral - a dynamic process attempting to explain how and when people change, and from what value system to what new one.

The search for patterns in society - past, present or future - is always dangerous. We approach this quest with considerable caution since no observer, critic or writer can be values-free. We see what we can see. Two people may look at or experience the same thing, but see and report altogether different interpretations. One sees a clearly defined trend and continually seeks out evidence to support his conclusions, often self-fulfilling his prophecies. The other detects an unrelated assemblage of anomalies, totally random and chaotic. One fixes on immutable laws of nature, claiming they are universal and unforgiving. The other lives in a pattern-less milieu and awakes to a different world every morning.

One sees history as a "science" that can be analysed, measured and tracked with absolute certainty and precision. The other regards the recording and interpretation of history as an art, the creative attempt to find meaning - not predictability or accuracy - in the past and in its impact on present and future.

George Will, the American syndicated columnist and social critic, offers this caution:

"History is a rich weave of many threads. Many of them, if pulled out, could cause a radical unravelling, setting the past in motion as a foaming sea of exhilarating contingencies. For more than a century we have been plied and belabored by various historicisms purporting to prove what happened had to happen, that history is a dry story of the ineluctable working of vast impersonal forces unfolding according to iron laws of social evolution. People, the historicists say, are mere corks bobbing on powerful currents. This demoralizing doctrine denies the possibility, ultimately, of meaningful self-government for individuals or nations."

What Will writes about history can likewise be applied to the interpretation of the present as well as to predictions about the future. An understanding of contemporary chaos theory confirms what George Will has observed about historical research. Events are much more complex than we realise they are; indeed, everything is "a rich weave of many threads". Yet order and chaos are not opposites; they are merely two sides of the same coin.

"No less than anyone else, students of world politics live and work in conceptual jails: while their frameworks, models and paradigms serve them well as creative guides to the framing and analysis of problems, the same conceptual equipment may blind them to change that lies outside its scope. Such is the dilemma we face today."
James N. Rosenau
Turbulence in World Politics.

Crucible of Chaos

South Africa is a dynamic crucible whose contents are - sometimes quite literally - exploding in the chaos of change. A crucible is a vessel in which elements are fused and transformed under intense heat, with high and focused energy. Millions of years ago the country was itself a geothermal crucible as volcanic activity created the physical characteristics we see today - mountain ranges, gold and ore-bearing reefs, diamond pipes, river valleys, agricultural lands. The man-made crucible - familiar to South Africans and so central to the country's economic development - is a reminder in miniature of those cataclysmic events so long ago: searing heat, the bubbling of minerals and molten metals, the pungency of escaping gases. It is also an apt metaphor for today's human crucible as the most disparate and often incompatible elements are forced by circumstance into fusion and transformation. A crucible melts down old systems, refines out impurities, forms new alloys, creates new entities, destroys old orders, contains and refocuses energy and sparks thresholds of change. It is a searingly hot and acrid process. The smell of burning is there as one reads of the body counts in parts of Natal and the Transvaal and tries to absorb the virulent rhetoric and the torrents of accusation and counter-accusation. A crucible is not a comfortable place to be.

Into this human crucible are being poured some of the most explosive elements and forces to have plagued the planet itself through history - the legacies of colonial dispossession, war, bizarre racial theories, perceived historical slights and injustices, warped religious cults, zealotry, ideologies with pretensions to transcendent truth. All the value systems which have developed over mankind's long psychological ascent are present in their pristine form in South Africa, impinging on one another. Iron Age man mixes on a daily basis with the High Technology / Information Age person, along with others at the various stages and gradations in between. While certain minds are at home with space age technology, others are just joining the agricultural or industrial revolutions. Time and geography make conditions all the more volatile. The time frame is compressed, South Africa being required to manage change, over years, which elsewhere has percolated over the centuries. The land area is relatively small and isolated, trapping expanding energies and unresolved dilemmas in a confined space from which there is no escape.

The crucible explodes with frightening images: children dancing the toyi-toyi* round a charred corpse; police armoured vehicles; neo-Nazi formations parading in uniform; rampaging war parties with shields and assegais; churchmen pleading; mass funerals, clenched fists; gunmen in balaclavas; angry mass marches; dwellings ablaze, women and children fleeing terrified into the night.

The crucible boils and bubbles with several critical destabilising forces and elements, any one of which is able to contribute to the unique turbulence and fluctuation. These destabilisers we call the Seven Gs: *gaps, gulfs, guilt, grudges, greed, glitches and games.*
Gaps exist in the close proximity of grinding Third World poverty and the conspicuous consumption of the First World sector. Ancient donkey carts and German limousines travel the same roads, affluent youths prowl modern shopping malls while impoverished children struggle in violent townships.
Gulfs exist in the multiplicity of languages and cultures; African, European and Asian, in thought processes which are centuries apart. These create deep-seated differences in perception, understanding and expectation. It will take generations to bridge these mental divides.
Guilt lies in the remorse experienced by many privileged individuals who contemplate decades of deprivation, oppression and mistreatment of others, based on culture or racial origin. It is both understandable and deadly. Decisions based on guilt are almost invariably bad, merely aggravating matters.
Grudges have been bred by the bitterness, resentment, anger and desire for revenge of those who have been deprived or mistreated. They are a breeding ground for demands for punishment, which solve nothing.
Greed is present in the "sinking ship" syndrome. Businessmen squeeze what they can out of the public, by fair means or foul, because "everyone is doing it" and this might be the last chance. Correspondingly, people in government abandon the ethics and norms of the past, enriching themselves and entrenching their interests while they can.
Glitches are the wild cards of social and political life, such as the Inkatha funding scandal, other unpredictable exposés, political violence and assassinations. They always have the capacity to destabilise unexpectedly, and may emanate from the outside world as

A triumphant rhythmic dance characteristic of politically radical groups.

20

much as internally.

Games are the activities of the players who use South African issues to their own ends, which often do not have a great deal to do with South Africa. Players include politicians, men of the cloth, the media and sports administrators all over the world. Americans off-load the guilt of their own racial feelings. Certain members of the Commonwealth vigorously play the anti-apartheid game because it suits their economic interests. African despots condemn apartheid as a distraction from their own shortcomings.

Has any society in mankind's long historical emergence had to deal with quite as much turbulence as South Africa while the rest of the world intervenes, exploits, condemns and exhorts? The chaos is awesome, the complexity overwhelming. Can there possibly be an order to bring sanity, stability and progress?

Out of Chaos, Order

Douglas Hofstadler, the American physicist and pioneer in the theory of artificial intelligence, noted:

"It turns out that an eerie type of chaos can lurk just behind a façade of order - and yet, deep inside the chaos lurks an even eerier type of order."

Can one find that eerie order lurking within the South African chaos? If so, where? Who will be its discoverers? One reads nothing of it in the press, academic journals or books by the experts. Is the cause then hopeless? Is the Southern African sub-continent doomed to repeat the sins of its past - and there has been no lack of cataclysmic conflict - or experience the eruptions that have tarnished other civilisations? The analyses of political scientists, sociologists and economists so far give no answers. There is a sterility, a sense of fatalism in the debate, little that is innovative. Politicians across the spectrum seem to be making yesterday's speeches, addressing yesterday's issues. One searches the sermons of the moralists and the commentaries of the pundits in vain for anything that is fresh and hopeful. The entire country appears to be in gridlock, destined to repeat the cycles of frustration and violence of an entire decade. Political stalemate threatens to increase the downward spiralling of the economy and standards of living.

Or is there a key by which the people of South Africa can discover a common language for an escape from the confusion of this Tower of Babel? Perhaps Albert Einstein gives us a clue:

"The world that we have made as a result of the level of thinking we have done thus far creates problems that we cannot solve at the same level as they were created."

If that is so, we surely have to address the issues in the crucible from a different level, within a new perspective. The entire world seems to be searching for solutions to the South African dilemma from the same level of thinking as produced the problems they are attempting to solve. And in that case the entire society must be trapped in a cruel and destructive cul-de-sac. If we are to follow Einstein's advice and solve problems from a higher level than where they were created, we need to operate within a New Paradigm.

Emerging Paradigms

In *The Structure of Scientific Revolutions,* Thomas Kuhn has popularised the term "paradigm" as simply a commonly agreed-upon model of society. He defines the expression as " ... a constellation of concepts, values, perceptions and practices shared by a community which forms a particular vision of reality that is the basis of the way a community organises itself."

Individuals have mindsets or value systems while entire communities or cultures share a paradigm - the basic operating assumptions that hold the social system together. The assumptions are seldom, if ever, stated explicitly yet they exist unquestioned and unchallenged. Once the paradigm emerges, we cling to it tenaciously since it impacts on virtually every area of our lives. But eventually new information enters our conceptual world, calling into question the older assumptions. At this point paradigm change becomes erratic, chaotic and discontinuous. Paradigms emerge from crucibles of the mind

Components of a Paradigm

Much like the genetic code on the DNA of any living organism, a paradigm is designed, formed and organised by a basic tool kit and set of instructions. Each new paradigm is created and tailored to the conditions produced by unique crucibles, through these instructional prescriptions and variables. By *organism* we mean a single person, a group, a team or organisation, or larger social systems such as cultures, communities, societies and nations. By *conditions* we refer to the elements within the environment - all previous paradigms in their residual forms - and the potential for emerging paradigms. The key components of a paradigm for consideration are:

World View: What is the world like? Is it a rain forest, an enchanted village, a dangerous jungle, a righteous cathedral, a market place of opportunity, a caring commune, a natural habitat, a global village or all and any of the above?

Command and Control Centre: This is a critical mass, centre of gravity or bottom line that emits signals and commands to the rest of the organism to provide the correctly coded information at the right time. What is the proper motivational balance? What ratio of reward and punishment will be appropriate? How will the children be taught? What form will justice take? What will be the view and role of science? Who will rise into leadership positions?

Degree of Complexity: How complex are the problems in the milieu? How can that level of complexity, or even greater, be created by the organism? The degree of complexity activated in the paradigm must not be too advanced or too primitive for the organism. First World systems and technology will fail within Third World environments.

Elaboration Stream: How are those principles reflected "downstream" in religion, politics, economics, psychology, architecture, community development, athletics, philosophy, common sense values and many other areas?

Organising Principle: What kind of organising system and model allows the paradigm to operate effectively? Should it be Tribal Order, an Empire, a Sacred Hierarchy, a Circle of Equals, an Integrated Network ... etc?

Potential: What are the available resources and competencies within the organism? Is the necessary thinking available, at least in its potential form? What happens if the demands in the conditions cannot be met by the resources in the organism?

Other Paradigms: Which other paradigms are represented in their residual form? How strong are they? How do they colour the dominant paradigm? How quickly can people downshift to the operating assumptions of the older paradigms?

Recognition Patterns: What messages and information patterns can be detected by the paradigm? What communication codes and media are used in the sending and receiving of messages?

Healthy and Unhealthy Forms: Does the expression of the paradigm contribute to the overall health and well-being of the entire spiral of paradigms? Or are the expressive forms selfish and self-centred? Do they absorb energy from the total environment without replacing it with something better?

Time Lines: Where is the time focus? Is it on the past, the present or the future? In what ratio? What determines how it measures time?

Flexibility Factor: What will trigger change in each of the respective paradigms? What are the early signs of impending change? How can they be recognised and by whom? How can each paradigm be successfully moved on from or subsumed in the next? Is the paradigm rigid or flexible? Is it open or closed? What anchors hold it back? What antibodies does it possess? Where is it in its life cycle? Is it emerging, in its nodal stage or in decline?

Edward Harrison, a physicist at the University of Massachusetts, describes a paradigm (or "universe") as a view of the Universe, a mask through which we perceive the world. "The universes," he wrote in *Masks of the Universe*, "are our models of the Universe. They are great schemes of intricate thought - grand cosmic pictures - that rationalise human experience. Each universe is a self-consistent system of ideas, marvellously organised, interlacing most of what is perceived and known."

When each universe or paradigm emerges, the believers are convinced it offers the ultimate view, the final word, the end of the quest, the last pinnacle. Everything now will become crystal clear. Pity the people of the future. They will have little to think about or do. But Harrison warns there is no end to the gallery of cosmic pictures. Each is simply the prelude to the next, then the next, then the next. He notes: "A universe rises, flourishes, then declines in the course of time and is superseded by another. Its decline and fall occur because the society is assaulted by an alien culture, or startling new facts and ideas emerge, or old problems erupt and refuse to stay suppressed."

To illustrate this, imagine if it were possible for your great, great grandfather to join you at your breakfast table. He would look a little like you - rather different also. He would speak the same language as you - but not quite the same language. What would you find to talk about? Last night's television? If you taxed him for not solving the race problem in his time, he would probably reply: "What race problem?" And if it were possible for you to have your great, great grandson at your breakfast table next day, he would look a little like you - rather different also. He would speak the same language as you - but not quite the same language. If he taxed you for not solving the problem of pollution in outer space in your time, you would reply: "Pollution where?"

The assumptions within our paradigms are expressed in religion, education, the marketplace, mores and traditions, sports, economic and political thought, virtually everywhere. Generational gaps may have little to do with time. They may have everything to do with contrasting paradigms.

Paradigm shifts, like major adjustments in the earth's tectonic plates, may be as turbulent and destructive as tremors and quakes. Everything is impacted on - both immediately and in a series of delayed after - shocks. Many established structures and landmarks are demolished, the rubble is cleared and new ones are constructed. This could have much to do with what is happening in South Africa today.

The New Global Paradigm

A new and entirely different pattern of thought is beginning to emerge world-wide and in various fields of human activity, driven by a fresh set of conditions and challenges. The New Paradigm is beginning to find expression in the natural and the social sciences, especially in education and philosophy and now in political thought as well. The end of the Cold War between East and West has unlocked forces which had been contained on both sides of the Iron Curtain. The Berlin Wall, focal point of more than 40 years of pressure and brinkmanship, almost overnight became the Berlin Mall. The Middle East erupted in a war which nobody would have predicted only months earlier. Operations Desert Shield, then Desert Storm, were successfully prosecuted under the auspices of the United Nations Security Council and with the blessing of the Soviet Union and China. Who could have predicted any such thing from within the recent paradigm of the Cold War? President Bush speaks of a New World Order, suggesting that the entire international system is being rethought and reframed.

The New Paradigm is being shaped by contributions from a host of new and revitalised academic and scientific disciplines. Insights from quantum physics and chaos theory are being applied in understandng the functioning of the brain, social behaviour, stock market cycles and weather patterns. Traditionalists within the fields of economics, political science, psychology, sociology and anthropology are being challenged by a new generation of integrative and open systems thinkers. New disciplines are emerging in political psychology, ecological evolution, general systems theories and a host of others. Everything is being called into question once again. The sacred cows are no longer safe.

The imagery of a crucible suggests that something new is created within the fiery mixture of chemicals, gases and base metals. Ilya Prigogine won the Nobel Prize in Chemistry for his concept of dissipative structures. A dissipative structure is an "open" thermodynamic (energy-processing) system that generates "order through fluctuations". When crucible-like conditions exist, torn by fluctuations or what are termed perturbations (things that literally perturb us), a threshold might be reached that will transform the system in the direction of more complex structural organisations and greater structural stability. In short, new forms of order emerge from the chaos, only to await the time when the process will repeat itself. When applied to large scale social systems such as cultures, nations, or the entire human species, the "new forms of order" are actually new paradigms. New thinking arises, then, out of crucibles, chaos, dissipation and fluctuation. The chaos of violence that has gripped parts of South Africa over recent years is, we contend, one of the more tragically spectacular instances of misunderstood paradigm change. In Chapter 8 we will examine this phenomenon in more detail.

The New South African Paradigm

South Africa is full of perturbations and is experiencing dissonance and dissipation at a dangerous level. If diamonds are created by pressure, the social landscape should be littered with them. Evidence of major dissipation is to been seen in the violence in Natal and on the Witwatersrand,* the turbulence within both white and black politics and the saintly, zealous discovery, in various quarters, of "the truth" (actually a new form of order) emerging out of doubt, turmoil and conflict (discontinuous fluctuations within thermodynamic systems).

What we may be seeing, therefore, is our collective intelligence setting up the conditions for change as we seek to escape the fiery hell of the crucible to embrace a new order. But how does one deal with a society whose population is encountering different expressions of dissipative structures all along the continuum of psychological time? Different kinds of mini-crucibles are bubbling and boiling all over the country. Mini-crucibles are there waiting to form authoritarian empires, to spew out the burning zeal of holy war. Others produce Dickensian squalour, still others are turbulent with conflicting ideologies, unscrupulous fortune-hunters and exploitative foreign interests. As with the blazing oil wells of Kuwait, the fires will burn for some time while society searches for the models to deal with the entire spectrum of evolutionary change. But if all the fires could be put out at once, that would surely release the pent-up energy for constructive purposes instead of wasting it into the atmosphere or in fruitless clashes with authority.

The emerging paradigm must therefore have the capacity to deal with complexities of a magnitude greater than what has evolved so far in South Africa's turbulent history. The New Paradigm must indeed be equipped to cope with multiple and often conflicting levels of development in contemporary society on a simultaneous basis. It must have the power, resourcefulness and range of operation to encounter each of the evolutionary crucibles while, at the same

*Major metropolitan region of the Transvaal, centred on Johannesburg.

26

time, acting to preserve the integrity and the future of the entire organism.

South Africa is in the throes of profound change as the older, racially discriminatory paradigm of apartheid and separate development disintegrates. Politicians, academics, church leaders, businessmen, in fact all responsible citizens, search for a glimpse of the New Order - the New Paradigm. As the pillars of apartheid crash down, what structures can be put in their place? What new wineskins can contain the new wine?

In the next chapter we will consider the key features of such a paradigm. In the remainder of the book we will describe, both theoretically and practically, the essence of this New Paradigm and we will apply this new thinking system specifically to the burning complexities of the South African crucible. Readers are invited to join us in a search for the New Paradigm, which is being forged at this very moment.

CHAPTER 2

Lead us, Evolution, lead us,
Up the future's endless stair;
Chop us, change us, prod us, weed us,
For stagnation is despair:
Grouping, guessing, yet progressing,
Lead us nobody knows where.
C.S. Lewis: Evolutionary Hymn

Mind is the eye with which the universe beholds itself and knows itself divine.
J.C. Smuts: Holism and Evolution

Paradigms Lost, Paradigms Gained: the quest for order

Smuts, that great South African thinker who lived and wrote a full half-century ahead of his time, discerned patterns in human history, holistic systems expanding along an evolutionary pathway. But in South Africa today that pattern becomes difficult to discern. Where is there any order or evolution in the chaos reflected almost daily on the front pages of South African newspapers? To be sure, there is a pattern in the similarly harsh and shrill language of extremists. But what can it mean when their causes are so diametrically and belligerently opposite? How is one to interpret the pattern that makes Buppies (Black Urban Professionals) in Soweto more like the Afrikaner Yuppies of Randburg than their brothers and sisters from the rural homelands? Does such a pattern have any meaning when - as all South Africans have been taught - blackness or whiteness are the overriding political factors.

And what is the nature of change? Are there steps and stages or is everything random, unpredictable, erratic? Are the Afrikaners who are presently leading a Third Trek of the mind simple carbon copies of their ancestors who struggled through the First and Second Treks (one from the Cape Colony to the hinterland, the second from the platteland to the cities)? Is the ANC today the same ANC as in 1912? Why is Africa dying instead of progressing? Is it the fault of the "white man"? What can be done to reverse the tide? Is it too late?

If we were able to answer these questions, would people want to hear the answers? Or would they instinctively prefer to cling to the familiar Old Paradigm? If a technology were offered which made it possible to see through the inflamed rhetoric, the sophisticated gamesmanship and the mind-closing ideologies that cloud people's judgment, would it be accepted? If we were able to develop X-ray vision to detect spectrums of natural difference and spirals of inevitable change, would it not be a great navigational aid as we enter the future? If a powerful solution to the South African (and global) riddle were to be lying right before our eyes, ought it not to be considered? One would imagine so. Yet there is a profound resistance to innovative thinking. People all the way along the political spectrum are comfortable with the Old Paradigm. "Rule or be ruled," say the extremists of the white right wing and the extremists of the black left wing. Their world is at least uncomplicated. "What can we do?" shrug those in the mid-range. But are we really prepared to continue with the Old Paradigm, to stagger through the minefields of time and accept whatever fate awaits us? If we are wedded to either classical Calvinism or Marxism, the answer is "Yes", believing that all will turn out right in the end - one outcome being in the hereafter and the other, in this life when those with "science" and "right" on their side finally and inevitably win the dialectical struggle. Nothing is worth worrying about. That is fatalistic thinking. We prefer the evolutionary thinking of Smuts and others.

Evolutionary views - the word means "roll out" - ebb and flow with the dominant paradigm of the day. An early version claimed that we run on invisible tracks, like a steam locomotive in the fog. While we blow off steam and make noises which suggest we are in charge, we are really just along for the ride. The fatalistic system has already written our script. If it is one's lot to ride into the Valley of Death with the other 599 members of the Light Brigade, that is fate and it has to be accepted. A recent television series on the Public Broadcasting Company network in the United States was entitled *The Civil War*. It graphically depicted the grim consequences of such an unquestioned loyalty to this fatalistic evolutionary paradigm. For future reference this will be called the Blue perspective. It is predeterministic.

A second set of evolutionary models is driven by the progressive, upward and onward ethic. In adapting the theme of survival of the fittest from the contributions of Charles Darwin in the biological sciences, this new social Darwinism promised that things were getting better and better in every way. *Laissez-faire* capitalism and chauvinistic imperialism were seen to be evidence of progress. Many did indeed encounter steady improvement in the human condition, as reflected in intelligence, morality and happiness. This positive and progressive evolutionary stream had tributaries in the social thought of the eighteenth century Enlightenment. Thus was created the Orange view of evolution. Mankind progresses along a continuum of improvement and future success is unlimited.

Social evolutionism's golden age was soon tarnished, however, by massive attack from a variety of anti-evolutionary forces. Human beings, it was argued, should not be stereotyped into rigid evolutionary schemes in which all cultural development is along a uniform track - especially not if this is used to justify the existence of different economic and social classes. The idea that certain individuals or groups were better adapted than others became anathema to those who hold to a "unilinear evolutionary" perspective. The seeds were sown for the egalitarianism which flourishes today in so many South African universities and religious groupings. Witness here the Green perception of equality and its rejection of any notion of elitism for specific individuals or groups.

However, the New Paradigm described in Chapter 1 brings with it a revisionist and scientifically updated view of the emergence of the species *homo sapiens*. The architects of this Yellow perspective have based their projections on careful study of the human brain's processing systems, the discontinuity insights of quantum physics, new advances in genetic and DNA analysis and the cycles of chaos and order that appear to permeate every area of our lives. This book is written with the New Paradigm in mind. It will not be popular in Blue and Orange evolutionary circles or in Green anti-evolutionary circles because it challenges so many of their basic assumptions. That cannot be helped. The New Paradigm stands or falls on its ability to provide meaningful insights to such phenomena as the turmoil with which South Africa is currently convulsed.

Pathfinder of the New Paradigm.

In the fall of 1952, Clare W. Graves, Professor Emeritus of Psychology, Union College, Schenectady, New York State, sat in his office in near-total frustration. This lanky man with an insightful and engaging mind and a powerful oratorical style of teaching found himself at a tipping point in his career. He found he could not go back to the classroom and act as a referee between conflicting schools of thought in psychology. After lecturing to his students on the various and mutually exclusive viewpoints of Sigmund Freud, B.F. Skinner, Karl Rogers and others, he would invariably get the question: "Well, Dr Graves, which one is right?"

He must have felt like a person trying to get the observers of the elephant mentioned in the Prologue to agree on something. None of them could. Exponents of each school of thought in psychology were altogether convinced that their theory accounted for the whole elephant. They had data to prove it and could call up legions of "true believing" graduate students who would echo their claims.

"How can this be?" Graves asked himself. "If this discipline has any integrity at all it should either face up to this unholy mess or close down shop." He had "had it up to here" with the whole field, he wrote, because he assumed psychologists, of all people, should be able to get their act together. The various schools of thought should at least engage in something less damaging than angry charges and counter-charges. He knew he had to either reframe the problem entirely and seek a new way to integrate all the differences into a single, broad-gauged theory or abandon the field altogether.

He did not abandon the field. Instead he undertook the enormous task of tracing humanity's human psychological spoor. He began an imaginative and open-ended research initiative, an extensive longitudinal project, asking all kinds of people to describe what they thought well-functioning and mature human beings were actually like. He collected these conceptions from thousands of people over several decades. He was in a position to observe if and when people changed their views, and in what direction. He amassed a huge pile of data and began to look for existing psychological theories to determine whether they could account for the patterns he saw emerging. He first attempted to make sense out of these thousands of viewpoints through the Hierarchy of Needs framework of his good friend Abraham Maslow, who taught at Brandeis University in Boston. He was shocked to find he had data left over. He found conceptions of the healthy human being that went beyond self-actualisation, the pinnacle and final state in Maslow's pyramid. Nothing made any sense of his data. There were fragments of this and pieces of that. He performed rigorous psychological validation studies, using both traditional and highly innovative assessment techniques.

He found that some people changed, others did not. Some responded to statements of authority, others to peer group pressure. His entire pile of data had become more chaotic and confusing. He feared he had reached the end of his research project and, probably, the end of his teaching career.

In September 1961, as he prepared his courses for the fall enrolment at Union College, he suddenly and spontaneously stepped over to the blackboard behind his desk and picked up a piece of chalk. He carefully erased the board and then, without conscious thought or hesitation, began to sketch a complex, multi-faceted and comprehensive model for the emergence of the human species. As with a brilliant mathematician who fills the blackboard with figures, formulae and schematics, suddenly it all came together for Graves and he finally wrote out the essence of his point of view. What had bedevilled him for an entire academic career was at last clear. The pathfinder had discovered the New Paradigm. He called it "The Emergent, Cyclical, Double Helix Model of Adult Biopsychosocial

This book presents a modern version of what Professor Graves drew on his blackboard. Do not be frightened off by its apparent complexity or its thunderous name. Rather stand with Oliver Wendell Holmes, the great American jurist who said: "I would not give a fig for the simplicity this side of complexity but I would give my life for the simplicity the other side of complexity." The New Paradigm will illuminate the whole elephant. Its elegance and simplicity will become apparent as this book progresses. But the reader first has to learn a new and colour-coded language, which is the key to a new way of thinking about everything. In this first exposure to the Graves Technology, we will describe the spectrums of difference in people - why and how we think and act in different ways and, in other cases, are astonishingly alike even though we might speak different languages and come from different continents. In the next chapter we will deal with spirals of change - when, why and how people, organisations and even entire societies deal with transitions and transformations.

Spectrums of Difference.

In *The Futurist* of April 1974, Graves wrote:
"The psychology of the mature human being is an unfolding, emergent, oscillating, spiralling process marked by progressive subordination of older, lower-order behaviour systems to newer, higher-order systems as man's existential problems change."

In short, we can change our own psychology. The brain can rewire itself. Society is not static. Evolution and revolution are part of our nature. We are on perpetual treks of the mind and only occasionally do we laager to collect our senses or get our bearings. Then we are once again on the move. This fourth generation evolutionary perspective (code it Yellow) has these components and characteristics. It is not our purpose to attempt to explain this complex new framework, but to provide enough information to deal practically with the issues of South Africa. (A list of resources is provided at the end of the book for those who might wish to explore more deeply into Gravesian theory).

It is important to remember that the Gravesian technology is "emergent". Crucibles (problems of existence) forge new solutions (paradigms) for the new problems. In time the New Order will run into difficulty because as it solves problems it creates new ones. Then a new crucible is reached and, once again, a fresh paradigm is formed to address those emerging problems. Such a process has continued throughout history.

CRUCIBLE-PARADIGM FLOW

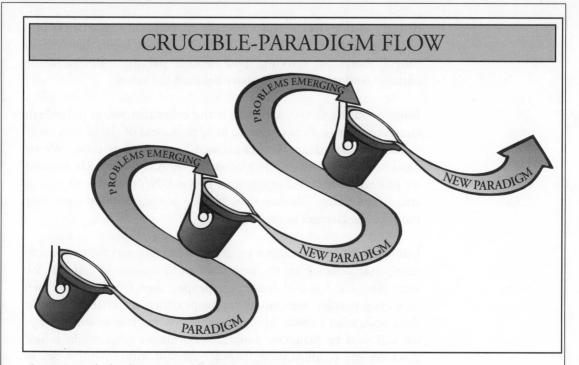

Graves used the language of the Double Helix to illustrate, as a metaphor, how crucibles and paradigms interact. Those who have seen a model of the *DNA*, containing genes and chromosomes, have seen a double helix. These are two strands which more or less wind together in a dance-like manner. The first helix (in the Graves technology) represents the problems of existence encountered by individuals, organisations and entire societies. The second helix reflects the coping methods necessary to deal with those problems of existence. Graves identified the problems as A, B, C, D etc and the coping systems as N, O, P, Q, etc. For the sake of clarity we use colours to reflect these different paradigms.

See Plate I, Colour Section

When the tribal (Purple) system faltered, a new crucible produced empires (Red). When the exploitative empires had run their course, what are known as the "living world religions" (Blue) emerged all over the planet - at about the same time. Whenever these purposeful and organised systems brought more stability, greater fairness and the guarantee of the afterlife, the restlessness produced a new crucible. This new paradigm (Orange) spawned the Renaissance, scientific method and the industrial revolution.

Yet the older and rejected paradigms do not vanish altogether. They remain within our individual and collective memories and repertoires in case the crucible conditions which gave them birth should fire up again. Consider what happened to the Kurds of Iraq recently when their conditions of existence deteriorated sharply. An orderly and moral society descended suddenly into theft and pillaging for food. Did civil rights mean anything when they were in mortal danger of starving? Did another paradigm not suddenly emerge? And who would not have behaved the same?

Inherent in the Graves approach is the belief that we, as individuals and even entire societies, operate in open instead of closed systems of values. Human nature, Graves claimed, is not a static thing. We are fixed neither at birth nor on graduation from university. He believed we possessed the coded programme in our DNA to enable us to shift among systems, to add new ones when appropriate and to constantly monitor the changes in the milieu.

Instead of being permanent types, or possessing specific personality traits, it appears we are the repository and processor of systems. We were once Ice Age and Stone Age people; then tribal people; then predatory people; then moralistic people; then materialistic people; then egalitarian people. Many are now systems people and perhaps we will next be planetary people. Who knows what might follow that? Yet any or all of these "people" are still within us; they are in reserve and always on call - types within us.

See Plate II, Colour Section

These "biopsychosocial" systems suggest how people think, not what they think. They suggest how people resolve problems, not what they value. Think of these paradigms as belief structures, as containers. What people value is the substance which goes into the container. Thus, two people might think within the same animistic/tribalist paradigm yet attempt to kill each other because one happens to be a Sioux Indian and the other a Pawnee. The film *Dances With Wolves* illustrates the point. The characters share the same paradigm, but the paradigms have diverse, mutually exclusive and conflicting content. The person who declares, "Kill a commie for Jesus!" has the same value system (thought structure) as his enemy who counters with "Necklace a capitalist for Lenin!" Both are dyed-in-the-wool absolutist thinkers. Be it Ku Klux Klan bigotry, radical black nationalist arrogance or neo-Nazism, racist viewpoints are similar because they emerge from the same value system, the same kind of brain, regardless of skin colour.

While none of the systems is inherently better or worse than any other, there is a hierarchy in the stacking of the paradigms, as illustrated. These do reflect diverse levels of complexity. The lower order systems will not understand the worlds within the higher order systems. A person in the power-driven, egocentric mindset of the Red system will have difficulty understanding the softer, egalitarian tones of the Green world view. In fact he will see it merely as an easy target for exploitation.

We have attempted to explain this difference by using the notation "to the power of". The second level system is "to the power of two" and has the complexity to function in an animistic society. The seventh level system operates "to the power of seven" and can handle greater complexity in life's choices. Yet the systems should not be compared in a sense of vertical priority.

In Graves' own words: "I am not saying in this conception of adult behaviour that one style of being, one form of human existence, is inevitably and in all circumstances superior to or better than another form of human existence, another style of being. What I am saying is that when one form of being is more congruent with the realities of existence, then it is the better form of living for those realities."

Think of these systems in people as Christmas tree light bulbs which are able to brighten or dim as dictated by the needs of the environment. When a person acquires a system, a light bulb has been screwed into his circuitry. That system is then available on call. If conditions in his life should worsen, the higher order light bulbs will dim while the more congruent colours will light up again.

Consider this schematic of how people cope with their problems of existence, depending on environment and consequent world view.

If the world is (Problems of Existence)	effective people (Appropriate Coping System)
HELIX I "Conditions"	HELIX II "Organism"
BEIGE a state of nature	act much like other animals
PURPLE mysterious and frightening	placate spirits and join together for safety
RED rough and hard like a jungle	fight to survive in spite of others
BLUE divinely controlled and guilt driven	obey rightful higher authority
ORANGE full of viable alternatives	pragmatically test options for success

GREEN
the habitat of all humanity

join communities to experience growth

YELLOW
in some danger of collapse

stand alone to learn how to be free

TURQUOISE
a single living entity

seek the order beneath Earth's chaos

Yet each system can express itself in positive or negative ways. The system itself is not inherently good or bad. This will become important in Chapter 3 as we look at various forms of value system change.

Note these examples in South Africa:

Healthy/Positive Expression	Unhealthy/Negative Version
AN - BEIGE	
Authentic San Bushmen - maximum coping within biological/emotional constraints. Subsistence lifestyle.	Profound retardation, serious drug problems, extreme shock conditions, malnutrition (eg.vagrants).
BO - PURPLE	
Warm, supportive nests Ritual, tradition and magic. Healthy use of sangomas. Belief in animistic spirits.	Witchcraft, curses and spells. War muti to encourage conflict. Faction fighting, grudges.
CP - RED	
Strong self-image. Expressiveness in sport, music, the arts. Break-ing free from barriers.	Warlords, violence, hit squads, gangsterism. Lack of guilt, excessive bravado, exploitation of the weak.
DQ - BLUE	
Truth, honour, justice, discipline, work ethic, sacrifice for greater good. (Seen in the Zion Christian Church and some forms of nationalism).	Rigid ideology, punitive holy wars, zealotry, depersonal-isation of "enemies". Heavy-handed bureaucracy.

ER - ORANGE

Entrepreneurialism, ambition. Desire to improve, to be the best. Attitude of thrive and help thrive. Expand the economic cake. Produce the middle class.

Crass materialism. dishonest government and business, shady dealing. Contamination of the environment for profit. Destructive, competitive gamesmanship.

FS - GREEN

Beyond materialism and dogma. Focuses on warm inter-personal relations. Promotes affiliation and personal growth. Supports consensus and community. Softens edges in conflict. Genuine concern for others.

Naive egalitarianism within moral crusades. Compassion becomes patronising contempt. Romanticises the under-privileged. Develops a narrow view of human diversity. Demands piety, harmony and understanding above all else.

GT - YELLOW

Big-picture view of life systems. Values what is natural - less can mean more. Focuses on competency, responsibility, and freedom of choice. Rejects status, conformity, authoritarian structures. Information and knowledge -based decision-making. Capable of fearless, creative problem-solving.

Often drops out, stays on sidelines or "does own thing" regardless. Shows little passion for others. Absorbed in self-interest. Pursues a variety of interests based on self-motivation. Often "lets things be" to excess.

HU - TURQUOISE

In tune with large scale of planetary concerns. Can "see" everything at once. Thinks in holo-graphic mosaics. Respects all life - and the impli-cit order within the uni-verse. Understands mega-systems in nature, social relations, evolution, business and the need to preserve Planet Earth for future generations.

Becomes abstract, other-worldly, tuned into frequencies and energy systems that transcend anything practical. Little use for people or community because of interaction with life forces in nature, through media and information net-works. Often condescending to those who are not "tuned in".

As long as there are new crucibles our genetic tool kits will create new paradigms - requiring new and quite different people to operate them. In that way the human brain/mind functions like our immune system. Christopher Wills, in *The Wisdom of the Genes*, notes that the immune system is highly complex and sophisticated. "It protects us," he claims, "against diseases that have preyed on our species for thousands of millions of years." We have known that for some time. But Wills adds: "More remarkably, we have found that it can protect us against diseases that we have not yet met. And it does so by an array of proteins, the immunoglobins, that can bind specifically to molecules that they also have never met!" The human mind is also able to reorganise and restructure its vast and powerful architecture to actually change its physiological state and adapt to new and complex challenges.

As early as the 1960s Graves was suggesting that the human DNA carries with it the genetic code that can instruct the species to radically change its internal programmes and priorities, thus producing new and different human beings. This process occurs within the chaos of the crucible. If this is so, new versions of our species, homo sapiens, could well be developing right now, right across South Africa. The peculiarities of the South African crucible could be about to produce men and women whose impulse for survival tells them to jettison the baggage of history and ideology and discover fresh modes of living. They would be the first such version to emerge on the planet. They would seek to integrate and creatively manage the other paradigms existing in South Africa, instead of attempting to obliterate them. A high priority would be quality of life and protection of the environment and life-sustaining resources. Because of South Africa's microcosmic quality, they would be the prototypes of Global Man. Their being freed from the shackles of the past would allow a harmony with the realities of their existence comparable with that of the San Bushmen. But these would not be little men with bows and poisoned arrows. To shift to the analogy of a musical score, these emergent thinkers would be exactly one octave higher, at home in the high-technology information age. Yet even this desirable outcome would not be the end of the story. Change would continue.

As Graves noted, "At each stage of human existence the adult man is off on his quest of his holy grail, the way of life he seeks by which to live. At his first level he is on a quest for automatic psychological satisfaction. At the second level he seeks a safe mode of living, and this is followed, in turn, by a search for heroic status, for power and glory, by a search for ultimate peace, a search for material pleasure, a search for affectionate relations, a search for respect of self, and a search for peace in an incomprehensible world. And when he finds he will not find that peace, he will be off on his ninth level quest. As

THE NATURE OF VALUE SYSTEMS

SOCIETIES AND CULTURES ARE SHAPED BY COLLECTIVELY HELD PARADIGMS.

PEOPLE EXPRESS THESE PARADIGMS AS INDIVIDUAL VALUE SYSTEMS.

PARADIGMS AS VALUES

Characteristics:

- **Ways** of thinking about something.

- **Means** of coping with Life's challenges and problems.

- **Filters** for perceiving and judging.

- **Patterns** for organising parts into meaningful wholes.

- **Views** of world: **Structures** of beliefs; and **sets** of the mind.

PARADIGMS AS SYSTEMS

Collections:

- **Spirals** of complexity.

- **Scaffoldings** of shifting priorities.

- **Levels** of psychological existence.

- **Degrees** of neurological activation.

- **Spectrums** of differences in people, organisations and societies.

PARADIGMS or VALUE SYSTEMS are expressed as views of religion, human destiny, the future and bottom lines. These are reflected in economic, social, political and philosophical theories as well as specific attitudes toward sex, marriage, health care, working, sport, social relationships, community development, race, ethnicity and human development.

he sets off on each quest, he believes he will find the answer to his existence. Yet, much to his surprise and much to his dismay, he finds at every stage that the solution to existence is not the solution he has come to find. Every stage he reaches leaves him discontented and perplexed. It is simply that as he solves one set of human problems, he finds a new set in their place. The quest he finds is never ending."

South Africa today and the rest of the world as well, is confronted with problems of existence to the Power of Seven and Eight. The New Paradigm reflects the cutting edge of the assumptions within the Yellow and Turquoise bands. It is a thinking, decision-making and problem-resolving system and process designed to deal with complex issues, diverse levels of complexity and rapidly changing conditions. Yet the path from past to present and into future is not a straight arrow, an unbroken line. Nor is it simply the next level on a symmetrical, equally steep staircase. The time line is discontinuous, broken, erratic, with sudden leaps, false starts and regressions, and shifting centres of gravity.

Suddenly, when a critical mass is reached, the stage is set for a major ratcheting forward. The tipping points will appear. Events will become catalytic and will appear to have impact far beyond their real effect. Many will, in error, believe they "caused" the paradigm shift, but they simply triggered the surface level version of the massive shift that has already occurred.

Suddenly a New Order is formed. A new thought collective containing consistent sets of principles and assumptions becomes visible. Typically these new clusters are first seen by physicists as they probe into the nature of the universe itself. Often they are treated as mystics who have come down from the mountains with strange visions of new universes. Then, in time, the new truths begin to flow like a streaking comet tail into other disciplines: the sciences, the arts, the social sciences, religion, politics and, ultimately, they reach the ordinary person in the street.

Clearly, the decade of the '90s is seeing the emergence of a new wine skin - the New Paradigm - engineered to contain the "new wine" flowing throughout South Africa and around the world as well. While this book will describe in more detail this emerging grand cosmic picture, the reader is likely to benefit from the following initial sketch so that its development and application may be followed more closely.

The New Paradigm has seven critical components. More will be detected as the account unfolds. A given person may possess parts of several components. A team, or brain syndicate, may have all components represented in some form between the individual members.

For the most part these components emerge naturally in people. They cannot be "trained in" or produced through manipulation of the opportunities and challenges in their lives, the carrots and sticks. Nobody knows how to "grow" people in the absolute sense. We have scientific evidence to suggest when and how these patterns of thinking appear to emerge in different people. The human brain is far too complex to think that one can easily insert these patterns through a command, lecture or even exposure to mentors or role models.

New Paradigm Thinkers: a Profile

Such people:

1. **Think in Open Systems in Contrast with Fixed, Ideal States**

   Fixed state thinkers in South Africa believe there is an ideal condition that, once put into place, will solve problems now and in the future. Once the ideal condition is achieved, it must be defended at all costs. The fixed state advocates carry the banners of African socialism, black nationalism, Marxist egalitarianism, free market consumerism, Western individualism and capitalism, "New Age" communalism etc. Whenever fixed state advocates become zealots for their particular cause, they lose perspective regarding the nature of change and become frozen and partisan in their view.

   New Paradigm thinkers think in flow states and recognise that society passes from one plateau to the next. In doing so, they integrate what is appropriate from the past with what will be congruent in the future to move the organism and its respective sub-systems along the human trajectory to greater complexity.

2. **Integrate Natural Differences in an Evolutionary Flow**

   Millions of people are passing through different levels of development simultaneously. There are literally different futures for different people. In South Africa, different segments of the population are ratcheting into different "final states" at the same time. And for them, at that stage, the state is "ideal." It is not ideal for the entire organism, however, not for the total human parade.

   New Paradigm thinkers therefore search for the integrated structures necessary to manage this long human march. Different population groups, with their differentiated needs and demands, are passing from pinnacle to pinnacle. Some are only now experiencing the trauma of detribalisation. Others are passing through a minefield of anarchy and anomie and the savage consequences. Not a few are riding the yeasty crest of becoming true believers, with all the associated senses of conversion, commitment and sainthood. Millions of others are leaving traditional orders in favour of pragmatic materialism, the quest for the best and the competitiveness of "the game".

New Paradigm thinkers have the scope, range, power and insight to manage the entire staircase of human history - a dynamic developmental spiral that characterises the South African microcosm. They think and act for the entire population instead of specific racial, ethnic, religious or class-based groups or interests.

They have the X-ray vision to see beneath the surface and detect the natural differences in people. As a result, they avoid being trapped in historic stereotypes and frozen categories regarding people and their values and priorities.

3. **Connect Everything to Everything Else in Quantum Chunks**
New Paradigm thinkers recognise that everything connects to everything else. One cannot deal with the "Young Lions" - the street kids of the townships - only through law enforcement. Everything has to be mobilised - the schools, the families, the churches, the business sector, community organisations. Major problems cannot be handled in a fragmented, *ad hoc*, piecemeal fashion.

Organisations which isolate functions in compartments, divisions, levels or territories are at serious risk. The new thinking in this decade points toward the need for common visions, integrated structures and focussed strategies and resources. Instead of becoming absorbed with small bits, the effective resolution of complex situations requires dealing with big chunks - therefore the use of insights from "quantum" thinking.

4. **Act for the Entire Organism in Creating and Distributing Abundance**
Practitioners of the New Paradigm focus on the whole instead of the parts. They recognise that to deal with any one thing or small part one must be prepared to understand and influence virtually everything at the same time. They take the panoramic, wide-angled view.

The commitment is to the organism called South Africa - the people living today and those yet unborn; the history, traditions and collective memories that provide safe and secure moorings and anchors; and the environment, natural resources and living conditions. Likewise, they recognise the interdependence of South Africa with the entire sub-continent, specifically, and the entire planet in general.

This positive thinking system is dedicated to the creation and distribution of abundance instead of the redistribution of scarcity. In this sense "abundance" refers to much more than material wealth or affluence. The standard of living and quality of life are impacted upon, as are the life of the mind, the health of the spirit and the wealth of the visions and dreams.

5. **See Everything by Holographic Scanning Before Acting**
New Paradigm thinkers are products of the Information Age. Their sensory systems are constantly open to the flow of data from all possible sources. They disdain political games, territorial defensiveness or other forms of information distortion and blockage. They have the capacity to navigate on past, present and future time lines - in all directions - to obtain a sense of perspective, continuity and receptiveness to new ideas.

6. **Employ a Full Range of Tailored Problem Resolution Processes**
Since New Paradigm people are skilled at dealing with different levels of development, competing "final states", the process of change and complex environments, they are adept at finding the right problem resolution package for the right situation at the right time.

They draw from a rich background in decision-making techniques that can be tailored to resolve issues in diverse settings. In all cases they act on behalf of the entire organism for the greater good. They employ compromise or negotiated processes where relevant; authoritarian conduits where absolutely necessary; and complex problem resolution formats where appropriate.

7. **Consist of Resourceful, Fearless, Tough, Competent yet Playful People**
A new kind of person is being forged in the crucible of the '90s, especially in South Africa. These people, of all ages, from all races, ethnicities, sexes and occupations, are experiencing quantum leaps in the quality of their thinking. The refining fire of the long ordeal of apartheid has charged the minds of an entire generation of South Africans with a creative power and range beyond that being produced in any other culture on the planet.

These 21st century San Bushmen are easily recognised. Status, the revenge motive, feelings of guilt or shame or the preoccupation with power are simply not valued. New Paradigm people rather display respect for competence - wherever it exists - a preference for autonomy and personal freedom, an interest in what is personally challenging and engaging and a passion and sense of joy in doing something which is unique.

They do not have blind, unconditional loyalty to causes, unthinking self-sacrifice. The New Paradigm thinker is his own man. Just as little will they have self-serving motives or lack of ethics and responsibility. New Paradigm thinkers are by no means perfect, but they cannot be manipulated. They will take up a cause only if they decide it is of merit - and it is they who make that choice.

New Paradigm thinkers may not be visible in the usual corridors of influence and prestige. They may be found on the periphery of power, among normal people doing normal things, and they may be found in any occupation. They may or may not have academic backgrounds, professional qualifications or certificates on their walls. One has to watch and listen carefully for them. They have no compelling urge to announce their presence until a problem draws them to respond. Having solved it, they tend to vanish from the scene.

In this chapter we have described the spectrums of thinking and the components of New Paradigm thinking, which are drawn from Levels Seven and Eight on the Psychological Map. In the next chapter we will describe the process of change in an evolutionary spiral.

CHAPTER 3

Panta rhei - All is flux
Heraclitus of Ephesus

Human value priorities stand out as the most strategically powerful causal agent now shaping events on the surface of the globe. More than any other causal system with which science now concerns itself, the human value factor is going to determine the future.
Roger Sperry
(Nobel Prize winner in Physics for innovations in mind-brain research).

Spirals of Change: Up and Down the Double Helix.

Plus ca change, plus c'est la même chose - the more things change, the more they stay the same. The nineteenth century historian Alphonso Karr could hardly have been more wrong. There is, of course, change of a circular nature which does seem to return to the same starting point. But even that is an illusion. The seasons come and go on some kind of time schedule, but no two winters are identical. In the winter of 1990 in South Africa, Natal won the Currie Cup rugby championship. The winter before, Northern Transvaal won it. Try telling any Natalian or Northern Transvaler that the winters of 1989 and 1990 were identical. No two minds are exactly alike either. Nor is the individual the same person today as yesterday, much less next year. In fact, like everything around us, we are in a state of constant motion. We are shaped by the Code of the Spiral.

It might be useful to think of two orders of change. This concept was introduced by Watzlawlck, Weakland and Fisch in their book entitled *Change: Principles of Problem Formation and Problem Resolution*. Change of the First Order stays within the givens, simply executes the next predetermined step or flows from the premises or beliefs already established. There are many cases where this mode of change is appropriate. The farmer rotates his crops to keep the soil fertile and productive. The coach alters his line-up to execute his game plan more effectively and efficiently. The pilot re-adjusts his fuel mixture or trims his flaps to stay within his flight plan. The mother changes the infant's diet to accommodate the nutrition needs. The best advice to be given in First Order change is, "Do more of the same." Better yet, do it in an improved manner, quicker, with greater efficiency - but do not change the basic plan. Stay within the same paradigm..

Change of the Second Order is different however. It involves a shift into a totally new dimension of thinking, a new order. Everything changes. When the commercial air industry shifted from piston to jet-driven aircraft, the entire aviation industry had to change, from the training of flight attendants to the design of airports. This mode of change is often chaotic, erratic, unsettling, full of danger, confounding to many and rather frightening at first. Second Order thinking is driven by the perceived future and, to the First Order mind, the new paradigms are puzzling, unexpected and paradoxical.

The initial attempts to resolve the problems flowing out of the apartheid dilemma were of the First Order - enforce the laws, shut down the country through emergency decrees, put more resources into Bantu education and draw more blacks into the homeland structures.

Likewise, many of the advocates of a transfer of power to the black majority may be within the First Order mode. To replace Afrikaner nationalism and its authoritarian structures with a black one-party state and its majoritarian mechanisms would not represent a change. The thinking would be identical. Only the names and faces of the people in the Union Buildings, in Pretoria, in the judicial positions in Bloemfontein and in the parliamentary seats in Cape Town would be different. Both represent monolithic systems.

The South African crucible we described in Chapter 1 is forging and fusing the elements necessary, and the thresholds of energy to spark Second Order Change. A new synthesis is in the early stages of being produced in workshops, seminars, conferences and informal interaction. When F.W. de Klerk cracked the whip for the Third Trek and led his wagon teams across the Rubicon, he dramatically announced change of the Second Order. He was determined to achieve it, at great personal and political risk.

The primary objective of this chapter will be to explore the Spirals of change: how, why and when major shifts occur in a complex social system. We choose the metaphor of a Spiral for a number of reasons. Spirals are found everywhere - they have an elegance in the enlarging architectural structure of seashells; in dynamic tornadoes and gravitational whirlpools; in the evolutionary coils that move in everything from cells of the human body to civilisations of greater complexity; in the Spiral staircase of the mind that connects floors containing different arrangements and memories.

The earlier world views, like rings on a Spiral, have been subordinated to greater complexity. They remain within the structure to give support, narrow the shape of the cone where necessary and add beauty and eloquence to the entire design. And, if the situation should dictate that they are needed, they are "on call".

The concept of the Double Helix has already been introduced. Helix 1, as will be recalled from the previous chapter, represents the problems of existence faced by people, organisations and societies. These have ranged from surviving in the bush to prospering in the global village. Helix 2 contains the responses we make to those problems in order to survive and prosper - under a myriad of different circumstances.

When the problems of existence worsen, we have to down-shift to a set of operating systems which were previously vacated but remain within our coping Spirals. When our particular belief system or collective identity is threatened, we close ranks, sing our cultural songs and return to the glorious days of yesteryear - at least in our minds. This is called a regression - a form of change of the Second Order to a previously embraced and congruent system.

If, on the other hand, we begin to experience problems from a more complex ring on the Spiral, we are under pressure to up-shift to the level that can address these emerging problems. Such change of the Second Order produces a quantum leap.

Second Order Change, consequently, is dependent on action within Helix 1. When our worlds are stable and predictable, we hold to the belief systems that work for us. Physicists call this a state of equilibration or homeostasis. When the environment is in the throes of major fluctuation, either down or up, we find ourselves metaphorically in white water, often grasping for ways to deal with these sudden eruptions, perturbations and uncertainties.
Clearly, South Africa is in a condition where up and down shifts are occurring virtually on a dally basis, all along the evolutionary Spiral. We have reason to believe this wind shear of chaotic eruptions will continue through the 1990s. We need help from thinkers within the New Paradigm to guide us through the turbulence. There are no maps, rule books or travel guides from any other culture that can assist South Africans to navigate the treacherous currents and minefields that lie ahead.

To understand the nature of change within this dynamic and chaotic Spiral, we must consider once again the contribution of Clare W. Graves, pathfinder of the New Paradigm. We will examine the conditions necessary for major paradigm shifts, as well as the phases or stages we experience in moving from one level of existence to the next.

Our intent here is to briefly describe the change process as set out within the Graves technology. We will highlight the ALPHA, BETA GAMMA, DELTA AND NEW ALPHA stages.

ALPHA is a condition where the current value systems held by individuals and societies realistically and effectively address the problems of existence. An individual "has it together". The company is doing well within its "niche". Society is meeting the needs of its citizens in a successful manner. The culture has created the forms and structures that match the problems.

The Zulu legions were certainly in ALPHA during the early nineteenth century when Shaka ruled supreme. His victims clearly were not. The English of Natal were in ALPHA during the heyday of empire when Britannia ruled the waves. Various hunting and pastoral societies were in ALPHA before Europeans arrived with guns to kill off the game and fencing to hem them in. The Afrikaners were in ALPHA during the heady days of Prime Minister John Vorster - Afrikaner nationalism at its zenith.

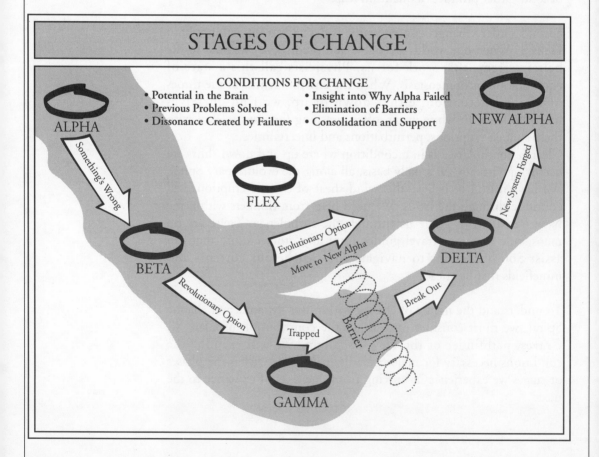

STAGES OF CHANGE

CONDITIONS FOR CHANGE
- Potential in the Brain
- Previous Problems Solved
- Dissonance Created by Failures
- Insight into Why Alpha Failed
- Elimination of Barriers
- Consolidation and Support

ALPHA

NEW ALPHA

Something's Wrong

FLEX

New System Forged

BETA

Evolutionary Option

Move to New Alpha

DELTA

Revolutionary Option

Barrier

Break Out

Trapped

GAMMA

Unhappily, although ALPHA societies can remain in that state a long time, the days are inevitably numbered. Institutions are weighed in the balance and found wanting. Meeting people's needs ultimately causes them to find others. Today's problems are yesterday's solutions. And nature has a way of introducing perturbations which range from changing weather patterns to threatening patterns of disease. Deranged dictators and malignant movements are dumped on the human tapestry and cause great damage and tribulation. It often takes the Spiral a long time to flush them out, often at great expense.

We first encounter the BETA state when we sense that something is wrong. At this point we do not know what it is - we lack the insight. We encounter evidence of dissonance and dissipation but we are uncertain as to what it means. The crime rate increases, the company loses market share, a marriage shows early signs of falling apart.

We intuitively respond with a series of counter moves. First we attempt "more of the same", under the assumption that nothing is inherently wrong with our system. We believe change of the First Order will clear up the symptoms and restore the homeostasis we previously enjoyed. We simply "hunker down", "rededicate our lives" or crack the whip to motivate people to work harder and better. We might pass more laws, communicate more crisply or even tighten down the screws to engender conformity and compliance with the system. We are not yet at the point of challenging the system itself.

When the change has been discontinuous and a critical mass has shifted, doing more of the same will make things worse, not better. The gaps separating people will widen, the sharper edges from the renewed commitment to the system will cut more deeply - causing even more haemorrhaging. The attempt to hold to the old paths speeds the day when they will be rejected. Nature plays tricks on us when we are stubborn and stand in the way of change.

Second in the BETA stage, we go on a regressive search. We experience a nostalgia for the "good old days" when everything seemed to work (we forget why it did not). This form of mild regression shows in the resurrection of cultural patterns from the past, the celebration of historic rituals and traditions and renewed study of the pioneers and pathfinders. South Africans recently witnessed such phenomena in one year of Afrikaner celebrations and re-enactments (The Great Trek, the arrival of the Huguenots and the Battle of Blood River). A sudden revival of interest in sangomas and other traditional healers and mystics is evidence of a BETA state. The individual needs guidance from these sources in surviving in the unknown and threatening world of the township.

Third, there is a point at which a window opens for a possible transition from BETA into a NEW ALPHA position. If we recognise that "the system", which we had thought came from Heaven or was the ultimate, final ideal state, was after all nothing more than "a system" (others being possible) there is the potential for a Second Order Change shift. This is what we call the evolutionary option.

Graves was quite specific about the conditions necessary for change of this kind to occur. This change process, remember, can flow from any of the value systems or specific paradigms to the next level of complexity. The ALPHA state will contain various combinations of value systems which have been activated by conditions in Helix 1. ALPHA might consist of Purple and Red systems. It might involve the dynamic tension between the traditional beliefs of DQ-Blue and the emerging materialism within Orange. At the height of Afrikaner power, for example, the authoritarian state of Blue was joined by the corporate state of Orange. Both colours represented centres of gravity producing the strength and power of the ALPHA system (and, by extraordinary coincidence, blue and orange were the colours of the National Party banner, deriving from the days of the Dutch East India Company).

Graves identified six conditions necessary for higher-level functioning on the part of individuals or entire nations. First there must be the potential in the brain. If the higher level structures are not present, change into that paradigm will not be biologically possible. (To assume that the entire human race, or the entire population of South Africa, exists at the same horizontal level of thinking capacity is both dangerous and foolish. If that were the case, it would imply that apartheid has done no damage to, nor artificially blocked, the development of people of colour. Few could accept such a proposition).

Second, the earlier problems of existence being faced must be resolved. Such a resolution releases psychic energy for an advance. If people are hungry or threatened by roving gangs of thugs, or have been blocked from entering the job market, the higher order systems cannot be expected to come on line.

In a later chapter we will describe how the potential of people can be released by guaranteeing the resolution of basic subsistence and safety problems. Failure to do so could trigger a downward Spiral, destroying the capacity of the entire society to leap into a new paradigm. Evolutionary change is sabotaged and the country descends into a revolutionary (GAMMA) holocaust.

Having the potential and actually solving existential problems at a given level are not in themselves sufficient to cause the next, higher system to develop. It was at this point that Graves disagreed strongly with the popular Hierarchy of Needs concept, as developed by his good friend and colleague, Abraham Maslow. Maslow contended that satisfaction of the earlier needs would automatically cause a shift in the direction of self-actualisation, the final state in his pyramid of needs.

Thirdly, dissonance has to be created by breakdown in the solution of current problems. As Graves noted: "None of my subjects made the jump to a higher level without a period of crisis and regression before the higher level system emerged." He believed the necessary triggers to be "the biochemical changes which ensue during a regressive search through past ways of behaving."

Fourthly, insight becomes critical, he claimed, because it provides the information necessary to understand why the old ALPHA came apart, why the regressive search was also doomed to fail and what it will take to construct a NEW ALPHA to deal effectively with the new problems of existence which have emerged.

Fifthly, when any insight is achieved there are other people around the individual and few of them may share the new insights. Thus the barriers - family, friends, the system and its way of thinking - must be overcome or ignored if the insight is to begin to propel the great psychological jump. It is at this point that new suggested models and proven patterns can be helpful. The mind is now open to new information from a number of sources.

The sixth necessary condition is the consolidation factor, when the individual or society begins to practice and affirm the new way of behaving. Obviously this requires commitment of resources, protection from earlier problems of existence and the support of others.

This entire book is dedicated to pursuit of this evolutionary option. Following chapters will sketch in a strategy for promoting this shift from BETA to a NEW ALPHA by detailing specific sets of actions that should be taken in South Africa and in other countries to facilitate such a positive scenario.

If this route is not taken, we face being trapped in the GAMMA state. GAMMA is a time of growing frustration, a feeling of being blocked, and it produces a range of anti-social, self-destructive behaviour. GAMMA can lead to violence and armed rebellion against the status quo. The anger is caused by (a) knowing what is wrong and why; (b) understanding what will relieve the tension and create a NEW ALPHA; but (c) fearing that powerful and often punitive barriers stand in the way. The barriers can be external such as the artificial restraints created by apartheid, lack of opportunity or restricted mobility. They may also be inside a person and self-imposed.

Genuine use of "struggle" rhetoric and illusions is evidence of a GAMMA condition. In some cases the external, oppressive "system" is accused of causing all the pain and suffering. Yet in many cases the real barriers that block movement are within the minds of people who have not yet crossed the Rubicon of change themselves. In America we continue to hear of the devastating impact of slavery on the condition of African Americans. Yet many enlightened black American intellectuals and political leaders are beginning to see this as a poor excuse for not extending oneself in a competitive environment. When things go badly the bloody shirt of racism is waved once again to put the blame back on a convenient scapegoat. The Red thinking band on the Psychological Map is incapable of putting blame on self. Such power gods always externalise their problems and create the barriers because they desperately need "to struggle". Others feel they must actually earn their liberation and insist on maintaining the barricades. The revolutionary option becomes tenable, then, when the barriers, real or perceived, block a person or entire group from advancing to their vision of the ideal state. They will demand fundamental change in structures and systems. Often they think in an unrelenting "all or nothing" mode as they launch major assaults on the barriers or obstacles. Actions are defended in the name of noble purpose, "the cause" or the righteous crusade. One detects this kind of change process if one swings from the French and American revolutions through to modern day Marxist-inspired upheavals.

When the barriers are removed, ignored or overcome, the DELTA state is reached. DELTA is a period of excitement and rapid change where the new energy is focused as the restraints drop away. People take charge of their own destinies. The past no longer controls the present. This DELTA energy surge is often raw, enthusiastic and unrestrained. Old ways of living give way to fresh solutions as unexpectedly different structures begin to emerge in a swirl of activity. This exuberance ignites creativity, resourcefulness and dedication to the task of designing a new age or person.

DELTA often brings stress into long-term relations as one party changes but the other remains in the old ALPHA. Too much DELTA too soon, too emotionally displayed, can produce a serious backlash that actually reinforces the old barriers.

South Africa may well be entering a DELTA period that can be as dangerous as it is exciting. The nature of a "post-apartheid" society has been the topic of many publications and seminars. As it begins to take shape, one has reason for concern at the rising tide of false (DELTA) expectations on the part of millions who believed "freedom" meant jobs, houses, safe neighbourhoods and affluence. Many genuinely expected Nelson Mandela to raise an army on his release and march on Pretoria.

New Paradigm thinkers will be in great demand during the DELTA phase as many of the expected rewards and opportunities, virtually guaranteed by "struggle" leaders, fail to materialise. It has not been uncommon, especially in Third World countries, for the enlightened leader to be replaced by the general, then even by the sergeant as reality begins to settle in following the emotive songs and anthems of liberation and nationalism. Ideal states are dangerous, as are the hopes and expectations of the "oppressed" in an age of diminishing resources and mounting pressure to do more with less.

Change is a complex, intricate and multifaceted process and it cannot be described in simple, cosmetic and quick fix terms. When one encounters advocates of change from the Orange-materialistic band, one gets an entire shopping list of manipulative techniques designed to implant into the empty minds of people the objectives of the persuader. When one learns about change from people in the Green-egalitarian range, one is told that anybody can change into anything at any time. If one mentions to them the mixed levels of thinking in people and the inability of many to respond to a sense of community and humaneness, one is ostracised and branded a racist. Ironically, one is likely to receive from these humane people the most inhumane treatment.

The Yellow-Integrative/Evolutionary assumptions about change coupled with commitment to the entire organism, right up to the Turquoise-holistic system, characterise the approach in thinking of the New Paradigm. People are indeed at different levels of development. To promise them something that is simply not in the stars for them, at least at that particular time, seems the worst kind of cruelty and irresponsibility.

Every person in South Africa is, at some level, a change manager. Since people are passing through different levels of development at the same time, the full range of change technologies is relevant - but must be carefully tailored to match different world views. The overall orchestration of change for the total society requires assistance from the New Paradigm thinkers. They see the Big Picture with greater clarity - and they have no secret or private agendas.

Finally, the following are key change triggers and transition elements. (Note that they are not predestined or fatalistic states as one finds in Calvinism and Marxism. Instead they are naturally evolving paradigms with all kinds of local and regional variations, especially in the content within the structures. This understanding of the evolutionary order has been impacted on by an insight to discontinuous change and chaos theory. The reader will discover an internal logic within the natural flow):

Forging The Spiral

AN-BEIGE: World to the Power of One

The automatic/instinctive "I survive" system of AN-Beige seeks only the immediate satisfaction of basic physiological needs. The individual lives only through the medium of his built-in equipment. When, as a food gatherer, he enters his Garden of Eden, that place in space which meets his Pavlovian needs, he begins to slip into the tribalistic (Purple) way of life. The Beige mini-crucible spawns the formation of tribal order.

Transition:

An awareness of self as different from a survival band emerges, a primitive version of cause and effect thinking develops and the population growth from Ice Age conditions produces more fear and threats to existence. This produces the need for a more complex organisation, a tribe. Systems in the brain, tuned in to animistic voices from a spirit-filled world, are activated, opening up a new world of magic, taboos, hexes, season time and ritual.

BO-PURPLE: World to the Power of Two

The animistic/tribalistic "we are safe" BO-PURPLE way of living produces a feeling of kinship and reciprocity. "We all share what we have since one will find food today, another tomorrow ..." etc. The tribal order consists of a chief, magic people, the circle of elders as a decision-making system. But then reliance on mystical spirits, the "warm nest" sense of being within the group and protection by the shaman and chiefs comes to be subordinated by the emergence of a dominant ego. "I am me" becomes more important than being part of the group and a "go it alone" view develops.

Transition:

More by chance than design, some men achieve relative control of their spirit world through their non-explainable, elder-administered, tradition-based way of life. Once the continuance of the system is assured with minimal energy expenditure, excess energy and resources leave people with time on their hands. This puts the system in a state of readiness for change. It then moves toward a threshold and its ultimate demise since it becomes overloaded with its accretion of more and more tradition, more and more ritual. This stifles those who are now yearning for personal autonomy, made possible by the meeting of their basic subsistence (AN) and safety (BO) needs. The dissonance arises, usually in youth, or in certain minds not troubled by memories of the past and who, because of the kind of brain they were born with, are capable of newer and more lasting insights to the nature of things. When this occurs it triggers man's insight to his own existence as an individual being, as an entity separate and distinct from others. He struggles to break free from predatory people, animals and even spirits within his physical world. He is no longer "one-with-all". Nor does he subject himself any longer to the Purple cultural programming which, as with a booted-up computer, forces him to fit in a self-sacrificial manner within the tribal order where the old people run everything. Instead he struggles alone for survival against the draconic forces of the universe. (The reader may begin to sense that we are already describing how the Purple mini-crucible spews out the street gang, the Young Lions of the townships, the rebels with or without cause, in the turbulence and trauma of detribalisation). He attacks those still within the older paradigm who lack the courage or strength to set out on an independent course themselves.

CP- RED: World to the Power of Three

In the Red band, raw, rugged self-assertive individualism strides on the scene. Since only a few are able to surge to freedom from Purple paralysis - a stagnant tribal existence - the many who were unable to break free accept the "might is right" claims of the powerful. They willingly submit or throw themselves at the feet of elites who have become the privileged few. This Promethean world view is based on the prerogatives of the "haves" and the duties of the "have-nots". Assured of their survival through vassalage, the "haves" behave as they please. The "have-nots" accept their fate in the resulting feudal order.

This spawns in time the absolute rights of kings, the unassailable prerogatives of management, the right of the lowly hustler merely to what he can hustle. It provides the *raison d'etre* for an entrenched colonial system. This is a world of the aggressive expression of man's lusts - openly and unabashedly by the "haves", more covertly and deviously by the "have-nots". Shame, loss of face or personal insult (often of a graphic physical or sexual nature) will provoke a violent response. Underlings have to pay tribute and homage and observe symbolic bowing of the neck to the privileged one.

Transition:

Death still faces the "have's". He may claim he will live forever but he cannot escape his mortality. The "have-not" has to explain to himself why he has to endure a miserable existence. Out of this mix in the Red mini-crucible, develops the DO-Saintly system. There has to be a reason for the "have" and "have-not" condition. This leads to the search for a directive design and identification of the forces guiding man and his destiny. He seeks to remove the pain from both the dominant and the submissive by finding a rationale that explains and justifies it all, while ensuring stability now and everlasting peace of mind in the future.

DQ-BLUE: World to the Power of Four

The seemingly endless struggle with unbridled lusts and a threatening universe and the need to prove oneself worthy of an afterlife spawns the production of rules, prescriptions, punishment for sins and the rule of law. This new paradigm, reflected in the emergence of the living world religions, also creates secular versions in ethnic and nationalist-based cultures, an elaborate code of moral conduct and "one right way" zealotry. Ideological movements form. Higher abstract thinking emerges in the brain, which is capable of fixing on a cause - even dying for the cause. A guilt system also develops, to cement people to the ultimate, ideal system which alone can bring order, stability and purpose to human existence.

Transition:

Once stability and security are achieved, and the afterlife is also guaranteed, the time comes when men begin to question the price. The saintly, puritannical, rigid, sacrificial lifestyle is devoid of pleasure, leisure or adventurous thought. Once again, as with the breaking of tribal bonds, man seeks to free himself from the restrictions and constraints of an authoritarian, punitive "suffer now to gain later" world view. New, excess energy is produced in the system, creating perturbations and, at first, subtle attacks on the established Blue Order. (Readers will probably recognise here the cautious emergence of the National Party verligtes in the 1970s). Deviation surfaces. The basic assumptions of "the system" are questioned. A new elitism is born. The evidence of the BETA state is everywhere, revisionist views abound. Blue thinkers attempt to regain control and stability by a frantic First Order Change mandate. Heretics are burned at the stake. Non-conformists have to leave hearth and home to pursue their personal destiny elsewhere. The hot, fiery Blue mini-crucible forges a new human species, such as those who arrived at the Cape in 1652 or today's black urban professionals (the Buppies) of Soweto.

ER-ORANGE: World to the Power of Five

At the Orange-materialistic level, man strives to conquer the world by learning its secrets rather than by raw, naked force as he did at the CP level. He develops and utilises objective, positivist scientific method to provide the material needs for a satisfactory human existence in the here and now. The DQ-Blue belief in the afterlife is not rejected. However, man feels compelled to master the objective physical world through analytical thinking, strategic goal setting and success-driven motivation. Such energies gave rise to the Renaissance, imperial ventures into the Americas, Africa, India and Australasia, the industrial revolution and the explosion of high technology. Heaven will be established here on earth.

Transition :

Once assured of his material satisfaction (not necessarily his neighbours') man discovers in himself a spiritual void. He has conquered the world, he has explored everywhere, even into space. He has all the human comforts that can be manufactured and purchased. Yet he has not achieved happiness. He finds himself a neophyte in a subjectivistic, humanistic world. He has achieved the good life but at a price. He is envied - perhaps respected - but not liked. Life becomes shallow, meaningless and jaded, his lifestyle has cost him health, family affection, self-respect and what he now perceives to be most important of all - people, community, sensitivity and human warmth.

FS-GREEN: World to the Power of Six

At this sociocentric level man becomes a being concerned for the relation of self to the selves of others. He becomes preoccupied with belonging, with being accepted not rejected, with knowing the inner side of living. He becomes absorbed with human harmony and his position within the whole, the total universe. He is driven to eradicate pain, hunger, division, racism, human disparities and all conditions which make some better off than others. He sparks crusades, mobilises causes and finds kindred spirits in religions, human rights and egalitarian movements. The Orange mini-crucible has forged a new human being - one who stresses his basic humanity above all. Credit cards are displaced by crystals and mantras.

Transition:

In spite of his good intentions and social programmes, man in the Green band of thinking does not produce the ideal state he envisages. After spending all the money, mounting the protest marches and boycotts and forcing "freedom and equality" into the law of the land, people are still not equal. Billions are still not free. Evil international troublemakers still emerge. AIDS threatens to destroy large segments of humanity. Available resources are shrinking. Nationalism and ethnicity re-appear, threatening the very fabric of community. His world is in shreds and he cannot understand why - it all felt so good at the time. At this point the Green mini-crucible produces a new alloy, a new paradigm - one that contains the elements necessary for a major quantum leap in the understanding of the species *Homo sapiens,* and at a level not even imagined in earlier systems of thought. In the Orange band the hidden secrets of the physical universe demand our attention. In the Green band the feelings of man are paramount. "Getting along with" is valued above "getting ahead". In the Yellow band a new self-interest returns, but in a higher form designed for thinking in natural, evolutionary, living systems.

GT - YELLOW: World to the Power of Seven

Having been hobbled by narrow, animal-like requirements of sustenance; by fear of the spirits; by the fear of predatory fellow-men; by anxiety about trespassing on the ordained order; by revulsion against personal excess; by anxiety about social disapproval - human thinking and processing of information is suddenly free. Man now focuses upon himself and upon his world. The picture revealed is disturbing because the world has clearly been abused. Triggered by this insight, man searches for a system of values which will allow him to be more than a parasite on the world and its inhabitants. He searches for a value system rooted truly in knowledge and cosmic reality instead of delusions brought on by animal and social needs. The mind is suddenly open for cognitive roaming over the entire human tapestry and evolutionary Spiral. The New paradigm, as described in Chapters 1 and 2, is born.

Transition:

Powerful insights gained in the Yellow band and implemented in an attempt to solve the global mess caused by the first six levels of human existence, lack means of enforcement. Destruction is still rampant. The ethic: "Recognise, truly notice what life is and you shall know how to behave" makes no sense at all to people with earlier world views. Therefore practicality. If it is realistic that an individual should suffer, suffer he should. If it is realistic to be happy, then it is good to be happy. If the situation calls for authoritarianism, then it is proper to be authoritarian. If the situation calls for democracy, one should be democratic. Behaviour is "right" and "proper" if it is based on today's best possible evidence. What was "right" yesterday may not be so today. The supreme issue in GT is restoration of the world so that life may continue - not just human life but life itself. For the first time man is able to face existence in all its dimensions, even to the point of valuing inconsistencies, oppositions and flat contradictions. The Yellow mini-crucible ultimately produces a human being who finds that the answers are not within "reality", currently available information or historical evidence. The scene is now set for the next paradigm to emerge.

This evolving mindset is still tentative, sketchy, uncertain. It does attempt to see everything at once in one dimension yet, in another, rejects the notion that one can understand existence itself. Instead, as Graves noted, "he values escaping from the barbed wire entanglements of his own ideas, his own mechanical devices, his own social forms and structures." The basic theme is: "Adjust to the reality of existence that you can only be, you can never really know."

This does not end the search. To many readers the GT and HU thinking systems will no doubt be remote, perhaps absurd; certainly unrealistic for the billions on the planet. But recall that the same was said around the tribal campfires about CP-Red; among the early barbarians about Blue; in monasteries when Orange first appeared; in the centres of trade during the mercantile age when Green was first talked about; and in university communes when Yellow first challenged the conventional wisdom and the pressure to be "politically correct."

The human Spiral is alive, vibrant, interactive, interdependent and healthy. It is an organism with a life of its own. We possess the coded systems in our brains that operate this Spiral, shape its direction, trigger its spin and establish its balances, chemistry and internal tension. The Spiral is full of mini-crucibles that continue to spew out new life forms. The process continues.

PART II

South of the Limpopo

To describe South Africa's historical setting as unique is to risk being glib and hackneyed. Nowhere else in the world has history placed together such a bewildering variety of peoples and cultures in close proximity and permanent settlement; in such numbers and with such great difficulties in assimilation. Africa, Asia and Europe have met before in East Africa, but never on this scale, never with the newcomers committed without reservation to staying on, nor with such demographic ratios as to make it impossible, in terms of raw power, for any one group to safely dominate. European colonists have made war on each other before, as in Canada, but never on the scale of the Anglo-Boer War and never with such a huge indigenous population as onlookers. Racial discrimination has been practised before in colonial and neo-colonial societies, but never until in South Africa was it encoded in law and made fundamental to a kind of civic religion. Other countries have discovered mineral wealth but few, if any (the oilfields aside), the richness of South Africa. With its mining and secondary industry, South Africa is a colossus in African terms, yet its productivity depends on the efforts of a workforce whose very legitimacy and permanence in their homes and jobs had been challenged for decades by government, which made every effort to denationalise them.

South Africa is at once an Eldorado of wealth, a cesspit of poverty, a Mad Hatter's Tea Party of ideology and a cockpit of violence. Strikingly, it is a microcosm of the world as a whole - even down to racial and ethnic ratios and wealth ratios - and if reason and justice are to prevail in the world and inform the relationship between North and South, between First World and Third World, answers will first have to be found in South Africa. They could then serve as a model for the world as a whole.

This book examines South Africa through the prism of Gravesian technology. However, the two chapters in this section provide brief conventional outlines (for the benefit of overseas readers in particular) of what South Africa actually is.

Chapter 4 provides the historical setting, focusing on events long ago whose effects are still felt every day. Chapter 5 examines the strengths and weaknesses of the industrialised, polyglot state which has emerged in this southernmost region of Africa.

Two minds, two worlds, one country: the kind of country H.G. Wells might have invented, or that Jonathan Swift might have sent Gulliver to, where people occupy the same space but live in different time frames so that they do not see each other and perceive different realities.
Allister Sparks: The Mind of South Africa

Boers, Britons and Blacks

The elements boiling and spluttering in South Africa's crucible got there through historical events which give the mixture an extra pungency and explosive volatility. It is not the purpose of this book to provide a detailed history, but a brief sketching is necessary for an understanding of the forces in contention.

South Africa's current geo-political configuration is the outcome of internal migrations and wars by the indigenous population, three major waves of colonial settlement, imperial expansion and dominion and - since 1948 - the ideology of apartheid.

The Dutch settled the Cape in 1652, originally to establish a limited victualling station for vessels sailing between the Netherlands and the Far East but later permitting a permanent settlement. Dutch settlers were joined by Huguenot refugees from France, who fused with the Dutch to form the present Afrikaner people, along with a significant admixture of Germans. Slaves were imported to work the farms, mainly from Indonesia and West Africa, and were the nucleus of today's mixed-race "coloured" community, which is still located mainly in the Cape. In the early nineteenth century the Cape passed to British control as part of the post-Napoleonic settlement. This was soon followed by significant British settlement in the Eastern Cape in an attempt to stabilise a frontier where the expanding pastoral Afrikaners had come into explosive contact with the also pastoral Xhosa people who had been gradually drifting south for generations. Another significant British settlement occurred at a later stage when the territory of Natal, on the north-eastern seaboard, was annexed. Meanwhile a series of cataclysmic wars centred on the expanding Zulu empire had sent shockwaves over the entire sub-continent, reaching as far as present-day Zimbabwe and Mozambique, putting entire populations to flight and leaving vast stretches of territory temporarily unoccupied.

This was to have important consequences, because when large numbers of the Afrikaner farmers (or Boers) of the Eastern Cape decided to skirt the Xhosa domain and migrate to the interior to escape British rule, against which they had various grievances, they found themselves entering what appeared to be virtually unoccupied territory. It was not until they crossed the Drakensberg mountain range into Natal, and others trekked further into the present-day Transvaal, that they came up against the Zulu military power and (in the Transvaal) an offshoot of the Zulus. Both indigenous forces were defeated after a series of engagements which seared deep into the collective psyche of the antagonists.

Britain had few real interests in the hinterland of Southern Africa until the discovery of gold and diamonds infused imperial policy with a new purpose. The Zulus were dealt with by crushing them militarily (though with the debacle of Isandlwana en route) and, 20 years later, the Boers of the independent republics of the Orange Free State and the Transvaal were to meet with the same fate (also with military debacles for the British along the way). The Zulu power was dismembered and Zululand was eventually annexed to the crown colony of Natal (along with the more northern territory of Tongaland). The Eastern Cape frontier was secured by annexing the Xhosa territory of Transkei to the Cape Colony. The imperial factor rode rampant. British protectorates were established in Basutoland (today's Lesotho), Swaziland and Bechuanaland (today's Botswana), whose leaders were eager enough to be protected against Boer encroachment.

This pattern of annexations and protectorates has had significant consequences. Whereas the numerically large and militarily powerful Zulu and Xhosa groups were defeated and incorporated with crown colonies which later became provinces of the Union of South Africa, the smaller and weaker Basotho, Swazi, and Botswana peoples followed a different route to sovereign independence (they spurned provisions in the South Africa Act for their eventual incorporation with the Union). The irony is great - and not just for the Xhosas and Zulus. If the architects of Union had in mind a white-dominated South Africa, they took with them the seeds of its destruction - the two largest and most militant groups of the sub-continent, who provide the core support today for the African National Congress (ANC) and the Inkatha Freedom Party.

Of course, black South Africa does not consist only of people of Zulu or Xhosa extraction. There are other significant black communities. And, as with the drawing of colonial boundaries all over Africa, ethnic communities were sundered without thought. The independent states of Botswana, Lesotho and Swaziland have left behind them, inside South Africa, what amount to ethnic satellite statelets, the despised homelands or bantustans (another homeland has a corresponding relationship with the formerly

Portuguese territory of Mozambique). Because colonial boundaries are regarded as inviolable in independent Africa, these statelets are part of the South African problem. They will not be joined to their independent ethnic heartlands. However, the KwaZulu homeland and the Transkei homeland are of an order significantly different. They are ethnic heartlands, not satellites. The difference is detectable in the slightly ambivalent attitude of the Inkatha leadership, which refuses to accept excision from South Africa yet insists that KwaZulu is an entity in its own right, the remnant of pre-colonial Zululand; also in the attitude of the ANC, which condemns the bantustan policy yet uses the nominally independent Transkei, and its government, as a sort of territorial/political base.

If diamonds and gold spurred the imperial factor in South Africa, ultimately bringing war and devastation on the Boers, they also had other crucially important effects. They set up the third great wave of white immigration, not just from Britain but from Europe, the Americas and Australia as well, as prospectors flocked to the diggings to establish roistering mining towns. And, for the first time, black South Africans went in great numbers to the towns for employment on the mines, setting up a pattern of migrant labour which persists to this day (encouraged in the past by government policy), as well as beginning today's urbanised black labour force as secondary industry developed.

The devastation of the Boer War was followed surprisingly soon by reconciliation (though a spirit of Afrikaner nationalism had been kindled and was to rapidly spread). A new British government, dismayed by the war, granted responsible government to the former Boer republics, now crown colonies, and very soon negotiations were under way for closer union. Yet the colonies which joined (Southern Rhodesia - now Zimbabwe - declined) were a disparate foursome. The Cape Colony had a colour-blind constitution where property and income qualifications in fact excluded the vast majority of blacks (tribal land is communal, not freehold). Natal had a theoretically colour-blind constitution where blacks could register as voters only with the permission of the governor; the sizeable Asian community (most of whom had arrived to work the sugar cane plantations) were excluded by constitutional sleight of hand. In the Transvaal and the Orange River Colony (soon to become the Orange Free State once again), matters were at least straightforward. The sturdy Boer dictum of "no equality in church or state" had been left undisturbed. The franchise arrangements of each colony were carried through into Union.

Many who participated in the National Convention which led to Union in 1910 expected a federation of some sort. Out-manoeuvred by the Transvaal delegation, they ended up with a quasi-federal compromise of central and provincial government, but with central authority unmistakably in control. This has had significant consequences. From the time the Afrikaner nationalists won political power in 1948, they have centralised decision-making and whittled away provincial democracy (which of course was available only to whites), a process which culminated in the abolition of provincial councils in 1986. It has had a profound effect on political life in South Africa. A culture of winner-takes-all has imbedded itself. There are no second prizes. Rule or be ruled. It is hardly surprising that the ANC tends toward a mirror-image of National Party attitudes of the past, envisaging only one locus of real power. Those in South Africa who espouse decentralisation and federal options find themselves fighting a rearguard action, encountering blank incomprehension on all sides. They are not assisted by the pseudo-federalism of the Nationalists' failed bantustan programme, which makes any argument for real federalism seem suspect.

Union saw battle joined between the "Cape liberals" and the rest. The blacks of the Cape lost their largely theoretical voting rights early on. After the Nationalists won power in 1948, Coloured men (their women had not been enfranchised along with white women) were first placed on a separate voters roll then lost their representation in parliament altogether. White "natives' representatives" disappeared from parliament. Two Land Acts, in 1913 and 1936, confined blacks to occupation of traditional tribal territory, prohibiting their purchase of freehold land outside, and provided for white-owned land to be purchased and added to the tribal holdings. This set up a configuration in which the minority whites own 87 percent of the land surface of South Africa. To be fair, a large proportion of that 87 percent consists of arid wastes which could not support a large population but the distribution remains patently out of proportion and unjust. The land issue is a focus of black anger and the emotional wellspring of the extremist Pan Africanist Congress (PAC). The abolition of the Land Acts is unlikely on its own to defuse the issue. The present government so far shows itself either unwilling, or politically unable, to make reparations to the dispossessed, and this is likely to be an emotional and bitterly contentious issue, whatever government rules in future.

From 1948 the Afrikaner Nationalists legislated into place the now notorious apparatus of apartheid, though the deeper issues were often obscured by furious controversy over such whites-only questions as joining two world wars on Britain's side or republicanism versus monarchy (which was settled when South Africa became a republic in 1961 and left the Commonwealth). However, apartheid operated at two levels - petty Jim Crow segregation and the Grand Scheme. The disfranchised coloured people elected councillors to a "Representative Council" with minimal powers; the never-franchised Asians had a corresponding "Indian Council". Both were prototypes of the coloured and Indian chambers in the present tricameral parliament. The tribal land allocated in the 1913 and 1936 Land Acts was to become the basis of a series of black statelets (many of them fragmented) which were to proceed to sovereign independence.

The ANC, which began as a conservative forum of chiefs and black urban professionals, radicalised but not sufficiently for an Africanist faction, which hived off to form the PAC. Protests and activism culminated in the Sharpeville shootings of 1960. Both the ANC and the PAC were banned and they went underground and into exile to launch an armed struggle. Internally, various groupings took over governing the black homelands. Four opted for independence, others - notably KwaZulu - refused it, frustrating the programme of grand apartheid. Yet at one stage the scheme appeared to be working reasonably well and South Africa enjoyed extraordinary prosperity behind the *cordon sanitaire* of its white-ruled northern neighbours, Rhodesia and the Portuguese territories of Mozambique and Angola. A radical coup in Portugal and precipitate decolonisation put an end to all that. Rhodesia fell and South Africa suddenly had a lengthy and problematic border to protect against guerilla incursions. Meanwhile, the giant black township of Soweto, outside Johannesburg, had erupted into youthful violence which soon spread countrywide and has not yet abated.

The response of P.W. Botha, a new prime minister and previously minister of defence, was twofold. The administration was militarised and cross-border strikes and destabilisation became the pattern. At the same time an attempt was made to draw the coloured and Asian communities into government in separate, and ultimately ineffectual, houses of parliament. The tricameral constitution had some startling effects. It split the ruling National Party. Apartheid purists hived off into the Conservative Party, which has gathered strength steadily among white voters and is now official opposition in parliament. And it galvanised black opposition. The United Democratic Front (UDF) formed in protest against the 1983 Constitution which for the first time, and irrevocably, excluded blacks from representation in parliament. Township unrest took on new dimensions while the UDF, a near-surrogate of the banned ANC, came into horrifyingly violent conflict with Inkatha, even though Inkatha also opposed the new constitution. Meanwhile, skills and capital left the country, investment dried up, sanctions were imposed and suffering intensified, in black communities especially.

This is the backdrop - in admittedly broad, generalising sweeps - to the position on February 2, 1990, when President F.W. de Klerk (who had replaced the ailing P.W. Botha in a palace revolution) rose to tell parliament the past 42 years of his party's rule were to be turned on their head with the unbanning of the ANC, the PAC and other organisations; early lifting of the state of emergency (since accomplished); negotiations with the ANC and others; and a dismantling of the legislative framework of apartheid so that a democratic dispensation could be ushered in. This has profoundly altered the political configuration, both parliamentary and extra-parliamentary, and introduced a new and powerful dynamic.

Within parliament, the parties of the House of Representatives and the House of Delegates (representing the coloured people and the Asians respectively) have been further marginalised. Elected on voter turn-outs so low as to be often farcical, they can for all practical purposes be ignored. The sturdiest among them, the coloured Labour Party, which had a long and distinguished record of opposing apartheid before it participated in the tricameral system - and has at times pressed its case vigorously from within the system - is likely, in a new, non-racial dispensation, to disappear and distribute its support between the National Party, the Democratic Party and the ANC.

In the white House of Assembly (where real power is located), there has been an acrimonious polarisation between the ruling National Party and the Conservative Party, which split away over the issue of the representation of coloured people and Asians in parliament at all - even in a subordinate capacity - and demands a return to the rigidities of Verwoerdian apartheid. The Democratic Party, bearer of the liberal tradition in South Africa and traditionally representative of the largely English-speaking business/professional classes, now occupies virtually the same political terrain as the Nationalists. By-elections have indicated substantial Democrat voter shifts to the Nationalists since President de Klerk came to power, compensating for a shift of traditional Nationalist support to the Conservative Party. It is very likely that the Nationalists and the Democrats will eventually combine in some form, though for the present they seem content not to oppose each other in by-elections, joining forces against the Conservatives. It was significant that in his early analysis of the 1989 general election, from which he claims a mandate, de Klerk lumped together the Nationalist and Democrat votes to achieve a total vote for reform, among whites, of some 70 percent. Since then he has appointed a Democrat frontbencher as ambassador to Washington, a departure previously undreamed of. The Democratic Party also has a faction in parliament which inclines toward the ANC, though white voter support for this inclination is uncertain and is not reflected in opinion surveys.

The Conservatives follow a strategy of mobilising white opposition to de Klerk's new directions and defeating him in a general election or a referendum on any new constitution negotiated. They are implacably opposed - officially at any rate - to participation in constitutional negotiations which do not have, as a non-negotiable bottom line, the right of the whites, Afrikaners specifically, to political self-determination within a partitioned off geographic territory. They reject negotiating with the ANC or the South African Communist Party. They maintain that de Klerk does not have a mandate as his intentions were not spelled out in the 1989 general election campaign.

Yet the Conservatives have a possibly fatal dilemma. Although they have made good electoral progress since breaking away from the Nationalists, and continue to make progress in by-elections, it appears to be not on a scale to defeat a combined Nationalist / Democrat vote (though continued political turbulence and violence, coupled with a declining economy, assists their cause). Also, it has become clear that de Klerk's objective is to have a new, non-racial constitution in place before he has to call another general election. In such an election the Conservative Party would command such a tiny fraction of the total vote that it would be swamped. What then are its options? To participate in negotiations and secure the best deal it is able for its constituency? To pin its hopes on derailing the reform process by winning a referendum against the Nationalists and the Democrats combined? Or to opt for "extra-parliamentary" action which, in the South African context and given relatively recent Afrikaner history, is a euphemism for rebellion?

The indications - hotly denied - are that a faction of the Conservative Party are edging toward considering joining negotiations, seeing no future in the other two options and possibly influenced by the orderly course of events in Namibia, where majority rule has been characterised by conciliation and reasonableness. They would no doubt be encouraged in this by all parties to negotiation, the ANC included, because a new dispensation which did not have the input of a significant and potentially militant sector of the white community could be inherently unstable. However, if such a grouping does exist it certainly does not include the Conservative Party leadership at this stage.

Bellicose yet ambivalent rumblings have come from the leadership about the consequences of de Klerk continuing on his present course. In South Africa they have to be taken seriously. In 1914 extreme Afrikaner nationalists went into armed rebellion in protest against entering the war on Britain's side and seeking to re-win their independence in alliance with the Germans of South-West Africa. During World War II their succeeding generation waged a campaign of serious sabotage against the war effort (again objecting to fighting on Britain's side) and established an armed fifth column so menacing that the government of the day had to keep a large portion of its armed forces in the country to guard against an uprising. Many figures who later reached prominence in public life were interned for their activities. If the issue of fighting on Britain's side in two world wars could rouse such passions, how much more so the prospect of the country perceivedly being handed to control by blacks and communists?

Yet there are serious constraints on the Conservative Party involving itself in anything so radical. One is the embourgeoisment of the Afrikaner population since World War II. The bourgeoisie are unlikely revolutionary material. Afrikaners have been drawn into the bureaucracy in vast numbers, a milieu where people tend to obey instructions. The pension could turn out mightier than the sword. And the Conservative Party is a sober, respectable parliamentary grouping, not a collection of hotheads. It is the spiritual descendant of the old National Party, which was in opposition when the country went to war in 1914 and 1939. However much it sympathised with the sentiments of the 1914 rebels and the Ossewa Brandwag (the underground fifth column) in 1939, the Nationalists would have no part of their activities and continued to operate as a parliamentary party. Nor is there any suggestion that the South African Defence Force, which is highly professional at senior officer level, would be sympathetic to rebellion. Although nothing in South Africa should be taken for granted, it does seem more likely that the Conservatives will vacillate between the options of joining negotiations and seeking to defeat the government in a constitutional referendum. Neither course appears particularly promising in terms of realising the Conservatives' fundamental objectives of partition and white self-rule, which makes the dilemma acute.

Outside parliament, de Klerk's actions have created political turmoil. Nelson Mandela has been released and lionised, locally and overseas, but the ANC has shown itself to be struggling with the transition from liberation movement to political party. Although it has undoubted mass support, surveys suggest this to be rather less than at first thought. In an election it might have difficulty defeating an opposing coalition. A membership drive has been disappointing. A welter of conflicting policy statements, the earlier ones couched in the language of an outmoded socialism, has caused confusion and scepticism. Continued sanctions are clearly hurting the black community yet, at time of writing, the ANC appeared unable to make up its mind whether to call for their lifting, giving the impression of being trapped in its own dogma. de Klerk is seen to be occupying the moral high ground and the ANC has to look on, no doubt with chagrin, as he is officially received in the very countries which have been its main sources of support. Violent conflict with

Inkatha has intensified (this will be analysed in depth in Chapter 8) in the Transvaal, taking on Zulu/Xhosa ethnic overtones. The ANC has proved no more effective than anybody else in halting it.

At time of writing, the ANC had yet to settle itself. Its support base varies from the activist township youth, the so-called Young Lions, to white university academics. At time of writing it had yet to emerge whether moderates or radicals would take control or what the future relationship with the Communist Party was likely to be. Ambivalences in the relationship with the trade unions have shown themselves. Much remains to be shaken out before the ANC is able to organise and project itself clearly. However, it is safe to say that in the present configuration the ANC represents the largest single constituency in the country and will be a major player in deciding the future dispensation and a major player in the new government that emerges, if not the dominant player.

Also outside parliament, Inkatha has staked its claim to a political territory whose extent is difficult to determine. Zulu-based, it is ideologically closer to the positions of the Nationalists and the Democrats than to the ANC, with a significant degree of overlap, suggesting that it could profitably enter an electoral alliance with them. Multi-party negotiations accord with what it has held out for all along. Yet there is fierce controversy over the real extent of Inkatha support. Some maintain it is a tribally-based puppet organisation which relies on patronage in the KwaZulu homeland to maintain the small support it does have. Opinion surveys give it a degree of support but well below 10 percent nationally. Inkatha figures protest that this in no way accords with what is clearly observable on the ground; that the survey methodologies are inadequate. Whatever the case, Inkatha does appear to have made ground lately. The ANC strategy of sidelining it has given way to grudging acceptance that it is a player; that without its participation, peace will not be restored to the townships. There have even been suggestions of the Nationalists, the ANC and Inkatha entering some form of interim troika arrangement. It seems likely that, whatever Inkatha's true numerical strength, its regional concentration in Natal/KwaZulu and its embodiment of the traditional Zulu ethos (anathema to non-traditionalists) will mean it continues as a significant player.

On the far left of the extra-parliamentary spectrum (though not as far left as the township nihilists) are the Pan Africanist Congress and the Azanian People's Organisation, with indeterminate though possibly fairly substantial support. Their ideological positions are very close, distinguished by the hair-breadth differences which assume such great significance among those of the left. AZAPO owes its inspiration to the Black Consciousness Movement of the 1970s, the PAC to the Africanist breakaway from the ANC in the 1950s over the involvement of communists and non-blacks in the nationalist movement. Fuelled by an irredentist demand for the return of the land to its original owners, the PAC has over the years developed a coherent, hardline Marxist ideology which it articulates in the most uncompromising terms. A PAC leader was able, for instance, to describe the Communist Party as "liberal quacks" who belong in the Democratic Party. The PAC never did have the international organisation or armed strength of the ANC, yet has survived as a factor. It has gained a foothold in several trade unions. Its hardline stance could well be a strategy to attract ANC radicals who are dismayed by the prospect of conciliation and negotiations, which makes it difficult to determine whether the PAC would, in the end, participate in multi-party negotiations.

A cluster of white extra-parliamentary organisations is to be found at the extreme right of the political spectrum. The now-miniscule Herstigte Nasionale Party (Reconstituted National Party) has lost the bulk of its once substantial support to the Conservatives yet still articulates ultra-orthodox Verwoerdism. To its right is the Afrikaner Weerstandsbeweging (Afrikaner Resistance Movement), a paramilitary organisation of unmistakable neo-Nazi tinge, which draws its support largely from small farmers and blue-collar workers. It is recruiting young men to its so-called Victory Commandos and threatens at emotional gatherings across the country that it will act to protect the Afrikaner Volk against betrayal. If any organisation poses the threat of a repeat of 1914 and 1939 it must surely be the AWB, yet it is difficult to distinguish real intent from bombast and the numbers of AWB enrolment are kept secret. It threatened to act to prevent the Namibian settlement, yet nothing happened. It appears to be riven by factions and the leadership is dogged by controversy. Still further to the right, various tiny splinter groups and cells have formed, some of them perpetrating violence of a sporadic, unco-ordinated nature. There have been horrific but isolated cases of mass murder of blacks by right-wing fanatics, some of them connected with the AWB, but apparently acting of their own accord. Yet whatever the real strength of the extreme right and the quality of its leadership, it has to be regarded as a potential threat which can disrupt the constitutional process. It looms ever larger with political unrest in the black community, worsening economic conditions and delays in achieving political settlement.

These, then, are the elements in South Africa's smoking crucible. Historical memories and outcomes combine with present-day realities. The mixture is inherently unstable and volatile. The above is conventional analysis. Chapters 6 and 7 will examine the crucible from within the Gravesian paradigm.

...all South Africans depend on an integrated economy which binds whites and blacks inextricably together. While ethnically segmented services of a country such as Lebanon can function under conditions of prolonged violence, South Africa demands stability because everyone in the country depends on a single, integrated economy.
Hermann Giliomee: "Rule By The Sword" (Leadership Magazine,1991)

The Place Called South Africa

If South Africa is to be likened to a crucible in which a new order is being fused, let us briefly examine the vessel itself, the physical characteristics and capacities of the country in which the changes are being wrought.

South Africa has a population of something like 36 million, of whom about five million are white and a few million Asian or of mixed blood. The rest are black, and about half these are younger than 18. A massive population bulge is bearing down on a society which already has an unemployment rate of something like 40 percent. Economists predict that if the growth rate continues at its present one percent, against a population increase of more than two percent, there will be eight million blacks unemployed by the year 2 000.

Society is diverse. Most whites, coloured people and Asians live in the urban areas, about half the blacks are rural. Eleven major languages are spoken and the rural blacks are mainly in a series of ethnic "homelands", four of which have taken a form of pseudo-independence not recognised by the international community and likely to be soon ended. Recent years have seen a massive migration to the cities from the rural areas. The newcomers have established vast, sprawling shack settlements where lack of sanitation and elementary health services, lack of schooling and crime have become critical issues. The authorities now speak of providing "shelter" rather than housing for these millions, so huge has the backlog become.

The Third World has in a very real sense spilled over into First World South Africa, yet it is only by sustaining and stimulating that First World sector that there can be any hope of providing the employment opportunities which can offer a reasonable lifestyle to the contents of the population bulge still bearing down.

South Africa's microcosmic quality is striking. As the British historian Paul Johnson has noted, in South Africa a small white minority, comparable with the societies of North America and Europe in terms of education, opportunity, affluence and values, exists side by side with a vast, disadvantaged black majority. And the ratio of the First World whites in South Africa to their Third World black fellow-countrymen is roughly that of First World North America and Europe to the Third World in total. The low birth rate of South Africa's whites is in much the same ratio to the higher birth rates of their black and Asian compatriots as are the ratios of North America/Europe to Africa and Asia. Income differentials appear to be correspondingly similar, according to Johnson, while, as in the world at large, it is the minority whites of South Africa who hold preponderant military and economic power.

The great difference is that whereas there is no credible demand for world democracy or a redistribution of wealth across the entire world, these are issues which South Africa has to address within its own borders over the next few years.

The critical question of the nineties is likely to be whether South Africa's developed First World sector will able to grow to the extent that it is able to provide employment plus expand its membership, taking in blacks and others at managerial, technocratic and entrepreneurial levels. Put another way: will the First World sector be allowed to grow. Continued sanctions are likely to blight the organic growth of the economy. Poor education prevents the development of a skilled and productive workforce. Educationists calculate that the state has the resources to educate all South Africa's children only through primary level. Secondary and tertiary education will have to be financed in future by the private sector. Can it be persuaded that this is in its own interests? And continued politically inspired violence is likely to deter the overseas investment capital without which the economy has no prospect at all of growth.

Yet, in spite of the current malaise, South Africa does have in place the infrastructure for growth. Its mining, manufacturing and agricultural sectors are of an order vastly different from anything else in sub-Saharan Africa. Freed from political constraints and stimulated, they could probably kick into life very quickly. Some analysts speak of a growth rate of 4.5 percent within three years, given a normalised society and normal access to overseas capital. That could turn around the malaise described above. Tourism is an undeveloped area of vast potential, given the country's great and varied natural beauty and its richness in wildlife.

South Africa has mines producing the bulk of the world's gold and diamonds, as well as a range of other metals and alloys - copper, iron ore, manganese, platinum, titanium, vanadium, uranium, chrome and antimony among them. The deep-level mining technology is the most advanced in the world. Secondary manufacturing industry has made a huge industrial complex of the Pretoria / Witwatersrand / Vereeniging region, on the Transvaal Highveld, while industry burgeons around the coastal cities as well. The economy is served by five major seaports, a rail infrastructure which has been largely in place since the 19th century and a sophisticated road network.

Electricity is supplied by one nuclear and a series of thermal plants (based on rich coalfields which also produce for export), operating in a grid which supplies the whole of Southern Africa, at times reaching as far as Zambia and Zaire.

Availability of water is a question which is critical to future industrial growth. It has been met by the building of strategically located dams, such as the giant Vaal Dam which serves the PWV industrial complex. However, the somewhat artificial location of the PWV complex (caused by the location of the gold-bearing reefs) means that water supply will always be a problem as population continues to pour in and new industries keep establishing themselves. The problem will be eased considerably when the massive Highlands hydro-electric scheme in Lesotho is completed, the water to be channelled to the PWV region.

South Africa's region best supplied with water, and very well suited to industrial development, has been inexplicably neglected for decades. This is the Tugela Basin, in Natal, a river system where detailed hydrological and other surveys have been conducted since the late 1940s, without ever having been put into effect. The Tugela Basin has the capacity to provide water and electricity for several large cities; it straddles the PWV/Durban economic and infrastructural axis and it adjoins the country's largest reservoirs of under-employed labour. The reason for its non-development probably lies somewhere between an influential school in the economics of hydrology, which argues for maximum centralisation of industrial activity, and a reluctance by Afrikaner nationalists to invest in a region inhabited by the Zulu people and English-speaking whites who did not support them politically. The Tugela Basin is a region which, if the political decision were taken to develop it and the funds could be raised internationally, would be a vast engineering project which would set up Southern Africa's second great industrial complex and would provide employment and wealth creation opportunities stretching far into the future.

However a price is paid for industrial development, in the form of pollution. This is reaching disturbing levels in the congested PWV region, while sulphurous pollution of the atmosphere from a battery of thermal electricity plants in the Eastern Transvaal ranks South Africa among the world's worst offenders. Much of South Africa's industrial development has a disturbingly Second World (or East European) appearance of lack of concern for the environment. A critical issue in future development will have to be a balancing of environmental concerns against the costs of "clean" industry in a society where the priority is job creation.

The country is largely self-sufficient in agriculture, with significant exports of sugar, fruit, wine, wool and, in times of surplus, grains. It leads sub-Saharan Africa in agricultural and veterinary science, the latter vital in a continent where livestock is the store of wealth of millions. However, soil erosion is an enormous problem which seriously threatens future productivity. It is especially bad in black rural areas where overcrowding and an almost complete lack of agricultural extension services have produced moonscape which in places will probably never recover. White farmers are far from blameless, yet successive governments have failed to initiate a proper and integrated programme of environmental conservation underpinned by legislation, nor even to properly enforce the legislation which does exist.

South Africa has the continent's most formidable defence force. It is large, highly professional and organised into a core permanent force and regionally based citizen units in a high state of training and readiness. As with economic capacity, South Africa's military strength is of an order different from its neighbours'. Although sanctions against military supply to South Africa have brought a degree of obsolescence to high technology branches such as the air force and the navy, the parastatal Armscor company has not only replaced overseas suppliers in lower-order weaponry, it has developed a range of armour and artillery which now finds export markets. With its nuclear technology in energy production, South Africa has the capacity - in principle at least - to produce atomic weapons. Until recently its political leaders cannily chose to keep the world guessing on this question, though it has now signed the non-proliferation treaty.

Units of the defence force have been involved in the past in commando-style cross-border destabilisation. The garrisoning of the Namibian/Angolan border was a drain on resources. But the defence force has never looked like being seriously extended in the conventional sense by its neighbours or by foreign surrogate forces. Internally it acts as an auxiliary to the police in the maintenance of law and order and, in the era of de Klerk, has come to be seen by wide sections of the community as a neutral stabilising force. Its intervention in strength to curb serious communal violence in black areas of Natal in 1990, for instance, had an immediate calming effect and the presence of the army has been welcomed by both sides in the conflict. Significantly enough, the extreme right has taken on a tone highly critical of the defence force, which it once supported without reservation and regarded as its own. Resignations from commando units - a system of rural militia - are frequent.

The defence force serves as a weighty stabiliser, ruling out revolutionary options launched from inside or outside the country, and making possible political and constitutional negotiation. A right-wing military coup to reverse the reform process is regarded as improbable. The senior officer corps is highly professional and there is nothing at all to suggest that it would disapprove politically of the government's present course. Also, the defence force's large citizen component means it is regionally spread and its members are likely to reflect a range of political values. There is no military monolith. Given a breakdown of law and order and administration - civil - war the defence force could, of course, be expected to intervene, and probably decisively. But while negotiations continue amid reasonable calm it is likely to remain very properly in the background. The defence force is really another aspect, corresponding to the economic, of South Africa's First World component and it further underlines the country's position as pre-eminent regional power.

South Africa trades with virtually every country in Africa, much of it through the back door and at some kind of cost. It is in a customs union with Botswana, Lesotho and Swaziland (who rely heavily on the shared revenues) and has a preferential trade agreement with Zimbabwe which (ironically, and with no apparent sense of the hypocritical) has been one of the most vociferous in demanding economic sanctions by the rest of the world. It seems likely to join the Southern Africa Development Co-ordination Conference (set up to develop the infrastructures of the other states of the region and reduce their reliance on South Africa's), as well as the Preferential Trade Area, which is comprised of various East and Central African countries. It has also signalled that it would like to join the Lome Convention, which allows the developing countries of Africa, the Caribbean and the Pacific preferential access to the markets of the European Community. However, whether South Africa's Third World component is sufficient for the country as a whole to be classified as "developing" is open to question.

South Africa is interlocked in many ways with its neighbour states. Hundreds of thousands of their citizens work in the country, mainly on the mines, remitting wages. South African railway trucks roll as far north as Zaire; Zambia at times ships copper through South African ports. Mozambique is connected as a supplier of hydro-electric power (though problematically, due to rebel sabotage) to the

South African energy grid. A massive hydro-electric scheme in Lesotho has already been mentioned. Political settlement in South Africa and a relaxation of regional tensions would, if accompanied by a surge in the South African economy, have beneficial effects reaching to the equatorial regions. South Africa's technology and managerial skills would once again become available; so would its veterinary and agricultural expertise in a continent of subsistence farmers who are stalked by famine. South Africa would also take a lead in re-establishing the health controls which have fallen into disuse. In fact, South Africa could be expected to play a dynamic developmental role in the entire region south of the equator, compensating for a waning North American and European interest in Africa. Dismayed and disillusioned by the corruption, brutality and bankruptcy which followed decolonisation, the developed nations of the West are also distracted by the needs of Eastern Europe and the Middle East.

However, whether South Africa will be able to play this dynamic role depends on the First World sector surviving and growing. If the crucible should fracture in the explosive heat, there would be no vessel in which to forge the alloy of the new South Africa; the contents would splash and dissipate chaotically, burning all who live in the sub-continent.

This is no fanciful notion. The First World component needs overseas investment if it is to grow and survive. Political turmoil and continued sanctions keep such funding away. And many of the individuals who make up the First World sector and drive it with their managerial, technological and entrepreneurial qualities happen also to possess the qualifications and skills which would make them welcome immigrants in most developed countries. Many actually hold dual nationality with Great Britain. Continued economic decline, continued turmoil, the threat of nationalisation of assets and punitive taxation - or a combination of these - could cause a flight of skills and capital from South Africa from which it would probably not recover. The vessel of the crucible, the First World economy, is weakened at great risk and with a high degree of irresponsibility.

An imponderable at present is the impact of the AIDS virus. This scourge of the continent has entered South Africa in strength and as a heterosexually transmitted disease. Several hundred thousand individuals are already carriers, mainly in black communities of low socio-economic status. Future years are likely to see the already over-stretched health services burdened beyond capacity and causing an increased drain on national resources. AIDS could alter the country's demographic ratios. It could also so deplete the workforce as to make economic recovery extremely difficult. It tends to occur precisely among those blue-collar workers of the black community who are achieving skilled and semi-skilled status in the workplace.

The South African economy is therefore fundamentally strong yet vulnerable. Continued economic sanctions, continued political turmoil, AIDS and the ever-possible flight of skills and capital threaten the durability of the very crucible within which a new society has to be wrought.

PART III

The Psychological Rosetta Stone

The terms First, Second and Third Worlds were coined by the non-aligned nations at a conference in Bandung in 1955. Calling themselves Third World, they designated socialist countries as Second and the free market milieu as First. While those categories continue to serve a useful purpose, we suggest there could be a need for a new way to describe emerging cultures in the decade leading up to the 21st century.

Unless First World societies are believed to be the final, ideal state, the question arises as to what the next stage should be called. On the current arbitrary basis of reduction in relation to complexity, would it be the Half World? The leaders in Bandung did not think ahead. Furthermore, if crucibles have the capacity to make something entirely new out of the old, South Africa could be destined to become something quite different from the First, Second or Third Worlds. Society will have to reconstitute itself from the mixtures of social chemistry which flow out of all South Africa, past, present and future.

Let us be realistic. The energy dissipation discussed in Chapter 1 could well cause this society instead to collapse into a condition such as that of Beirut. In such case the horrendous violence in parts of the country is simply a message from the future. Dissipative and disruptive forces could cause this already troubled country to regress into convoluted, burned-over wasteland. Parts of society would then down-shift to the First Level of human existence, the AN survivalistic state.

But the opportunity does exist for society to be reframed into a new and positive order. The New Paradigm will provide the instructions for producing that kind of environment. As the New Paradigm exists at the Seventh Level of human development, we will be considering a World to the Power of Seven, a system with insights and values so different from what has gone before in the First, Second and Third Worlds that it might as well be known as the "Seventh World", consistent with its position on the Seventh Level of thinking.

The only realistic common ground around which 90 percent of South Africans are able to rally is within the Law of the Spiral - the natural, evolutionary process that actually shapes society into its complexities. At some later stage a more complete version, the

Eighth World, will begin to form as the insights and problems solved and created within the Seventh Level (GT-Yellow) pattern come to be realised.

Graves was convinced, in his original work, that human societies evolve in sets of six, much like symphonic themes which repeat themselves an octave higher every time they appear. Level Seven, he believed, would start a new series of six. Graves wrote:

"Human existence can be likened to a symphony with six themes. In a symphony, the composer normally begins by stating his themes in the simplest possible manner. In human existence, our species begins by stating in the simplest way those themes which will preoccupy us through thousands of variations. At this point in history, the societally effective leading edge of man in the technologically advanced nations is currently finishing the initial statement of the sixth theme of existence and is beginning again with the first theme in an entirely new and more sophisticated variation."

Just as early man at the most primitive level of subsistence (AN), had to use what power he could command to stabilise his individual life functions, so GT (Yellow-Systemic-Seventh Level) man, the individual who has reached the first level of being, must use what knowledge he can to stabilise the essential functions of interdependent life.

The shift into the Seventh Level represents a quantum leap, not simply an incremental step from Level Six to Level Eight. Yet First, Second and Third Worlds, in the popular sense, function within the first set of six in the Gravesian symphonic theme. (Their proximity explains the fear of many that South Africa's delicate and fragile First World system is in danger of being overwhelmed in a sea of Third World problems and demands.)

Both South Africa and the larger macrocosm - the planet - are becoming so integrated and interwoven that it is unrealistic to think of a single linear flow from Third World to Second to First. Nick Green and Reg Lascaris, in *Third World Destiny*, acknowledge that "black" and "white" markets no longer exist as South Africans blur into a series of non-racial marketing bands. Yet they still designate this new social arrangement "Third World". The emotional and potentially biased question then becomes one of how to shift everybody into the First World. We maintain it is more realistic to seek what we have just termed the Seventh World, a dispensation where First, Second and Third are creatively managed in a synergistic and open-ended manner.

We are now in a position to see the first set of six levels of human existence as a single dynamic and interactive organism. The issues of race, haves and have-nots, competing ideologies and a history still fresh with insults, inequities and grudges cannot be resolved, as Einstein cautioned, at the same level at which they were forged. One attempts at one's peril to "solve" problems created within the first six levels by thinking on one of those levels.

The creative leap necessary to discover the pathway toward a new South Africa is possible only from the perspective of the Seventh Level in the Graves formula. This entire book is written from that perspective. South Africa is seen as a single organism. Through the holistic filter of this wide-angled lens, everything is discernible at once. The consequences of initiatives all along the psychological tapestry (Levels One to Six) can be assessed. The entire organism can be seen as a living entity as different systems interact on the developmental Spiral. Future chapters will locate all the major economic, political, religious and social models in South Africa on their evolving landscape. It then becomes clear that only the Seventh Level system of thinking has the complexity to manage the entire Spiral.

The New Paradigm therefore provides the thinking necessary for the next "world". It will not be the First World in the Eurocentric, capitalist, elitist, Westernised sense. Nor will it be the Third World in the Afrocentric, socialist, communalist sense. The Seventh World, in the dynamic, holistic, evolutionary and synergistic sense, will be the command and control centre within the World to the Power of Seven. In this Part of the book we will illustrate the power and precision which result from examining South Africa from this perspective.

In Chapter 6 we will translate the Graves Technology into a model of currents flowing across the sub-continent. These powerful streams have shaped virtually every facet of social life from the time *Homo sapiens* first appeared in the region. We will revisit the history of conflict recorded in Chapter 4, placing it within this analytical framework.

Chapter 7 will examine the deep structures (value systems) of the various political groupings along the entire spectrum of thought in South Africa. In a sense this will serve as a guide to the personalities, the parties and their likely positions in any serious process of negotiation or nation-building.

Chapters 8 and 9 will address two of the most difficult and complex issues which plague South Africa. Chapter 8 will reframe the question of political violence and point toward practical solutions. Chapter 9 will examine the highly contentious and volatile issues of

VALUE SYSTEMS MOSAICS

	AN	BO	CP	DQ	ER	FS	GT	HU
	Survival Sence	Kin Spirit	Power Gods	Truth Force	Strive Drive	Human Bond	Flex FLow	Global View

South Africa

United States

Europe

Sub-Sahara Africa

SOUTH AFRICAN MANAGERIAL AND ORGANISATIONAL MAP

GT	Integrated Structures	Systemic Thinking Value Management Training The Graves Technology Systems Thinking
FS	Circles of Equals	Sensitivity Training Corporate Cultures "Z" Orientations Quality Circles Wellness Programes
ER	Enterprises	Achievement Motivation Management By Objectives NLP Training Maintenance & Motivational Factors "X" & "Y" Orientations Strategic Planning Situational Management Managerial Grid
DQ	Hierarchies	Plan, Control and Do Training Moral Education - Boy Scouts Systematic Thinking Behaviourism - Negative Awards Seniority-Based Systems
CP	Empires	Behaviourism - Positive Award Tough Love Positive Discipline Authoritarian - Colonial Management
BO	Tribal Orders	Oral Traditions
AN	Bands	See and Do

race and ethnicity, demonstrating why these are confounding to so many, both in South Africa and in the world at large. We will discover in Chapter 8 that violence cannot be resolved only by addressing violence. We will note in Chapter 9 that issues concerning race are really not about race at all.

CHAPTER 6

Currents of Conflict and Change

Major ocean currents meet off the coasts of South Africa. The warm Mozambique and Eastern Madagascar currents sweep southward down the East Coast from the Indian Ocean to form the giant oceanic river of the Agulhas current, which interacts with cold water swells from the Roaring Forties to create vast gyres, eddies and counter-currents and seas as turbulent as anywhere in the world. The cold water Benguela Current drives up the West Coast.

Correspondingly powerful human currents have cut deep into South Africa's political and social topography. They spring from the mind of *Homo sapiens*, who has inhabited this part of the world since the earliest times. The descendants of earlier *Homo sapiens* today wrestle with the legacies of those currents which now flow with increased velocity through the narrowing gorges of new conditions, new values, new paradigms. The turbulence is often comparable with that of the physical currents offshore.

The Currents:

Colour Code	Popular Name	Current
AN-Beige	Survival Sense	Reactive current of subsistence and survival
BO-Purple	Kin Spirits	Animistic current of safety and security
CP-Red	Power Gods	Exploitative current of power and action
DQ-Blue	Truth Force	Moralistic current of stability and justice
ER-Orange	Strive Drive	Strategic current of materialism and success
FS-Green	Human Bond	Humanistic current of equality and community
GT-Yellow	Flex Flow	Naturalistic current of knowledge and change
HU-Turquoise	Global View	Living systems current of order and renewal

Before we begin this analysis of South African psychological history, we need to review two critical aspects of the nature of these systems. First, each system arises in response to a highly complex set of circumstances. Peter A. Corning is a pioneer of applying biological perspectives to the social sciences. In *The Synergism Hypothesis* he concludes:

"In sum, the evidence is overwhelming that the dynamics of social life are the product of a complex interplay between nature and nurture, internal and external variables, micro-leve genetic and organismic phenomena and macro-level cultural historical, ecological and even geophysical phenomena."

The migration of Bantu cultures to the south, the appearance of Europeans at the Cape in 1652, the expansionism of Shaka's conquests and the Boer treks, the rush to the diamond and goldfields, the yeasty emergence of Afrikaner nationalism and the contemporary rise of economic and political activity among the African populations are all products of this complexity. No single factor caused these movements or events to explode on to the scene. Always there are multiple causes.

Secondly, each system has to be evaluated within its unique context. It should not be compared with other systems in isolation from that context. There is, without question, a hierarchy of complexity within nature - and in the evolution of societies. Jonas Salk, discoverer of the vaccine which bears his name, put it this way:

"As a process, evolution seems to be nature's way of finding means for extending the persistence of life on earth. This involves the elaboration of increasingly complex mechanisms for problem-solving and adaptation. The ability of the human mind to solve the problem of survival is part of this process."

This does not imply a hierarchy of personal value, intelligence, temperament or quality of the human experience. It is possible to be bright or dull, pleasant or boorish, open or closed, dedicated or irresponsible all along the psychological landscape. Each value system, as we noted in Chapter 2, can be expressed in positive and negative terms. When it contributes to the life of the Spiral as a whole, it is healthy. When it disrupts that process, selfishly absorbs energy or introduces venom to the Spiral's bloodstream, it becomes a menace.

Psychological Views of South Africa

When Napoleon's armies discovered the Rosetta Stone in 1799, they made possible the unlocking of the mystery contained in Egyptian hieroglyphics. This in turn opened up the world of Ancient Egypt to modern inquirers. The stone (which can be viewed in the British Museum today) had the same message in two languages and three alphabets, two of which the scholars already understood. The discovery broke the hidden code of hieroglyphics and allowed us to explore that ancient world in a profound and realistic manner.

We maintain that the Graves technology is such a Rosetta Stone. Its living systems framework allows us to observe and evaluate human relationships, key decision points, the emergence and significance of ethnicity and culture and large-scale societal change in a different and provocative light. Worthwhile recent publications such as *The Mind of South Africa* (Allister Sparks), South Africa In Search of a Soul (Graham Saayman) and *White Tribe Dreaming* (Marq de Villiers) are designed to probe the psyche of South Africa. We suggest that these and other analyses be read with the Psychological Map of South Africa alongside so that their observations and findings may be assessed and interpreted from the viewpoint of this fourth generation evolutionary model. It should be a rewarding exercise, though some individuals are prevented by their personal value system profiles from understanding the whole Spiral.

South Africa's Psychological History

For purposes of simplicity and clarity, we use this linear version of the complex Double Helix model to chart the key historical trends and developments in South Africa.
The issues are obviously far more complicated and involved than we will be able to portray in this chapter. The Graves technology in fact describes 27 levels, not eight. Each system can be expressed in an open, closed and arrested format. And since these are types in - and not types of - people, a given person or grouping will possess a number of systems simultaneously. Our intention is to identify the critical mass of the various South African sub-cultures as they move along this evolutionary trajectory.

Phase I: European Exploration of Africa

When Europeans arrived at the Cape in 1652, they brought with them a psychological package that would enable them to survive and prosper. Subsequent waves of immigration strengthened this brain syndicate substantially, thus setting the stage for the processes described in Chapter 4. They encountered populations who were functioning mainly within the AN and BO currents but with clear signs of the CP and DQ systems emerging. The expressions of these AN and BO systems were quite complex, healthy and tailored for the environment. Beware of such misleading terms as "primitive" and "savage". Note also the difficulty egalitarian thinking (FS) has in seeing these historical vertical differences.

See Plate III, Colour Section.

EVOLUTION OF AFRIKANER THOUGHT

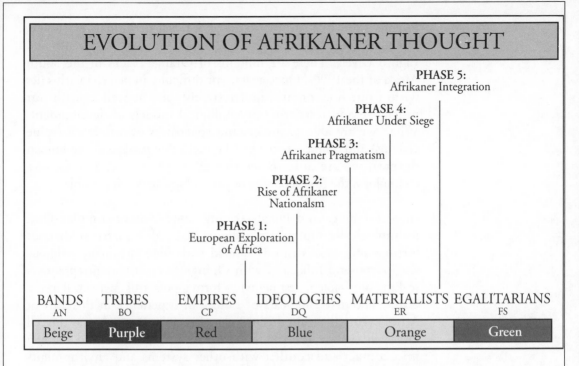

					PHASE 5: Afrikaner Integration
				PHASE 4: Afrikaner Under Siege	
			PHASE 3: Afrikaner Pragmatism		
		PHASE 2: Rise of Afrikaner Nationalsm			
	PHASE 1: European Exploration of Africa				
BANDS	TRIBES	EMPIRES	IDEOLOGIES	MATERIALISTS	EGALITARIANS
AN	BO	CP	DQ	ER	FS
Beige	Purple	Red	Blue	Orange	Green

For a perspective of what we are suggesting, note the careful and sensitive language of Dudley Kidd, a missionary who spent several decades living with what he called "natives". He wrote *The Essential Kafir* in 1904 (at a time when the word "kafir" was not considered pejorative or insulting).

"The whole mental furniture of a Kafir's mind differs from that of a European. His outlook upon life is different; his conception of nature is cast in another mould. It is quite common for Europeans to think that they can soon sound the depths of a Kafir's mind; but maturer experience always reveals the shallowness, not of the Kafir's but our first and hasty impressions. There are depths beneath the shallows of a native's thought. The most incompatible things seem to be able to dwell together in harmony and peace in the muddy and turbid stream of his thoughts. He is a complete stranger to western conceptions of clear thinking, and is as ignorant of logic as he is of the moons of Jupiter. His conceptions of cause and effect are hopelessly at sea, and, as all primitive religions are based on such conceptions, his religion is a confused mass of ancestorship coupled with dread of magic. He cannot distinguish between coincidence and causation; he will argue that because he had a headache yesterday and a cow did something unusual, therefore the headache was caused by the weird action of the cow. One of the commonest generalisations made by hasty observers is that the natives are but overgrown children. There is, of course, some truth in the statement - just sufficient to make it very untrue."

What is being described here is neither "black" nor "African" but

Purple - the BO-Animistic Second Level of human existence. Obviously today there are Africans functioning at the Seventh and Eighth Levels. There are millions of Orange-blacks in the South Africa of the 1990s. Once again, our difficulty in perceiving this lies within our horizontal, bipolar stereotypes, as well as with our restrictive and restricting psychological models of development. When we are able to understand spectrums of difference (value systems) and Spirals of change (the inevitable passage of the human drama), we are able to see things more clearly. The Graves technology, the Rosetta Stone of psychology, makes it possible.

Into this Beige and Purple setting came a more complex (and technologically superior) paradigm. Red (adventurers, soldiers of fortune and social cast-offs) joined with Blue (staunchly religious and purposeful folk) and with Orange (mercantile entrepreneurs seeking profitable investments) to form a powerful energy cell at the Cape. The first 200 years of European experience in this part of Africa occurred within this turbulent crucible. Not only was the cell internally chaotic, it began to expand toward the hinterland, coming into contact and conflict with other systems and environments which were both attractive and hostile.

At the height of the Anglo-Boer War, A. Conan Doyle, creator of Sherlock Holmes, captured the qualities of this crucible in *The Great Boer War* (written in 1900):

"Take a community of Dutchmen of the type who defended themselves for fifty years against all the power of Spain at a time when Spain was the greatest power in the world. Intermix them with a strain of those inflexible French Huguenots who gave up home and fortune and left their country forever at the time of the revocation of the Edict of Nantes. The product must obviously be one of the most rugged, virile, unconquerable races ever seen on earth. Take this formidable people and train them for seven generations in constant warfare against savage men and ferocious beasts, in circumstances under which no weakling could survive, place them so that they acquire exceptional skill with weapons and with horsemanship, give them a country which is eminently suited to the tactics of the huntsman, the marksman and the rider. Then, finally, put a finer temper upon their military qualities by a dour, fatalistic Old Testament religion and an ardent and consuming patriotism. Combine all these qualities and all these impulses in one individual, and you have the modern Boer - the most formidable antagonist who ever crossed the path of Imperial Britain. Our military history has largely consisted in our conflicts with France, but Napoleon and all his veterans have never treated us so roughly as these hard-bitten farmers with their ancient theology and their inconveniently modern rifles."

Once again, if we replace Doyle's descriptive phrases with the language of our Rosetta Stone, the critical mass of Afrikaner thinking in 1900 existed within the Red-CP to Blue-DQ range. The immigrants brought with them the technological advances of the ER-Materialistic wave which was beginning to flourish in Europe. Sparks (*The Mind of South Africa*) offers a vivid description of the cultural alloys, with their historical antecedents, that formed this emergent power cluster. He searches for the reason this system developed in this part of the world in the minds of people of this type. We believe the answer is to be found in contemporary knowledge about the human brain, multiple intelligences and the way in which value systems form within the neurological architecture.

At the same time the BO-Purple populations were responding to these and other perturbations by shifting into Red-Empires with elements on the horizon of thinking in terms of nationhood. With the exception of Shaka with his rampaging impis in the remote north-east, European firepower and discipline consistently blocked this natural development. The Shaka Zulus of this world do cause major change. As George Bernard Shaw wrote in *Man And Superman*: "The reasonable man adapts himself to the world: the unreasonable one persists in trying to adapt the world to himself. Therefore all progress depends on the unreasonable man." Shaka moulded a cohesive military empire whose echoes are heard to this day.

By the turn of the 19th century, however, the might and technology of European-oriented structures had dominated the indigenous groupings. The more complex system had the strength to constantly thwart any attempt on the part of the African population to move to greater sophistication. Thus a ceiling was created by the more advanced and aggressive European-based system. Of course, African kingdoms and empires had a similar effect on weaker tribes. And constant feuds between Afrikaner and English cycled through various issues in succeeding generations. The Boers found themselves constantly frustrated by English imperialism, materialism and arrogance; the English by the Boers' stubborn refusal to accept the ethos of empire and the benefits of the Pax Britannica.

Phase II: The Rise of Afrikaner Nationalism

By 1948 the necessary elements were in position for the emergence of a powerful and pervasive edifice of Afrikaner-based thinking. A powerful religious ideology combined with worldly interests to create a Colossus-on-the-veld. Afrikaners had a common language and religion, the common holocaust of the Anglo-Boer War and a common vision of the future. One discovers in Afrikaner nationalism underpinnings identical to modern Israeli culture and in any other nationalism where an inner core of "chosen people" perceive themselves to be under pressure and attack.

The Afrikaner nationalist electoral victory of 1948 meant displacement of the until then dominant Blue-Orange British-centred paradigm. The Third Level-Red British colonial adventurer had been subsumed in the Fourth Level-Blue of imperial mission and discipline. As the British (in partnership with a substantial number of non-nationalist Afrikaners) constructed the framework of South Africa's economy and infrastructure, Fifth-Level Orange emerged - material abundance and confident entrepreurialism. Sixth Level-Green egalitarianism had shown itself briefly in the liberal constitution of the Cape Colony, but was eclipsed during the 1930s. Blue-Orange was a powerful paradigm. The power of the Blue ideology of empire and commonwealth is illustrated by the fact that in 1939 Smuts (one of the great Afrikaner leaders of the Anglo-Boer War) was able to argue honour and duty to the British Commonwealth in persuading parliament to vote for war with Germany.

The Afrikaner-centred paradigm which displaced the British came in Blue-Red - ideology and struggle - but by the apogee of Afrikaner nationalism in the 1970s had become Blue-Orange. Ideology remained but Fifth Level pragmatism, and materialism had displaced the element of struggle. By the mid-1970s Afrikaners were thinking in much the same paradigm as the British-centred United Party had been in 1948, though the content of the ideological Blue thinking - nationalism as against commonwealth - was entirely different.

Neither paradigm provided in any meaningful way for accommodation of the country's black majority (apart from the brief flickering of Green in the non-racial Cape franchise). South Africa was to be a white man's country. The argument was over which white men should rule. Yet present-day commentators ought not to be over-judgmental about this. The British colonials and the Afrikaner nationalists inhabited systems of thought in which they were simply not equipped, in terms of political, social and psychological insights, to behave otherwise.

From 1948 Afrikaner political leaders found themselves under constant pressure from their "Third World" rural constituencies who demanded access to "First World" urban opportunities. Afrikaner academics and political thinkers, caught in the zeal of this meaningful movement, searched Europe for models to preserve its purity and integrity. The solution was grand apartheid, which was appealing on paper, felt good in spirit and was to be financed by extracting wealth from English business interests who would forever be a minority in the new country. The impact on the indigenous populations was barely considered. When Afrikaner political thought eventually did progress to considering such questions, it was presumed that a corresponding spirit of separatist nationalism would take hold in the bantustans and Afrikaner culture would be preserved in perpetuity.

This huge energy cell absorbed everything in its path in producing the Afrikaner monolith. In terms of our analysis it was Fourth Level DQ-Blue - truth, ideology and authoritarianism. (And it is interesting that, in its authoritarian characteristics, the monolith approximated closer to what is today described as "Second World" than the "First World" the poor rural Afrikaners set out to seek. Such is the course of any shift from "Third World" conditions). The Afrikaner nation was - and to an extent still is - separate and self-contained. Its banners, symbols, music, traditions, holidays and patriotic displays are for the Volk. Others participated only by invitation (and only if they were interested). As recently as 1980, Afrikaner South Africa had a flavour of America of the 1950s, where sovereignty, Old Glory, the Fourth of July and the anthem were potent and unquestioned symbols.

Every African political development which arose naturally in response to this scheme of apartheid appeared instantly on the Volk's radar screen and was targeted for attack. The ANC appeared in 1912 as an early expression of non-tribal, pan-Africanist Fourth Level Blue-DQ development. Though it was benign, non-threatening and natural in its evolution, its further growth within a common structure could not be tolerated by the Afrikaner monolith because it had the capacity to cause cracks which would ultimately bring down the structure. African nationalism activated the anti-bodies of Afrikaner nationalism - and still does.

Phase III: Afrikaner Pragmatism

Success in meeting the needs of people clustered about the Blue-DQ system (stability, hope for a better future, purpose in life) of necessity sparked a shift out of the rigidity of Fourth Level thinking with its racial and absolutist categories. This was to launch in Afrikaner business and certain political circles, within academic settings, and even among Afrikaners in general, a quest for affluence and materialism within the next level, the Fifth-ER-Orange, a pragmatic, materialistic and status-driven system. Afrikaner ideology came face - to face - with Western science and technology and global markets. Television brought images of the good life and material abundance. (And not without reason did a cabinet minister, who went on to found the extreme Herstigte Nasionale Party, dig in his heels for years against the introduction of television). The growth of Afrikaner middle class communities on the Witwatersrand and elsewhere testified to the growing economic and technological capacities of the Volk. No longer were they poor, peasant class Europeans with the ox wagon as their heritage and symbol. They drove the latest limousines and took pride in walking tall in the world community.

The world's response to events inside South Africa began to make a difference to Pretoria. The Sharpeville and later massacres were a stain on the national reputation which embarrassed businessmen and diplomats who had dealings in the world's capitals. International opinion had an impact on the availability of global markets for South Africa's raw materials.

The infusion of Orange thinking into Afrikanerdom forced a re-assessment of the black population in several ways. The growing industrial base required a thinking working class, hitherto stultified by a system of deliberately inferior black education which had been introduced by Verwoerd. Blacks represented a huge mass market to add to the cumulative wealth of the larger society, and it was in society's interest to increase their wealth and earnings. It made sense to develop a black middle class who would discover contentment among their own kind, especially if they were able to afford the creature comforts of relative urban affluence. The Wiehahn Commission recommendations of 1979 gave expression to this new pragmatism. Black labourers were to be perceived in an entirely new way. They were to be allowed to unionise and, in conjunction with the accompanying recommendations of the Riekert Commission, their permanence in the urban areas was recognised. No longer would they be temporary sojourners or foreigners. The die was cast and the surge into Orange thinking by the governing Afrikaner elite was to forever change the face of Southern Africa.

Phase IV: Afrikaners Under Siege

By the 1980s the Colossus-on-the-veld was under serious attack, both internationally and from within South Africa's borders. The shift into the Fifth Level system was not just by the ruling Afrikaners: leadership was awakened among black communities also, many of whom had fled the country after Sharpeville and the banning and suppression of the ANC and the PAC. As expectations were raised in the townships surrounding the industrial and financial centres, it would no longer be possible to keep their inhabitants content with their lot. The stage was set for a major migration of African thinking out of the Purple and Red systems, and benign versions of Blue, into the full array of Orange needs and aspirations. Once again, the South African crucible was at work.

Equally significant was the growing pressure from western countries, the United Nations, the independent Afro-Asian countries and other societies which could not tolerate the injustice inherent in institutionalised racial discrimination. Many of the reservations and unhappinesses about the apartheid system had a long history, but two major value system changes transformed the anti-apartheid movement into a mighty wave.

Much western thought began to abandon the materialism of the Fifth Level system of values, to embrace the Sixth Level. From this Green perspective, all are equal; racial or ethnic differences are anathema. A powerful Green movement began to flow through the American churches and made an impact on political values in Washington. As whites in America began to experience egalitarian Green thinking, they became aware, many for the first time, of attitudinal and institutional racism at home and even in their own neighbourhoods. This set the stage for the Civil Rights Movement and the highly effective social activism of Martin Luther King Jnr. Yet the Civil Rights Movement, so pervasive today, would not have been possible in the America of the 1940s and 1950s before the Green current emerged. In Europe, the current was equally powerful, emerging as it did in the aftermath of the racially-based perversions of Nazism. The wave of world opinion crashed against the Afrikaner monolith, while the citadel was awash on the inside as well from identical currents of Green thinking within certain churches and political parties, as well as a spectrum of educators and opinion leaders.

The second major value system change was in America, where certain black leaders entered the Orange current, with access to the media, growing affluence and greater political sophistication. The search was on for high visibility issues to serve the internal political cause, and the plight of black South Africans provided such an issue. The anti-apartheid campaign in America is in many respects an expression of the Orange system, South Africa providing an issue of opportunity. The way Nelson Mandela's tour of the United States was managed by local political interests to their own advantage, and with little obvious lasting benefit to the ANC, illustrates the degree to which the black American political leadership rides the Orange current.

The fusion of egalitarian Green with opportunistic Orange currents caused an international high tide of pressure, with economic, political, cultural and academic isolation of the "white, minority, racist apartheid regime." The Afrikaner dream of a safe and secure future behind the political monolith had become a nightmare.

When F.W. de Klerk spoke to the world from the South African parliament on February 2, 1990, for all practical purposes he announced the demise of racially based political and social structures and signalled the approach of a value systems-based society. He sounded the death knell of the Colossus-on-the-veld, which had inspired Afrikaners since 1948, simultaneously ringing in what has been termed the New South Africa. In 1838 the Afrikaners set off on the Great Trek to the hinterland. Today they - and all South Africans with them - have been inspanned for another Trek. Obviously it cannot be a physical migration this time (though many skilled and valuable individuals have departed South Africa's shores, to its great loss): it will have to be a Trek of the mind. de Klerk, and those about him, have departed the Blue psychological level of authoritarianism and ideological certitude; they have departed the Orange level of opportunistic gamesmanship and material advantage. Where then do they find themselves?

It seems likely some have entered what Graves termed the GT-Yellow level of integrated thinking, a higher order of complexity which has the capacity to manage the entire evolutionary Spiral, creatively drawing together every level which exists in South Africa, extracting from them their positive contribution to the whole, controlling the negative. If that is so, they have begun thinking in terms of what we have called the New Paradigm - and, quite obviously, the Afrikaners will not succeed on their own. They will need the contribution of all major players.

The intention of this chapter has been to sketch, without detail, how the first six levels of the Spiral interact on one another and on the Spiral as a whole. Movement at one level, either forward or backward, impacts profoundly on the other levels. The management of South Africa (ultimately of the planet, for that matter) will require the capacity and insight to manage the entire Spiral. Isolated, piecemeal, fragmented approaches simply will not work. To return to the analogy of the elephant, one has to be able to see and act on behalf of the entire beast, at the same time communicating to those who experience only one part of it why their concerns are real for that part only. They have to be persuaded that their very existence depends on the health and well-being of the entire animal.

In the remainder of this book we will suggest how the South African Spiral might be managed. The New Paradigm will be our vantage point, the Seventh Level observational and problem-solving system which oversees the six preceding value systems which continue to splutter and explode in the crucible.

Political Spectrums and Psychological Spirals

Draw a sketch of the South African negotiating table. It can be any shape. Which individuals and political entities will be seated there? What positions will they take on the critical issues? Who will say what about the economy, the future political order, the distribution of resources, the quality of life, national holidays and symbols, the management of communities, the education system? These are only some of the questions.

How will decisions be made? By majority vote? By the give and take of political gamesmanship? By political horse-trading? By some form of mystical consensus? By Divine guidance? By threat and intimidation? These are matters of great concern to South Africans - also to a great part of the rest of the planet, which does not have to live with the outcome and has not been spectacularly successful in resolving similar problems of a lower order in its own domains.

The Political Spectrum

Chapter 4 concluded with a brief analysis of various positions on the South African spectrum. Let us assume this particular version will still be operative whenever negotiation actually begins. We intend placing the various groups about the table even though some, at time of writing, deny any intention of participating. Since they are a part of the South African equation, for our purposes they have to be involved. It is important that they do so because they provide the necessary counter-balance to the process. We position these entities along the traditional "left-wing" and "right-wing" continuum merely to set the stage. Then we illustrate what happens to them when they interact.

See Plate IV, Colour Section.

Let us assume this represents an accurate, objective and non-partisan placement of the various positions. Because of their levels of ego-involvement, the parties on this spectrum probably would not construct the continuum in the same manner. They would be subject to a perceptual distortion process known as the "assimilation and contrast effect".

By "assimilation" we mean that entities tend to deny the differences between their own and other positions, attempting to pull or displace other views toward their own anchor. Coalitions or common fronts form in an attempt to increase bargaining power, yet these are often entirely artificial and opportunistic and can make for very strange bedfellows.

Clusters do tend to form naturally in the centralist positions and often on the wings as well. Yet they tend to be tentative and fragile. Readers will recall the difficulty with which the Democratic Party was able, in 1989, to "assimilate" three different spheres of interest - Wynand Malan and the National Democratic Movement; Dr Denis Worrall and the Independent Party; and Dr Zach de Beer and his long-established Progressive Federal Party. They will recall the frustrations of the political Right in attempts to achieve an electoral alliance of the Conservative Party, the Herstigte Nasionale Party and the more radical Afrikaner Weerstandsbeweging. The anticipated black unity has not developed either. Yet should it be surprising that blacks are subject to the same differentialist tendencies as whites? Black society produces its own Eugene Terre'blanches and white society its own Nelson Mandelas. There are black as well as white versions of the so-called Third Force.

By "contrast" we mean a process by which entities enlarge or exaggerate the differences between their own ideal position and all the other possible positions within the universe of discourse. This is not to infer dishonesty or deviousness, it is simply part of the natural phenomenon of social judgment. People in "our" group are decent, upstanding and responsible - all of them. People in "their" group are evil, have been duped or pursue self-enrichment.

This contrast effect skews political judgment. A person views all positions and stances from the perspective of his own, which serves as an anchor or viewing point. The extreme positions on the left and right wings see moderates on their respective wings to be further skewed toward the opposing side than they actually are. The champions of a Boerestaat see F.W. de Klerk as belonging in the same camp as the ANC. To those of the radical Left persuasion, Buthelezi is simply a spokesman or stooge of the white racist regime.

Furthermore, each extreme end-position tends to see the opposite extreme end-position as the true articulator of that entire wing. Moderation therefore becomes a myth or a smokescreen to hide the true motives of the opponent. The other wing has designed a conspiracy to destroy "us". It is only the more radical voices from that wing that tell the truth about it. This sets up a foil and counter-foil relationship, an extremist "dance" between the proponents of the two end-positions. Since each desperately needs the other, they may even create the illusion that the other exists in order to prove to their constituencies how dangerous and threatening the other side is to their interests. They may even reach the point of believing that elements on their own wing - the "moderates" - are part of the conspiracy. It becomes all or nothing - you are either 100 percent for "us" or 100 percent against.

Those who operate in the mid-range are subject to very similar distortions. They tend to lose patience and perspective regarding the shades of difference among the positions on the wings and to place them all around the more radical positions. They often play to the strength of these extreme positions, forcing them into a defensive posture and generating publicity for them beyond what they could achieve on their own.

When extreme polarisation occurs, the mid-positions virtually disappear (qualitative shift) and population support (quantitative stacking) skews out toward the two end poles. Note the tendency, during protracted negotiations, for politicians of the mid-range to attempt to counter this tendency by mobilising along racial, ethnic and ideological lines. There is no guarantee in any conflict as explosive as South Africa's that the mid-range will find enough common ground to maintain preponderant popular support. If the polarisation should deepen, and both sides resorted to justifying their rationale by higher powers and principles - and blood were shed - the dispute could then enter an irreconcilable stage. At this point we may expect holy wars with all their fury, cruelty and lack of reason.

What is it that really differentiates the personalities, and their supporters, all the way along the spectrum? Why do those of the more radical persuasions think in the same patterns, whether they are of the Left or of the Right? And when a radical voice changes - why does it so often skip across the entire continuum to identify with the opposite radical position? Why do the so-called moderates speak in such similar tones and display such similarities in mien - even down to style in dress - whether they are labelled "liberal" or "conservative"? Why are mid-rangers so similar, even though they have different visions of the future in South Africa and serve very different constituencies? Do we have here the makings of the melting pot, or are these often unique entities destined to preserve something of their identity in a greater whole? We believe the preliminary answers to these riddles may be found by reference to what we have described as the psychological Rosetta Stone.

The Evolutionary Spiral: the only Common Ground

Suppose we had the X-ray vision to look beneath the rhetoric, the posturing, the gamesmanship and the concealment of real intent to gain temporary advantage; suppose we were able to peer into the real depths of the various advocates. What should we see? What would be the true "bottom line" in each case?

See Plate V, Colour Section.

Before we analyse the various political and psychological positions, it would be useful to define terms. By First World we mean: a Puritan, Confucian, Muslim, black nationalist or other form of work ethic; a capacity to engage in scientific, analytical thinking; a skill at visionary, strategic projection; a strong commitment to progress and improvement; and the capacity to think pragmatically about issues. The political framework of First Worldism is, of necessity, multi-party pluralism - a system which has not yet properly developed in South Africa or elsewhere in the continent. Afrikaner nationalism has for the most part expressed itself, over the past four decades, in a *de facto* one-party state.

In the Second World one discovers a commitment to a more structured, authoritarian system with fairly tight and inflexible rules and regulations; a robust nationalist and patriotic fervour; restrictions on deviant, alternative viewpoints; and a more straitlaced lifestyle. Examples are Cuba and other socialist-inclined societies. In the language of Graves, "the pathway between tribalism and democracy has always gone through autocracy."

In the Third World one encounters far less of First World characteristics and rather less of Second World. It has a character of its own. Clock time is less important than personal relationships. Strong people (chieftains, warlords, Mafia chiefs, god-kings, ecclesiastical potentates, neighbourhood gang leaders) dominate. Mysticism and superstition are rampant. Money changes hands in an informal manner. Battles for political or economic territory are frequent. The music is frequently louder and more strident, major events tend to occur in the streets and a lack of attention to detail or scheduled maintenance is apparent.

For a definition of the Fourth World, simply imagine Ethiopia in the worst days of famine.

While these are the outward manifestations of the stereotypes, they actually exist in the minds of people and in the collective intelligences of communities, not in material possessions or physical structures. First World, then, is a way of thinking. First World thinkers may be placed in an under-developed milieu and they will find ways to alter conditions in the direction of First World standards. Place Third World thinkers in a First World milieu and conditions will soon enough approximate the Third World. However, we suggest that it should be possible to get all these elements working together to create not the First, Second or Third Worlds but what we have termed the Seventh World - the World to the Power of Seven, directed by Seventh Level thinking with the capacity to creatively manage the entire evolutionary Spiral, and to the benefit of all.

We have already defined and illustrated the differences between and among the six value systems within our Spiral. At this point it is necessary to briefly illustrate how each makes decisions since all will be represented, in one form or another, around the negotiating table.

System	Thinking	Critical factors
AN	Reflexive	Instincts and survival senses
BO	Animistic	Traditions, mystical signs, reciprocity
CP	Egocentric	Dominance and instant gratification
DQ	Absolutistic	High authority and orderliness/logic
ER	Strategic	Competitive advantage and risk-taking
FS	Relativistic	Harmony and collective pressures

Since we do not anticipate the AN system becoming a factor around the negotiation table (in its modern form it is represented mainly by vagrants and addicts to drink and drugs), we shall not discuss it in this context.

The BO-Purple system uses elements of communal decision-making, along with varying degrees of autocracy on the part of the chief, king or spiritual leader. In the traditional tribal system the chief will hear contributions from various parties, then, after discussion with the elders, announce a decision. Since Purple thinking is rooted in the mysticism of land and the magic of the soil, its practitioners are in no position to negotiate property or assets in the traditional western way. Purple-thinking leaders perform an elaborate social ritual between one another and are attuned to nuances of relationship which Westernised First World thinkers often miss.

Observe the manner in which the ANC makes decisions, the painstaking way in which every individual on the National Executive Committee has to be involved. The same communal process is to be found in Inkatha, especially in the way its leaders bring a large group to any negotiating session. Each organisation has in it enough of the BO-Purple influence to make it necessary to observe the conventions of that system, whether the leaderships find it necessary or not. At time of writing elements of the former United Democratic Front had hived off from the ANC to form a new association of civic organisations, and this is possibly due in large part to frustration experienced in dealing with the ANC's slow-moving process of decision-making. Elitism in the western sense does not show itself and there is little of the quick-reacting information age understanding of nano-seconds and the need to think and act within a commodities-trading environment.

In the Red-CP approach to problem resolution, "power gods" demand everything on their terms. If their terms are not met, these egocentric elitists will employ intimidation and threat to have their way. The *Godfather* film series gives an idea how the system operates. Godfathers can "deal" with one another on occasion, they divide territory where expedient. There could well be honour among thieves, but the agreements are often temporary, sealed in cash or in blood. No Red-CP leader ever sits with his back to the door. Such leaders often facilitate intermarriage between the power groups to ensure some kind of peace, but typically their willingness to negotiate implies a willingness of the other party to turn over power. They will gladly engage a competitor or opponent regarding the time and place of surrender.

When the Blue-DQ system makes decisions, it does so within an authoritarian structure. The primary objective is to determine what is "right" or is mandated by a higher source. There are appeals to higher authority, the law of the land, the law of nature, the need for justice and honour and the respect due to elected representatives. The rules of negotiation are carefully followed. Compromise of principle is not an option. Traditions, holy places, deep beliefs and other expressions of the absolutist order are not for trading away, and any such suggestion will be met with firm resistance and cold self-righteousness. The purpose of negotiation is to establish what is right - not what is expedient.

In the Orange-ER world one encounters negotiation, horse-trading and deal-making as an advanced art. All is negotiable. Every person has his price. Deals are struck at the last moment after protracted haggling. Every party plays subtle games to increase leverage. The winners take the spoils - but the losers do not leave entirely empty-handed either. The most skillful at negotiating win the most. All kinds of power alliances may be struck, often behind the scenes. The run-up to negotiations is used to set up and influence an entire political climate. After the deal is struck there is an elaborate ceremony of celebration by all involved, to create the impression among their constituents that everybody "won". While the negotiators might confront one another with emotional rhetoric over the work table, they might well socialise afterwards. It amounts to a kind of game and they are professionals at it.

While the ER-Orange model of power negotiation can be useful in certain settings, it has limited capacity when called on to deal with great diversity in the positions about the table. It could produce a compromise decision which might - but equally might not - be the best decision within the potential of the parties involved.

Green-FS thinking produces a reliance - even insistence - on a consensus decision. This has in it aspects of Purple. Each person is accorded an equal right to be heard, there are no hierarchical rankings or differences in status and very person has an equal vote. Such a negotiating group will normally sit in a circle and opinions are frankly expressed. Deviousness and self-serving motivation are disallowed. The decision-making process is lengthy because everybody has a say on every issue and the edging toward a compromise which all can accept is necessarily a time-consuming process. Such a process is sensitive, communal, participative and harmonious. However, it works best where the people and issues are essentially homogenous; when the participants are largely from the same social strata. When there are major developmental gaps, as with the staircase between the Third and the First Worlds, such a negotiating system tends to break down.

Some of the conflict resolution models which have been presented to South Africa by Western governments and academic institutions and think-tanks have been designed out of the Green set of assumptions. They assume a horizontal level of development and speak in soft tones; they spend time facilitating relationships and expect the potential participants to enter with mutual goodwill. They are ill-equipped to deal with vertical levels of development, issues involving human ego or with deep historical resentments. They can become dangerous because they programme the parties for failure, producing frustration and a lack of faith in any process of problem resolution.

Now that we have defined the benchmarks on either side of the spectrum, it is appropriate to comment on the positions of the various parties. Note that both Inkatha and the ANC have been identified in four bands - Orange, Blue, Red and Purple. Each reflects a quite different picture of those organisations and they are likely to co-exist for some time to come. Inkatha has a rich base of Purple because of its traditions and its large rural population base. (The ANC also has this Purple base though it is not always evident, being hidden from view in the remote, tribally ordered Xhosa heartland of the Transkei). Inkatha supporters within the Purple band are inclined to think and behave primarily as Zulus. The ANC was, at time of writing, still in transition from being an anti-apartheid movement to becoming an entrenched and clearly-focused political party. What appears on the surface to be major conflict between the two organisations is actually conflict at different levels within each group (Purple versus Purple or Red versus Red), which spills over into inter-party relationships.

Both the ANC and Inkatha are likely to display their different faces - Purple, Red, Blue and a small degree of Orange - at the conference table. We already see evidence, however, that if the ANC and Inkatha continue to fight physical battles within the Purple, Red and Blue bands, a significant number of blacks and black groupings might jettison them for the more complex thinking of Orange. Cosatu has already served notice on the ANC that it will not support authoritarian controls which curtail freedom of speech or the right to organise into unions. There could be further spin-offs if the process of negotiation should mire down in the Purple, Red and Blue ranges. Furthermore, many black leaders have become increasingly influenced by participation in conferences, workshops and seminars sponsored by the local business community and American and European agencies. These are rooted in from a strong tradition of Orange thinking.

The Red-CP elements within Inkatha, the ANC and the AWB are identical in terms of their belief structures - it is only their respective contents which are mutually exclusive. All three are quite obviously sparring for battle, anywhere and at any time. If the critical mass of decision-making were to begin down-shifting to this range, the Beirut scenario would become reality.

Note the commonality across the Blue to Orange tier of parties. The CP, the Bophuthatswana government, the ANC, Inkatha, the Labour Party and parts of the conservative Christian churches have much in common. As a group they are more congruent with the developing communities of South Africa than the National Party, especially under its present leadership.

The location of F.W. de Klerk in the nodal Orange position, with elements of Green beginning to appear, will surprise many. We believe he has been misunderstood all along. As the Dutch Reformed movement begins to mature in its more progressive stages, its rock-ribbed Old Testament rigidity is likely to shift into a Green, humanistic expression of service, equality and a rightful place for all in this Kingdom on Earth. This is one version of early Green, and it seems unlikely that all of de Klerk's cabinet are anywhere near nodal Green. Contrast de Klerk's paradigm profile with that of Dr Andries Treurnicht, and the variations out of Blue in the president are still there in full force in the Conservative Party leader. Their respective expressions of religious conviction are likely to be correspondingly different. It is perhaps significant that de Klerk is a product of the Potchefstroom University of Higher Christian Education, an institution which espouses a strand of austerely logical Calvinism which produced a brand of innovative political thinking years in advance of the other Afrikaans universities.

Note also the continuing split in the Democratic Party between the Orange free marketeers and the Green humanists. The Orange element seems likely to shift to the National Party, whose values now make it its natural home. The Green Democrats seem likely to side with the ANC - for the time being at any rate - while others in the party are thinking within the GT-Yellow system and are likely to spin free to act as honest brokers, in conjunction with others in that system.

As we analyse the deep value structures of the parties likely to find themselves about the negotiating table, there is cause for concern. Unless there is significant agreement ahead of time between the leading parties to negotiation, the process is likely to be inordinately complex and difficult. With the vast differences between the parties, the deep conflicts and mutually exclusive motivations and demands, it might not be possible to achieve any kind of accord so long as the decision-making system flows out of any of the first six levels of complexity identified on the Psychological Map.

In Part IV we will attempt to re-organise the entire problem resolution process around the GT-Yellow and HU-Turquoise systems of decision-making, from the vantage point of the New Paradigm. We call this process the Table Mountain Summit. All are invited to attend.

CHAPTER 8

The population undergoing drastic change is a population of misfits and
misfits live and breathe in an atmosphere of passion, imbalance,
violence, explosiveness and are hungry for action.
Eric Hoffer: The Ordeal of Change

The treson of the mordring in the bedde;
The open werre, with wounds al bibledde;
Contek, with bloody knyf and sharp manace;
Al ful of chirking was that sory place.
Geoffrey Chaucer: The Canterbury Tales

Misfits and Mayhem

"Take your guns, your knives and your pangas and throw them into the sea. Close down the death factories. End this war now!" These were the ringing words of Nelson Mandela, deputy president of the ANC, as he addressed a huge rally in Durban soon after his release from prison. He was speaking in Natal where thousands, most of them innocents, had already died the most grisly deaths in conflict between his own supporters and those of the rival Inkatha movement. Many expressed relief at this statesmanlike pouring of oil on troubled waters. If Inkatha could be persuaded to reciprocate, who among the rest would defy the authority of the saintly Mandela?

Next morning the news editor of a Durban newspaper received a telephone call from Umhlanga, an upmarket dormitory town and seaside resort just north of the city. "You must get your photographers out here fast," said the caller. "A whole lot of blacks have arrived at the beach with trucks just loaded up with weapons, tons of them. They're down on the rocks now near the lighthouse, throwing them into the sea - spears, pangas, guns, everything you can think of ..."

A news team sped to Umhlanga to record this major event. It was only after tramping about the near-deserted beach and receiving looks of astonishment from those they asked about a mass dumping of arms in the sea that they realised they were probably being observed with sardonic amusement from one of the high-rise balconies just behind them.

Of course, it was all too good to be true. Such is the fate of any attempt to quell the turbulence of South Africa, based on a single-cause analysis of the violence on the ground. Appeals from the pious for peace, a hard line from the authoritarians, hand-wringing by the business community, finger-pointing from all quarters - every one is doomed to failure. The violence is too deep, too pervasive, too systemic.

The hoaxter's motivation was probably cynicism. We seek a different explanation why communities who had endured generations of deprivation without surrendering their humanity should suddenly become so tragically convulsed with violence. Many analytical models - economics, sociology, criminology and political science - yield useful results. However, we believe the new level of thinking possible from within the New Paradigm may provide fresh and powerful insights to this national tragedy, as well as point toward a fresh and comprehensive programme of action to stem the tide of terror and brutality. This sort of exercise does nothing to diminish the horror of such events as a man being dragged from his car, stabbed to death and soaked in petrol and set alight before being thrust under the vehicle so that it too bursts into flame and his children on the back seat are burned to death. It does nothing to diminish the moral culpability of those responsible. But we believe the exercise does give us a better understanding of how and why such things are happening and therefore equips us better to stop them happening in the future.

This chapter will broadly sketch the occurence of communal violence in South Africa, and its changing character, then consider it in terms of Gravesian technology and the New Paradigm.

The Course of Political Violence

The cycle began with the Soweto schools uprising of 1976 when children of the sprawling townships adjacent to Johannesburg took to the streets in protest against their inferior system of education. The police reacted harshly, firing on protesters. Casualties were high and the fact that they were mainly children fed fuel to the flames of anger. The minister of police of the day was quick to attribute the upheavals to agitation by the ANC and the PAC, though both organisations were in fact internally dormant and themselves taken by surprise (though no doubt gratified to be credited with an uprising which owed more to the Black Consciousness Movement, which thrived in institutions of education). Revolt by the youth spread fast to the Cape Peninsula, where coloured children also became involved, and to the Eastern Cape. Natal was a significant exception, its vast black townships and schools remaining relatively calm under the leadership - at that stage undisputed - of the Inkatha movement. The disturbances had the distinct character of youthful revolt by blacks against white authority and, as it was gradually brought under a semblance of control by the police, thousands of black youths slipped across the country's extended borders into neighbouring states to seek out the ANC and the PAC.

However, once ignited the conflict has smouldered for years, spreading into other communities as well, such as the shack settlements which had sprung up around Cape Town. The conflict began to take on an intra-communal quality rather than direct itself solely at the state. Conservative vigilante groups, the Xhosa "Witdoeke" - so named for their white headcloths - of the Cape would attack and burn out the homes of neighbouring communities perceived to be politically radical. In Soweto, Zulu impis* formed from immigrant workers housed in hostels, who went on terrifying rampages (15 years later this was to be repeated on an amplified scale). Suspicions were strong that *agents provocateurs* of the government were at work, implementing a strategy of divide and rule. In the townships of the Witwatersrand and the Eastern Cape especially, a vicious polarisation occurred between blacks perceived to be "collaborating with the system", such as policemen and township councillors, and a fast-swelling Jacobin Left which dispensed swift street justice in the form of the infamous necklace - a blazing, petrol-filled tyre placed about the victim's neck. Large sections of coloured youth in the Cape Peninsula were in a seemingly endless running battle with the security forces, while elsewhere the unrest spread to all kinds of hitherto obscure townships across the country. From exile the ANC preached the doctrine of "ungovernability" as a prelude to seizing power. The response of the authorities was repression: a state of emergency and certain actions by the security forces which were as singularly brutal as they were unintelligent counter-revolutionary tactics.

However, this mayhem was to pale in comparison with what was to come in Natal as the established Inkatha movement was challenged by the ANC and its internal surrogate, the United Democratic Front (UDF). The UDF had formed in response to the overwhelming acceptance of a new constitution in a referendum among white voters. This gave coloured and Asian voters representation in subordinate chambers of parliament (subordinate in the sense that they could not overrule or frustrate the white-dominated executive), while blacks were seemingly debarred in perpetuity from parliamentary representation.

It is worth examining underlying conditions in Natal in some detail because it is here that the large explosion occurred and it is here that the elements of conflict which are so illuminated by New Paradigm analysis are present in all their complexity. It is also from Natal that violence has been "exported" to the Transvaal, where it takes on the disturbing characteristics of inter-ethnic conflict.

*War parties, regiments

104

The Background to Political Violence

When we speak of Natal we really mean the Natal/KwaZulu region. KwaZulu is a fragmented entity which was carved out of the province of Natal to create a Zulu homeland in pursuance of the ideology of grand apartheid. KwaZulu does in a sense represent the remains of the old Zulu kingdom which once existed beyond the Tugela and Buffalo Rivers while the British ruled the colony of Natal. However, it now also includes large patches of territory lying in what used to be the colony. It includes the huge, teeming dormitory townships of Umlazi and KwaMashu, on Durban's doorstep. Geographically speaking (and politically and economically as well), Natal and KwaZulu are closely intertwined.

Anthony Minnaar, of the Human Sciences Research Council, has produced a useful study of the historical forces which have been at play in the region since the early nineteenth century. Among these were a series of tribal migrations from old Zululand into the colony to escape the Zulu imperium. British rule also saw the return to their old territories of various small tribes and clans who had fled the turbulence of the Mfecane, the domino effect set up by Shaka's conquests. Zulu groups in Natal came into contact with British traders, farmers and missionaries. Many became Kholwa (Christianised) and adopted Western values. They tended to gather in church settlements on freehold land and earned the contempt of their brethren north of the Tugela for going into paid employment. They had a corresponding contempt for the backward traditionalists who had not taken on the new ways.

The cleavage should not be exaggerated. There always were tribal societies in British-ruled Natal, whose descendants today are administered by KwaZulu. These tend to be strongly and vibrantly traditional and loyal to the Zulu throne. But there are significant localities where the opposite is true. One such is the Kholwa settlement of Edendale, outside the Natal capital of Pietermaritzburg, which raised a regiment to fight on the British side during the Zulu War of 1879. Edendale has been the scene of probably the most intense and brutal fighting since the focus of conflict shifted to Natal.

Dr Minnaar also provides an interesting perspective on what has come to be known in Natal as "faction fighting." These inter-clan conflicts tend to smoulder interminably, revenge being a potent factor, and at times they produce horrifying casualties. Minnaar traces back two faction fights for more than 100 years (one of which, at time of writing, had again flared up fiercely on the South Coast). The conflict is shrugged off by many whites with stereotype explanations such as "tribal war" or "a warrior race letting off steam."

Yet the fighting is often traceable to early colonial policy. Clans were moved about and consolidated in reserves. Recalcitrant tribes had their land made over to others. Chiefs were appointed and deposed by the colonial authorities, which caused distress and friction. Meanwhile, the colonial intrusion and the allocation of land to white farmers and the crown exacerbated a land shortage which caused competition for resources and enhanced the authority of the chiefs. Their role in allocating land to subjects gave them a power not enjoyed by earlier chiefs, whose subjects would simply walk away, if dissatisfied, and establish themselves under the authority of another. There had once been enough land for such a system.

The real causes of faction fighting are generally to be found in competition for resources, revenge and - at times - disputed chieftaincies. What makes faction fighting relevant to our analysis, rather than a quaint if bloody relic of times past, is that the conflicts often overlap with more modern struggles. The fighting on the South Coast mentioned above appears to have its origin in grazing rights, yet coincides with an intense struggle in the area between Inkatha and the ANC. Fighting on another part of the South Coast appears to be rooted in a disputed chieftaincy, but is difficult to distinguish from an adjacent urban conflict. A prominent chief assassinated in Pietermaritzburg was politically active - but also embroiled in a long-standing territorial dispute. And if revenge is a potent factor in rural faction fighting, it is likely to be as much a factor in urban conflicts.

Such is the historical backdrop. To this has to be added mass migration to the urban centres. In Natal this had been happening for many years, even before the government dropped its influx control policy and machinery in 1986. Parts of KwaZulu adjoin the city of Durban, other parts adjoin the Kholwa settlements of Edendale, Pietermaritzburg's black satellite. Hundreds of thousands of people have moved from rural poverty, whose extreme conditions are best judged by the degree of squalor in the shack settlements which they nevertheless find preferable. Even without the mass migration, urban Natal would have experienced a housing crisis because the ideology of apartheid decreed that blacks were "temporary sojourners" in the "white" urban areas and their presence was discouraged. Additional housing for blacks had not been provided by the authorities for many years. The formal black townships are overcrowded to bursting. They are surrounded by insanitary, crime-ridden shacklands. Greater Durban is estimated to have something like two million squatters and is one of the world's fastest-growing conurbations.

Poverty-stricken people of rural origin, their tribal values intact, are thrust into close proximity with others who urbanised long ago and are relatively more affluent. Law and order of a kind is imposed by strong-man vigilante figures, many of them also involved in gangsterism. Conventional policing is inadequate in the formal townships, non-existent in the shacklands. The burgeoning shacklands expand into formerly rural chieftaincies, where chiefs and their counsellors are outraged to find uninvited strangers in their territory, who do not even respect their authority. Such incursions are often aggravated by waves of refugees from unrest deeper inside the conurbation, often people of explicitly radical and anti-traditionalist conviction. The traditionalists attempt to re-impose the order they grew up with.

Add to this economic recession and an unemployment rate of something like 50 percent and a combustible mixture reaches flashpoint. Competition for political support set up friction to ignite Natal into a conflict which has burned fiercely since 1985.

It is not our intention to provide a detailed account of the course of the violence in Natal, though a brief sketch is appropriate. It began with a serious fall-out in 1979 of Inkatha and the ANC (which was still banned and in exile). Until then the relationship had been reasonably cordial, the Inkatha leadership having ANC origins. Many had regarded Inkatha almost as an internal wing of the ANC.

In 1985 serious disturbances and arson were perpetrated by youths in the Durban townships of KwaMashu and Umlazi, which were firmly put down by Inkatha using traditional Zulu regiments. The conflict moved to Pietermaritzburg (the Kholwa settlement at Edendale) where it took on a new ferocity and Inkatha were dislodged from much of the Edendale valley, though the UDF (acting for the ANC) were hemmed in by Inkatha's strength in the surrounding rural districts of KwaZulu. The conflict moved also to Mpumalanga, a large township serving an industrial area roughly midway between Durban and Pietermaritzburg, then back again to KwaMashu and Umlazi, as well as the shacklands.

The ANC's broadcasts from Zambia urging "ungovernability" were directed particularly at Natal/KwaZulu, where Inkatha was in large part the governing authority. Inkatha has in fact been dislodged as a force in several areas though by no means removed altogether. An extremely violent stalemate set in. The schools were in chaos, services were widely disrupted and the geographic juxtaposition of the two sides - Inkatha supporters often having to travel through UDF territory to reach work or to shop in the cities - posed a constant threat of friction.

Ignition came with the unbanning of the ANC and the release of Nelson Mandela. A huge Inkatha force swept down into the

Edendale valley, killing and burning, sending thousands of refugees into Pietermaritzburg. It was a new and escalated phase in the conflict. Almost simultaneously Inkatha went on the offensive in Mpumalanga and in a new theatre, Table Mountain, a rural area near Pietermaritzburg where a chief had declared himself for the ANC. Inkatha was accused of a massive and co-ordinated offensive. It retorted that it was doing no more than retaliate for provocations and attacks along the transport routes of its supporters, who were being throttled economically.

The government's response was massive military intervention which soon restored peace and, at time of writing, had managed to maintain it. In spite of initial ANC misgivings, the army's intervention has been generally welcomed. As mentioned above, the conflict has since shown itself most prominently in a fierce and horrific struggle in the rural areas of the South Coast, where small children have numbered among the victims.

In late 1990 the focus of conflict shifted from Natal and into a new and still more menacing phase. Zulu impis from the migrant worker hostels of the Transvaal clashed with groups of Xhosas from the Transkei, mainly in the squatter camps. It echoed the Zulu impis which suddenly and inexplicably raged through Soweto during the schools uprising of the late 1970s. It also echoed the attacks of the Cape Witdoeke on squatter settlements, which had nothing at all to do with Zulus or Inkatha. And whereas the conflict in Natal had been between Zulus parading different political allegiances, here suddenly was an ethnic element, Zulu versus Xhosa. The Zulus form the core of Inkatha support, the Xhosas the core of ANC support. Here was conflict with the potential to rend not just a region but virtually the whole of South Africa.

The ANC maintains that the ethnic conflict in the Transvaal has been engineered by a sinister "Third Force" which seeks to derail the process of negotiation set in train by de Klerk. It has to be accepted that this would be an effective way to derail the process if such were desired. The major black participants can hardly negotiate while at each other's throats. Whites are likely to look askance at them as prospective partners in a new political dispensation. It also has to be presumed that the security forces, rooted as they are in an ethos of securing white domination, would still contain individuals with the incentive - and the means - to engineer such conflict. Some find significance in the fact that while P.W. Botha's hardline administration appeared content to allow the Natal conflict to rage on interminably with an inadequate security force presence, de Klerk did not hesitate to send in the army in strength to smother it.

However, it is not our purpose to pursue these intriguing questions.

We are more concerned with what it could be that sets community so viciously against community. What it could be that can rouse Zulu hostel dwellers in the Transvaal and Xhosa Witdoeke in the Cape to paroxysms sufficient to send them off as rampaging war parties. This is surely more central to an understanding of the problem of violence than whether the antagonists are or are not urged on by *agents provocateurs*. Such agents could operate with success only in a conducive climate.

Has a climate conducive to violence been created? Developments outlined above would suggest so. Mass urbanisation, competing value systems among the urbanised, competing ideological certitudes and competition for the highest political stakes combine with the *frisson* of excitement and expectation which has charged black society since it became clear that the old apartheid order was to be dismantled. The stresses are most severe at the psychological levels of Purple-Tribal Order, Red-Power Empire and Blue-Ideology / Absolutism, all of them value systems with a high degree of volatility and an inherent propensity to employ violence as an instrument. These factors also combine with economic decline and a dawning realisation that expectations are not going to be met. Economic sanctions, and the palpable decline in opportunities for blacks which have resulted, are like a great piston compressing black society to flashpoint. Sanctions could turn out in the end to have been as destructive to South Africa as apartheid. It illustrates the mirror-image quality of "the system" and "the struggle". They need each other, they are of the same paradigm.

White society is not immune to the stresses of change. Right-wing organisations also display Purple, Red and Blue characteristics and, as they perceive their values and traditional orders to be threatened, they too are capable of erupting into violence. This had, at time of writing, shown itself to be sporadic and limited to individuals and very small groupings.

Violence explodes at diverse psychological levels, creating spirals of turbulence up and down a fiery funnel. There is no single form or context of violence, multiple forms with different triggers and degrees of intensity exist simultaneously at diverse levels. Deep belief structures exist within individuals, as described in previous chapters, and can be recognised as complexities of thinking within organisations, which reflect layers of the value systems within society. These mosaics of world-view systems, in their various mixtures of peoples, technologies, environments and communities, determine the patterns, thinking and forms of social unrest rather than race or ethnicity.

The violence in the townships, on trains, down the Free State mines and virtually everywhere is misleadingly classified "black on black." The conflict rather pits Purple against Purple (clashing tribal orders), Purple against Red (tribalists against gangsters), Red against Red (warlords in combat, often spuriously under the banners of political groupings), Red against Blue (rebels attacking authority or traditional structures), Blue against Blue (conflicting models for society, conflicting nationalisms or ideologies) or Orange against Orange (competition for limited niches and pre-eminence in the post-apartheid society). It is these deep structures which give the violence its pervasive quality.

If Dr Minnaar's study suggests that many of the explosions in Natal are the echoes of unresolved conflicts which have been at play in the region since the early nineteenth century, it is also true that localised confrontations have meaning at different levels on the psychological stack. A century-old dispute over grazing rights (Purple) is conducted at the same time as an adjacent dispute between two rival chiefs (Red), while people throughout the region argue the abstractions of competing (Blue) truths (free enterprise versus Marxism), flying the colours (Orange) of two competing political entities, Inkatha and the ANC. Small wonder that the results have been so horrifying. The conflict is at four distinct levels and the motives of all the wars of human history are compressed into one struggle.

However, the important theme of the violence is that all the systems are in flux, millions of people are entering and leaving them. They leave older systems to embrace new ones. The differences between the people of these different systems is becoming painfully apparent as they come into collision, but they had been there all along, disguised by apartheid and the artificial isolation of entire communities. Now that the barriers are being removed, all the pent-up anger, the contained aspirations and the raw energy of excitement and change have been released.

Detribalisation is painful as the Purple structure disintegrates before a new, ordered system appears to take its place. The Young Lions of the township streets did not experience the rites of passage of the tribal order and are trapped in Red. Millions of people abandon Third World thinking and struggle for freedom in Blue, the cause and revolutionary crusade which characterises the Second World and aims for the authoritarian "people's democracy" where the omniscient "party" directs events. Others at different levels of complexity reject the constraints imposed by Calvinist or feudal conformity and struggle to break free as individuals striving for affluence and material possession within First World assumptions. Meanwhile, still others continue to cling to the values of tribal order and attempt to re-impose them, as in the peri-urban areas of Natal where tribal authorities find their territory invaded by strangers who do not recognise that authority. Conditions of uncertainty and danger cause people to down-shift to more primitive levels of operation, as described in Chapter 3. Impis form and go on the rampage. Such conflict is both vertical and horizontal - directed upward at levels of thinking which challenge the old values and sideways at established adjacent urban communities which have a degree of affluence and privilege in comparison with the migrant communities of the hostels.

Political Violence in Gravesian Terms

Examined in terms of New Paradigm thinking, it becomes apparent that political violence has a dynamic of its own, the flashpoints occurring - possibly quite spontaneously - where the different value systems identified as Purple, Red, Blue and (sometimes) Orange come into collision. It is therefore pointless to accuse Inkatha of being responsible for the activities of warlords - these have their own agendas; pointless also to brand the ANC as the "common factor" in violence countrywide, including regions where Inkatha has no presence. Simply by being present, the ANC will be caught up in the turbulence.

If the crucible of change in South Africa is as complex and explosive as all this, it becomes clear that simple, cosmetic and single-valued peace-keeping initiatives are doomed to failure. What then might work over the short and the long term? Can any order at all lurk behind this chaos?

It should be understood that when society contains a large number of misfits - people who do not see a place for themselves in the emerging order - turbulence and conflict are inevitable. When there is a serious gap between the decay of the old order and the emergence of the new, violence is usually the result. The misfits are seized by a sense of claustrophobia and panic, they kick violently to escape. To raise the expectations of "the oppressed" without providing meaningful outlets only creates greater barriers than existed before hope was kindled. The township streets display raw, unfocused energy, fueled by anger, hopelessness, poverty, exploitation and a lack of any sense of guilt. The energy strikes out at any perceived barrier. Friends and strangers are attacked without provocation, random victims suffer attacks which are really directed at the system. Anarchy reigns.

The shameful and saddening thing is that this explosive condition has been exploited by various self-serving interests across the entire spectrum - black leaders as well as white, radicals as well as right-wingers, church leaders as well as secular moralists. There is guilt enough to go around. Let alone a "Third Force" - there could also be Fourth, Fifth and Sixth forces sowing mayhem and destruction among the innocent.

Much of the violence is like a viral infection which hides within the cells of society, making every institution vulnerable to infections of opportunity. Until the contours of the next order are put into place, providing a vision of hope for all South Africans, the episodes and patterns of violent upheaval are likely to continue. Far too many elites are jockeying for individual power and privilege and are playing reckless and irresponsible games with the lives of millions who live on the brink of disaster.

A caution: beware those who offer simplistic solutions cloaked in the language of "democracy", "socialism" or "free enterprise". Alvin Toffler's new book, *Power Shift*, validates this warning. He says the newly emerging mosaics surfacing everywhere on the planet cannot be managed by monolithic or mass democratic structures. Unless South Africa's leadership discovers a way to manage society as a living, complex organism, violence will not just beget more violence - it will eventually "square root" on itself.

Grand apartheid, no matter what its architects might say they intended, failed because it did not address the realities of difference and change in people - all people. Anti-apartheid leaders, no matter how genuine and honest, could make the same mistake by demanding a system which would be just as rigid and destructive for the entire South African human and technological Spiral, even though it seems eminently fair and just.

Finally, much of the violence is like a bacterial infection which can be reduced by a number of therapeutic and preventive measures. Among these are more effective training and management of law enforcement agencies and the creation of command and control centres within local communities to anticipate and contain violence. The Young Lions might well need (and desire) special service unit/kibbutz-style sponges to draw them through positive and productive authoritarian conduits. Sanctions and boycotts need to be ended. Society desperately needs the common goals, values and symbols provided by sports and cultural events, as well as an influx of finance to provide jobs, education, housing and health care. Such measures would be the equivalent of antibodies, calculated to cool down the patient without impairing the creative tension of pulling society to a greater complexity of thinking, producing new and unexpected results.

Anger and violence emanate from the deeper wells of fear and depression. Unless these deep frustrations can be allayed and all can see a meaningful place for themselves in the new order, it matters little what constitution is imposed. Violence cannot be redressed only by dealing with violence. Misfits must be given a place. When that happens, perhaps weapons will indeed be cast into the sea.

CHAPTER 9

The Pigmentation of Politics

Present: Hennie Burger, 39-year-old Orange Free State farmer, member of the Conservative Party and the Dutch Reformed Church; Ms Ann Thompson, 55-year-old Capetonian, member of the Democratic Party, the Anglican Church and the Black Sash, supporter of numerous worthy causes; Joseph Khumalo, 29-year-old economics graduate of the University of Zululand, supporter of the ANC and recently returned from an exchange programme in the United States; Dr Don Beck; Graham Linscott.

Burger: Look, I've read this book of yours and I don't know what to make of it, whether it's liberal rubbish or not. You seem to be saying race isn't important in South Africa. Is that what you're saying?

Beck: What we're saying is that it's an irrelevant category. The colour of a person's skin doesn't determine the way he thinks and sees the world and behaves. That is what is important.

Thompson: How can you possibly say race is irrelevant? It underpins the very system in South Africa. It decides a person's chances in life. Are you trying to say it doesn't matter what race you are?

Beck: I think we're looking ahead to a post-apartheid South Africa. If the constitution is going to enshrine non-racialism, wouldn't it be an idea to get race out of our thinking and our vocabulary as well?

Thompson: Easier said than done. You have to bring justice and equality to the blacks before you stop talking about race. And how can we be sure your values analysis isn't some clever divide and rule tactic? I'm very suspicious of anything that divides the black community into different categories, and that's what you seem to be doing. When you write about differences between First and Third World blacks, aren't you just as bad as the Nats exaggerating tribal differences? The only way we'll get justice in this country is to let the majority rule. Don't try to divide them.

Burger: Can I get a word in? I reckon there's not much where I agree with Ann, but here we do. Race is what it's about. It's rule or be ruled. Look at the rest of Africa. Do we want that here? My Volk bought the land with their blood. We're not going to give it away.

Linscott: Hennie, do you have a black farm foreman?

Burger: My bossboy, Herklaas? What about him? I pay him well, treat him well. His family have been with us three generations. They'd leave if they didn't like it.

Thompson: I've never heard such paternalistic drivel.

Linscott: This man, Herklaas. Do you let him drive your combine harvester?

Burger: Let him? That's one of his main jobs.

Linscott: How much did it cost?

Burger: The harvester? Close to a quarter million. Why?

Linscott: Do you let Herklaas drive your car? Is it a Merc?

Burger: Well, sometimes he fetches the kids from school for my wife. Yes, it is a Merc. What are you getting at?

Linscott: You must trust old Herklaas quite a bit. You trust him with an expensive bit of machinery and an expensive car, you trust him with your kids. He must have something going for him.

Burger: Look, he's a good type. Respectable, he goes to church on Sundays.

Thompson: A separate church, I'll bet.

Linscott: But you couldn't share political power with him. I'm getting quite interested in this man. Did you know his grandfather? Did he also drive the combine harvester?

Burger: I remember him only a bit. No, of course he didn't drive a harvester, we didn't have one in those days. He was raw anyway, straight from the kraal.

Linscott: This Herklaas - does he have children? Where are they? What are they doing?

Burger: He's got two sons. One is an electrician, he did some course at the tech. The other one is at university studying law. The daughter is a schoolteacher. They all live in Johannesburg, they say the farm's too quiet for them. But they wouldn't have got anywhere if we didn't look after Herklaas decently.

Linscott: You seem quite fond of Herklaas.

Burger: Of course. He's almost like part of the family. We Conservative Party types aren't brutes, you know.

Thompson: What on earth is the relevance of all this? I thought we were talking about race.

Beck: No, something interesting is coming out here. In one black family we've got these different levels of complexity emerging, generation by generation. Increasing levels of complexity. Yet Hennie believes these achievements and attitudes are less important than their race. I wonder what those individuals believe. And at the same time there's a degree of affinity between Hennie and Herklaas. You could say they inhabit the same world. You've been sitting there very quietly, Joseph, what do you think?

Khumalo: Well, I've been listening. I think we need to get away from race and ethnicity, that's why I support the ANC. They're non-racial and they want a just society. Dividing the country along lines of race has brought it down. I'm Zulu by background but I don't support Inkatha because they're too tribal and traditional, it's embarrassing. I just want to work and get on in life.

Beck: What do you do?

Khumalo: I'm in management with one of the multinationals.

Beck: We know the ANC is a broad church, but don't some of its more socialistic outbursts bother you a bit: its commitment to sanctions?

Khumalo: I'll be honest, they do. But what else is there?

Beck: Who knows what's coming? Maybe the ANC will turn out right for you after all. That's for you to decide. But I think we're getting somewhere. It's our values that count, not our genes.

Thompson: No, no, no! You can't just alter the agenda like that. It's blacks as a race who have to be freed. I've spent my life fighting injustice and I know about it, the things that have been done in the name of apartheid. You can't just wish away the past.

Linscott: Perhaps you're suffering punchbag withdrawal symptoms, Ann?

Thompson: I find that remark offensive. But here's another thing: just by coincidence, the people at the top of your so-called Spiral happen to be whites. They are the ones who should take the decisions, you say. This is elitist arrogance, just disguised racism, another form of apartheid.

Beck: By no means all of them are white, Ann, they're emerging from every group. But we have to agree that at present most of them happen to be white.

Thompson: Exactly!

Beck: But that's the legacy of apartheid, of deliberately blocking people's development. If you don't believe apartheid has blocked people in this way, most of your objection to it has to fall away surely? And you seem to have misread our book. We're not advocating a ruling class or caste or anything like that. We're talking about harnessing all South Africa's talents in a creative way, drawing on talents at all levels for the common good. That's true liberation, allowing people to develop as they wish and at their own pace.

Thompson: And what about democracy?

Beck: We're all for democracy. But it has to be a special kind, a special structure to manage a society as complex as yours. That's for the political leaders to sort out. All we're doing is offer a framework to cater for the needs of all sectors of society, Hennie's included, so they can develop in a free flow. You mustn't get bogged down in racial categories - that was the Nats' big mistake. There are probably as many First World black South Africans today as First World white South Africans. That's got to be taken into account.

Burger: Thanks, you can count me out! You're really Progs, wanting to swamp us in black numbers. Man, you don't live in the real world. Look what's happened in Africa. Look at Ethiopia. Look at the Zulus and Xhosas killing each other. No way! We fought the English and we'll fight anyone else who wants to take our land.

Such a discussion could continue indefinitely and in ever-widening circles. It is interesting that two whites, members of a racial minority, insist on the primacy of race yet a black man who has numbers on his side declines to do so. Is Hennie a racist? Is Ann an inverted racist? Is Joseph a non-racist?

It is more useful and illuminating to describe Hennie as DQ-Blue authoritarian, ideology-bound and knowing what is best. He categorises everything and everybody yet is unable to detect Fifth Level thinking in blacks such as Joseph. Ann is FS-Green, an exaggerated egalitarian who cannot believe the struggle against apartheid is actually over. Without a system to struggle against, her reason for existence has been challenged. So has her belief that Afrikaners are all bad and blacks all good (she is appalled and stunned that the people whose cause she has so long espoused should show themselves capable of such frightful violence). Joseph is ER-

Orange, a pragmatic materialist who seeks results and the good life. He has First World aspirations and sets about achieving them in a strategic manner.

It would be comforting to believe that racism and ethnicity have been safely consigned to the museum of history. Many naively believed such thinking patterns had in fact been so retired. In an age of secularism, materialism, humanism and globalism, such primitive motivations appeared to have been eliminated. How could the emotionalism of cultural supremacy co-exist with high technology in the Information Age?

Yet since the collapse of communism in the Soviet Union and Eastern Europe, and the joyous tearing down of the Berlin Wall, it has become clear that racism and ethnicity are once again on the rise. The constituent republics of the Soviet Union seek secession under the banners of language and culture. The Kurds are persecuted in the Middle East for retaining their identity. Certain black Americans now call themselves African-Americans and gather behind the banner of what amounts to an inverted apartheid. The Gravesian formula warns of the possibility of such developments. Few have paid heed.

Racism and ethnicity have become, in the 1990s, two of the most powerful driving forces in shaping political and economic trends and realities. Our purpose in this chapter is to use our psychological Rosetta Stone to decipher the origin and development of thinking and theorising about race, and to examine the basic human elements involved in the resurgence of ethnicity and nationalism.

Racial Theories

Racism is really not about race. Rather, it is about value systems. Skin pigmentation, the shape of hair follicles or ancestral origins are not really what separate us. All brains are grey and pink. Differences are systems of thinking within brains; they are not types of brain. This runs contrary to conventional wisdom because of the belief that race is about race, which is thought to create deep, foreboding fissures in our social order. Racism continues to raise its ugly head almost everywhere, even in the decade running up to the 21st century when people ought to know better. We believe that the colour of value systems, as we have coded them in the Graves Formula, ought to replace the distortion of shades of skin colour. This is a far more accurate and reliable indicator of differences in people and societies.

Racial Theories, by Michael Banton, traces the emergence of different theories about the concept of "race." He contrasts race as Lineage,

Type, Sub-species, Status and Class. At each developmental, historical stage "race" is seen in a different light, serving the interests of those who wish to claim superiority in their own kind and weaknesses in others. In each of these stages "they" are not like "us", for different reasons.

In Lineage, it was because of divine intervention at source by the Sun God, the Sea Dragon, the Mountain Deity, the Earth Lizard - whoever it was who made "us" unique.

In Type, a number of different typologies were invented, with a focus on physical characeristics and cultural traits. Thus the Negroid, Caucasian, Mongolian, Malayan and other categories surfaced.
In Sub-species, races were different because each was a snapshot classification at a particular moment in time.

In Status, the differences were accounted for in terms of the social contracts, deference and demand and trade-offs between racial groups. One would be the feudal provider and master, the other the stereotyped "Sambo" or "Rastus" of the plantations of the American Deep South.

In Class, the variations are best understood as print-outs of power, oppression, privilege and opportunity.

The common thread that has impacted on all five racial theories, but has been hidden from each viewpoint, is the hierarchy of values, the manner in which operating systems have risen in population groupings. Racial differences are, in all five theories, artefacts of the movement of the Gravesian Spiral through time and space. Each value system level imposed a definition of race that either liberated the privileged or restricted the victims. Thus the San Bushmen at AN-Beige Survivalist level were perceived by both black and white to be altogether primitive (if not sub-human vermin) and their fate was virtual extermination. Blacks first encountered by European settlers at BO-Purple Tribal level were stereotyped at that state as tribalists. Others who had shifted to the CP-Red level of conquest and empire (such as the Zulus) were stereotyped a "warrior" race. Conversely, CP-Red colonial adventurers from Europe were stereotyped by the blacks they encountered as land-grabbers and ruthless exploiters. There was little provision for anybody to shift or flow out of those fixed categories.

Banton quotes Robert Chambers who, in 1864, established the "Principle of Progressive Development" in *Vestiges of the Natural History of Creation:*

"Our brain ... after completing the animal transformations ... passes through the characters in which it appears in the Negro, Malay, American and Mongolian nations, and finally is Caucasian ... the highest type."

Chambers altogether missed the real evolutionary flow. These stages are not at all linear or sequential as he suggests. Instead, the unique matrix of value structures and content, from AN-Beige through to HU-Turquoise, has emerged in different ratios and mixtures in the groups he identified. For reasons which we will touch on later, "Caucasian" developed the Fourth and Fifth Level value systems more quickly. Today millions of Negroes, Malays and American Indians are moving through those ranges. Millions of others are either trapped in or moving through the Third World value spectrum, unable to break through their respective barriers. They are trapped either in BETA or GAMMA.

Banton explains the superiority accorded the Caucasian by noting that "popular beliefs in white superiority were probably conditioned by the success of Britain and other European countries in extending their influence over so much of the world." But what caused this aggressive expansionism? If one is to translate "white" as the DQ-Blue and ER-Orange value systems - Puritan-like values coupled with scientific and strategic thinking - one understands, once again, that the issues are about underlying belief structures, not racial or ethnic classifications.

The real question, therefore, is why European-based societies experienced Fourth and Fifth Level systems before other cultures? What was there in the experience of Europeans, in contrast with that of Africans and others, that contributed to such a pattern?

Laurens van der Post says, in *The Dark Eye of Africa:*

"The white man could not have been less prepared for what he was about to find (in Africa). A long period of pure reason which had begun with the Reformation and been stimulated by the French Revolution was deep at work in his spirit, setting him at variance with his intuitions and instincts. The materialism of the industrial revolution already dominated his values and motives. His mastery of the physical means of life and his increasing annihilation of distance together with the conquest of what he understood to be time, had already brought man far down the broad way to exceeding his humanity and setting himself up as a god and controller of destiny. Walking into Africa in that mood he was, by and large, quite incapable of understanding Africa, let alone of appreciating the raw material of mind and spirit with which this granary of fate, this ancient treasure house of the lost original way of life, was so richly filled."

Van der Post wonderfully captures how far the European mind had travelled along a certain trajectory before encountering Africa, but the perplexing reasons as to why it should have happened that way lie beyond the scope of this work. Many attribute the rapid development of the European on the psychological map to a function of cold, inclement conditions in that part of the world, where strategic thinking meant the difference between survival and extinction (compared with Garden of Eden conditions in Africa). Others point to luck of the draw in the discovery of the Phoenecian alphabet or the heritage from the Ancient Greeks of clear reasoning. Others have produced pathologies of "master race", which have plagued European history.

The literature on race is voluminous and diverse. For example, Karl Vogt, a German professor of anatomy (1817-1895), echoed the Darwinian doctrine in examining variations in cranial capacity. He found American slaves to have smaller measurements than their African counterparts. He believed the whites of the American South would have less intellectual capacity than their Northern brethren. He blamed slavery for having an injurious effect on both master and oppressed. And in 1864 he observed:

"The Anglo-Saxon race is itself a mongrel race, produced by Celts, Saxons, Normans and Danes, a raceless chaos without any fixed type; and the descendants of this raceless multitude have in America so much intermixed with Frenchmen, Germans, Dutch and Irish as to have given rise to another raceless chaos, which is kept up by continued immigration. We can readily believe that from this chaos a new race is gradually forming."

Such lines of investigation today have a curious ring to them. Our intention is simply to suggest that at each location on the Psychological Map, our species has thought about race in a different way. It still does, repeating racism from the past and projecting it into the future.

In the AN-Survivalist Beige system, race was neither a concept nor a dividing point among the original bands of hunter/gatherers. Band identity might have been critical but not race *per se*.

In the BO-Animistic Purple system, one often encounters mythical and mystical beliefs in the origin of the tribe, the people and the ancestral traditions. In Zululand today members of the Shezi tribe will point out the cave from which their troglodyte ironsmith ancestors crept, lured by the smell of a roasting ox, to be pressed by the Zulus into manufacturing spears for their armies. "Dreamtime" beliefs among Australian Aborigines contain a number of creation epics which locate the origin of their "kind" deep within the bowels of the earth. Race becomes important as origin.

In the CP-Red-Exploitative system, racial dominance is translated in terms of raw power. Power Gods select whatever allows them to dominate and causes others to be weak. If racially-based differentiations serve that purpose, racism will be both rampant and insidious. Race as power divides the strong and the weak.

Racism began to expand exponentially within the DQ-Blue Fourth Level belief system. The values structure itself invites classification of people into rigid, unchangeable categories with varying degrees of goodness. With Aryan and Untouchable types as end points in the Indian chain of privilege, race was a factor in differentiations and social opportunity. Americans did even better with exact classifications based on percentages of "black and white blood" in a person. The South African system of apartheid classification was able to flourish because of the strength of Blue thinking within the Afrikaner Volk. Individuals were classified from birth as white, black, Indian or "coloured" - the latter category containing an abstruse range of sub-categories. Absurdly (in terms of any doctrine of racial purity), blood brothers would find themselves on different sides of the racial divide, on grounds of appearance, and the law made provision for individuals to move through a cumbersome, bewildering - and inevitably humiliating - bureaucratic process of reclassification on grounds of appearance and acceptability by members of the new category sought.

The content of Fourth Level structures can also mandate racially-based stereotypes. If a person believes God condemned blacks with the curse of Ham to be perpetual hewers of wood and drawers of water, or if he believes God mandated that races and nations should forever be separate, he will no doubt view race very differently from others who reject that interpretation of the Bible.

It is ironic that many of the African-American community in the United States should themselves have moved into precisely this Blue perception of race. Whites are perceived as "ice people" and therefore inferior to blacks, who are "warm". Leaders insist on a version of apartheid partitioning in order to preserve the purity of the Afro-centred culture. Only blacks should teach blacks. Only black police officers should enforce the law on blacks. Certain politicians perceive themselves to be exclusive and enlightened leaders of the Black Diaspora. They have therefore been "chosen" to lead the entire continent of Africa into the "New Order". In such cases race becomes ideology.

The Fifth Level (ER-materialistic, scientific and achievist) value system captured the race issue in two ways. Pseudo-scientists turned their relatively primitive instruments on to racial differences in the attempt to prove one theory or another. Cranial size, blood typing, hair density, hormone balances and other manifestations were brought into racial type-casting. If these things were "proved" scientifically, who would be bold enough to argue against science? In addition to this, the incessant quest for competitive advantage has exploited racial classification to allow the privileged to justify their position. Through job reservation in South Africa, Bantu Education (wholly inferior) and exclusion from private ownership of property, blacks were locked into menial, labour-intensive jobs reserving the privileged occupations for whites in general and Afrikaners in particular. A ceiling was placed on the absorbtion of blacks into the normal and natural spin of the Spiral. Every attempt at protest, rebellion or insurrection was put down by force of arms and the terror of imprisonment.

As millions of African-Americans surge into the Orange-materialistic system of values - and compete vigorously for affluent niches in society - they too exploit racist imagery and make racist accusations in order to get ahead. Explosive and controversial issues surrounding affirmative action and quota systems reflect this tendency for relatively affluent American blacks to utilise race as a way to enhance opportunities for their children. The poor and deprived black underclass seldom if ever benefits from these well-publicised initiatives. Race, in such cases, means "advantage".

In the egalitarianism of the FS-Green Sixth Level of thinking, race disappears as a classification and is fiercely rejected in the name of people-centred humanity and affiliation. When this thinking pattern emerged in white Americans, the campaigns of black civil rights leaders were significantly strengthened. As FS thinking began to dominate Scandinavian and other European cultures, South Africa's system of apartheid came under massive attack. Ann Thompson, in the panel discussion at the beginning of this chapter, quite clearly has no use at all for any system which declares differences in people. She and others like her in South Africa have opposed racial definitions for decades, often suffering personally and professionally for their position. Ann Thompson finds difficulty distinguishing between differences based on race and differences based on life experience, immediate needs and aspirations. She consequently finds herself in the anomalous position of appearing to defend race as a category because she is suspicious of any form of differentiation at all.

Finally, in the GT-Integrative Yellow system, racial categories are purely arbitrary and meaningless. Yet when others impose them, they have to be addressed. Hennie Burger's dogmas and his anxieties should not be ignored, still less ridiculed. They are real to him and have to be acknowledged and engaged. He has to be persuaded that there is a place for him in the emerging South Africa, that he is not in danger of being ploughed under. However, having said that, the entire thrust of the Seventh Level system is the emergence of "types in" people rather than "types of" people. The pigments with which we have coded the Gravesian Spiral are more important than the pigments in the human skin.

However, relatively few have reached this level of complexity. Many "whites" still see "blacks" as Purple and Red. Many "blacks" see in "whites" Blue and Orange. Green-thinking critics of Afrikaners stereotype them as Red and Blue - old-style Boers and bureaucratic mandarins. Communists see capitalists as exploitative Red. Free marketeers see Marxists as rigid Blue. Conservatives see liberals as soft-hearted Green. Radicals see businessmen as greedy, grasping Orange.

Racial views consequently reflect different stages of thinking along the spectrum of value systems. When individuals or groups pass through specific ranges on the Psychological Map, they become vulnerable to specific racial beliefs or practices - both in the way they perceive others and the way they are perceived by others. Managers of the evolutionary Spiral have to exercise constant vigilance and caution in dealing with this tendency to reduce human beings to destructive and demeaning stereotypes based on racial origin or racial characteristics. What should matter is the content of character and the quality of thinking.

Ethnicity and Culture

Ethnic sensitivity ebbs and flows in societies as pulsating colour mosaics - often hidden, sometimes surfacing, occasionally forming alloys and alliances, constantly in a quest for power, privilege and permanence. Groupings along ethnic lines tend to share common myths and memories regarding origin, feats of discovery and conquest. They usually have common language and religious expression, some sense of common territory, common enemies and threats, webs of family and kinship, common cultural habits and celebrations and common visions of future grandeur and glory.

Ethnic groups are sometimes culturally distinct communities within a state. They retain their cultural identity while accepting the larger state and operating within its institutional framework. At other times a political dispensation is forced on them by a more complex system, entrapping them within a coercive and punitive state. When the external force is reduced or removed, the ethnic groups bubble and boil back to the surface, demanding autonomy and independence. This has been the experience of the Soviet Union, India, Canada,

Iraq, Sri Lanka and other societies.

Some view ethnic attachments as being frozen in time, pervasive and permanent characteristics or traits of the individual or group. Such ethnicities are seen to exist on a horizontal level, to be closed and rigid and to develop a hard and impervious surface. In this view the Zulu ethnicity is seen by many to be chauvinistic and in an almost Teutonic mould, demanding the allegiance of members within a closed, tribalist order. The Afrikaner Volk is likewise perceived by some to be a "white tribe", a dedicated and self-contained monolith with a fixation on volk, fatherland and the Voortrekker tradition.

Others view both the Zulu and the Afrikaner ethnicities as flow states, open systems and steps on the staircase, responsive to threats and the surrounding environment. In times of tolerance, prosperity and generally benign conditions, ethnic attachments are buried deep within the psyche. But when the trumpet sounds the call to battle and the drums beat, the ethnic attachments may instantly surface and all the trappings of more complex systems may drop away.

Both forms of the Zulu and the Afrikaner cultural/ethnic groupings (as well as those of all others in South Africa) appear on the value systems spiral. They cluster essentially around the BO-Purple Second Level and the DQ-Blue Fourth Level collective systems. Ethnicity clothes itself in Purple and Blue, depending on the problems or challenges of existence being confronted on Helix One.

As has been demonstrated so vividly around the issues of violence and intimidation, when the Zulu system is under siege the assegais appear and are rattled as a prelude to battle. The imagery of a King Shaka is invoked, the impis form and attention tends to shift from the "civilian" leader (in this case Chief Minister Buthelezi) to the traditional king, Zwelethini, the Ingonyama or Black Lion. Yet millions of "detribalised" Zulus live in urban settings with Westernised urban values. They remain aloof from such events. Although they might be linguistically, and by extraction, "Zulu", their collective systems are likely to coalesce about a different Blue content - religion, the ANC or even versions of common South Africanism.

It is at great peril to society as a whole that communities are driven by events about them to redefine their worlds in terms of perceived threat. It is easy for elitists, self-serving politicians or groupings with a hidden agenda to wave the bloody shirt of racism to serve their ends; to define the world in terms of ethnic particularisms or exclusivist ideologies. But it causes the other components of society to react, displaying corresponding characteristics. When the PAC injects extreme black nationalism into the bloodstream, the antibodies of white or Afrikaner nationalism are activated, introducing a polarising element to the conflict. When the AWB marches under neo-Nazi banners, hard-core members of the Communist Party flaunt the hammer and sickle in response. When Afrikaner nationalists show preference to the Volk in employment opportunities and access to finance, they spark exactly the same behaviour in the ANC and others as to future distribution of the spoils.

In short, if one group paints the world in the colours of the Purple and Blue value systems, others do likewise though the content of their Purple and Blue systems differs and is usually in conflict. South Africans can avoid many of the excesses of racial and ethnic hostility by going out of their way to paint the environment in Orange and Yellow - signalling a readiness to strike deals, as well as a concern for the well-being of the entire social organism.

South Africa is a kaleidoscope of floating mosaics, each with different content (for instance differences within the Blue-DQ system in the Asian community - Muslim, Hindu and Christian, the castes and gradations among the Hindus), as well as different hierarchical structures (such as the different vertical pictures of various groups that disclose more Red and Orange in some, more Purple and Blue in others). It is not enough to define South Africa in terms of traditional categories such as English-speaking, Afrikaner, Zulu, Xhosa, Asian, coloured etc. Such descriptions fail to accurately portray the reality of this microcosm of the planet.

By profiling society's psychological geology - as levels, layers, pressure points, flashpoints, centres of gravity and critical masses - one is able to begin filtering the confusion of rhetoric, the confoundment of conflict and wildly different views of the future. But can it be possible to actually manage such a hotch-potch of differing Purple, Red, Blue, Orange and Green groupings?

In *Power Shifts*, the final book in Alvin Toffler's trilogy (the others were *Future Shock* and *Third Wave*), this social critic claims that:

"Under the impact of the new production system, resistance to the 'melting pot' is rising everywhere. Instead, racial, ethnic and religious groups demand the right to be - and to remain - proudly different. Assimilation was the ideal of industrial society, corresponding to its need for a homogenous workforce. Diversity is the new ideal, corresponding to the heterogeneity of the new system of wealth creation."

In the place of monolithic structures such as Afrikaner nationalism or the mass democratic mandates of liberation movements, Toffler insists we should create "mosaic democracies". The real challenge confronting South Africans in this global microcosm is to find the models, mechanisms and methodologies for the design of such a version of democracy. In Part IV we will outline an approach to the management of both horizontal (Purple, Blue, Green and Turquoise) mosaics, as well as vertical (Red, Orange and Yellow) as we describe a dynamic process of managing the complex, multifaceted and explosive South African Spiral.

Designing the Seventh World

Project yourself well into the future. Man has succeeded in colonising the moon, but all is not well on Planet Earth. Global nationalism has been shown to entrap people in arbitrary and artificial geographic enclaves which stultify their development and cause great discontent. The United Nations has declared national boundaries and self-seeking national economies to be a version of "global apartheid", and you are among the global citizens who have been invited to the first Indaba on the moon with the purpose of drafting a constitution for Planet Earth.

You are there looking at the blue orb suspended in space and you have to consider all its nationalisms, ethnicities, ideologies, collective memories, hopes and aspirations, technological triumphs and disasters. All have to be synthesised into one.

If you happen to be a South African you could have an advantage. You could have with you a copy of your own constitution, forged in the chaotic crucible of the 1990s. Other delegates could well turn to you for guidance in designing a Seventh World which is democratically managed to optimal benefit of all its constituent parts.

The future has to play a greater role than the past in shaping the present. Every time we, as the species *Homo sapiens*, have reached the end of the prevailing paradigm, we have begun to search frantically for what will be next, the New Order. Only a new complexity of thinking has the power to address problems created in part by the previous paradigm. We are fated, as human beings, to a never-ending quest because it is this, more than any other characteristic, that makes us human - this constant and pervasive search for meaning, fulfilment, freedom. Every time we think we have found the ultimate we discover it was a sandcastle all along, destined to be washed away by the next massive wave of change. If ever we discovered true happiness we would seek the nearest cliff to leap from. We cannot endure boredom. Our minds are designed to solve problems, and in doing so create new problems in their place.

Societies caught in the cusp between what was and what will be are at great risk. They can implode as the parties contending internally destroy one another in a mad orgy or feeding frenzy. They may collapse under external attack, especially if internal discord makes them vulnerable. An 800-strong Inkatha impi caused massive casualties in May 1991 when it attacked a squatter camp on the West Rand in the very early hours. The authorities explained later that the impi managed to penetrate in that way because it caught the heavy police contingent in the middle of a "shift change". The incident is mentioned because South Africa as a whole is in a major "shift change" and the resulting power vacuum has resulted in levels of violence as described in Chapter 8.

There can be no guarantee at all that life as we know it on the planet will continue to exist. History is full of the shadows of civilisations and empires which flourished, only to disappear. How audaciously arrogant we must be to imagine we are in control of these processes. We are like millions of ants riding a log down turbulent rapids, each arrogantly believing it is in control and knows best how to steer.

Beware those who proclaim they have discovered the road to Utopia, the key to Nirvana, the pathway to the enchanted garden. Rather heed such as the pragmatic American philosopher, Eric Hoffer, who loaded ships as a longshoreman most of his adult life in San Francisco and cautioned:

"Better to be bossed by men of little faith, who set their hearts on toys, than by men animated by lofty ideals who are ready to sacrifice themselves and others for a cause."

In Part IV we intend to describe a way of thinking designed to address problems to the Power of Seven and Eight within the Graves technology. We offer this psychological Rosetta Stone as an aid to negotiators who, in crafting a new constitution, will reconstitute society in its entirety. We trust that both friends and critics of South Africa abroad will find this a useful compendium of alternatives and strategies as they watch from a distance. But we have written this section specifically for bright and knowledgeable South Africans, right across the spectrum. They are only too keenly aware that their future, and that of their descendants, is on the line.

In Chapter 10 we describe how New Paradigm thinkers view the South African Spiral and what assumptions they will make in suggesting new options, processes and strategies.

Chapter 11 identifies the critical superordinate goals necessary to pull together conflicting elements into a common cause.

Chapter 12 designs strategies for facilitating the natural and inevitable flow of value systems through steps and stages.

Chapter 13 addresses the issues surrounding the establishment of the next political and economic order.

Chapter 14 concentrates on innovative and appropriate models for managing both the public and the private sectors.

Chapter 15 highlights practical application of this technology within South Africa.

CHAPTER 10

Bushmen of the 21st century

The San Bushmen who roamed Southern Africa three centuries ago were people who lived on the very edge of existence. Survival depended on the ability to locate and hunt down game, to detect the presence of water. Failure to do so - or to anticipate danger in the bush - meant certain death. The San accordingly developed a harmony with their environment which meant they were able to read it intuitively, as easily as modern-day man reads a book. We maintain that 21st century man has to become the modern version of a San Bushman because his very survival depends on it. Whereas the threats and challenges which confronted the San were relatively simple, the threats of today and tomorrow to our survival include thermo-nuclear war, the AIDS pandemic, degradation of the environment and its life-sustaining resources, population growth outstripping economic production and political turmoil which threatens to tear society apart. Twenty-first century man has to develop the intuitive capacity to handle these challenges, otherwise he will not survive in a meaningful way. In his favour are the positive achievements of science and technology such as medicine, a dawning understanding of man's place in nature, an unprecedented flow of information and access to a vast store of computerised knowledge and experience. Highly developed systems of ethics are encoded in law and religion, while various societies have developed effective and stable structures of decision-making and government. But 21st century man will not be able to relax for an instant. The challenges are so enormous and the have-nots confront the haves so consistently across the world that the fabric has frayed and torn in various places, South Africa included.

Let us return, for purposes of analogy, to the San Bushmen and consider what it was that gave them their remarkable instinct for survival. They existed three centuries ago in their pristine AN (First Level) and BO (Second Level) environment. Those we see today are scattered, often pathetic, remnants of a social system once well suited to its milieu. What remains is trapped in a time warp of history, unable to let go of the old ways but with little hope of integrating into the new. The film *The Gods Must Be Crazy* might have been more fiction than reality but it did make a point. The First and Fifth Level value systems are cultures and aeons apart.

Yet Louis Liebenberg, in *The Art of Tracking: The Origin of Science*, paints a picture of the original San being anything but primitive. He describes a survivalist system which is the antecedent of contemporary scientific thinking and of what we have called the New Paradigm.

The San developed an intuitive, holistic and dynamic anthropomorphic sense by placing themselves within the thinking processes of an animal. Perceptive trackers could think as the game thought. They would vicariously enter the decision-making world of the animal, creating a "virtual reality". Since they were able, in their communal and reciprocal society, to rely on others to supply meat when they failed, they had the freedom to experiment and explore new hypotheses. In a sense it was they who invented free-ranging "academic freedom". These so-called primitives inductively assembled an elaborate body of knowledge, what one might term a "collective research programme", a perpetual learning society. Every child learned through observation and practice and from fireside story-telling sessions where knowledge was disseminated. Liebenberg dispels any false impression that these hunter-gatherers were savage killers who ravaged the bush, savannah or tundra. They appear, on the contrary, to have been gentle and co-operative with others.

The San were simultaneously elitist and egalitarian. They did not have to choose between individual and communal needs. They were remarkably free of authoritarian thinking, which produced the flexibility and adaptability appropriate to a nomadic society. Their science of spoor-tracking was simply that - a science - without the baggage of "truth" and "certitude" that go with ideology. The San were also the first environmentalists. They demonstrated an almost child-like awe and enchantment with nature and all living things and, unlike practically all other societies, they left no trail of litter or destruction, only their marvellous rock paintings.

Liebenberg concludes that the modern brain had fully developed by the time of the San, and that it is this same brain which grapples with modern complexities. "A fully modern brain had evolved at a time when all humans were hunter-gatherers. Yet the same brain that has been adapted for the needs of the hunter-gatherer subsistence today deals with the subtleties of modern mathematics and physics."

In the Graves technology, the Seventh Level (GT-Yellow) system is one octave higher on the societal development scale. As such it harmonically reflects many of the First Level (AN-Beige) world view assumptions, though it obviously elaborates principles and processes at a higher level of abstraction and complexity. The seven characteristics of New Paradigm thinking, as described in Chapter 2, announce the beginning of a new set of six value systems in the Gravesian symphony. Those who have emerged into this New Paradigm (GT-Yellow) are the harmonic reflection of the First Level

(AN-Beige). They have the same characteristics of holistic information-gathering, an instinct for survival, an impatience with ideologies and self-proclaimed transcendental truths. Hence our analogy with the San Bushmen. They are the Bushmen of the 21st century.

As sketched earlier, the World to the Power of Seven contains elements a lot more threatening than the Kalahari Desert ever was for their psychological forerunners. The Bushmen of the 21st century confront a world which has been impacted on, both positively and negatively, by the experience of value systems which the San never encountered. The World to the Power of Seven is more complicated than the World to the Power of One. We are not saying it is better or worse - only different. The excesses of ER-materialistic thinking threaten to poison the environment. Advanced technology of mass destruction is easily available on the arms market. We continue to suffer from the activities of human predators in the form of modern-day warlords or robber baron capitalists. Competing ethnicities and so-called holy wars continue to plague and undermine civilisation. Millions starve while food rots in the breadbaskets of America. Lopsided planetary development spawns wars of national liberation and a parasitic struggle industry. Racism still haunts us, almost a half-century after Hitler. The inner city ghettos in parts of the world are given over to drug-fuelled barbarism and gangsterism, and the symphony of gunfire and sirens tells us Utopia is not here, nor around the corner. Explanatory theories, from rigid Marxist dogma to humanism, seem only to make matters worse. It is a very different world from that experienced by the San.

These and other problems exist in the South African microcosm in a compressed and highly explosive form. The theme of this book is that, no matter hard we try, we cannot resolve these problems by viewing them from any, or in a combination of, the first six levels of human existence. But we do have a "collective research programme" available, which can tell us what each system contributes to the human Spiral and what each detracts from it.

We know the BO-Purple-animistic system brings us a sense of mysticism and enchantment. It also paralyses us with superstitions and fear.

We are aware that the CP-Red-exploitative system empowers us with feelings of strength and invincibility. It also makes us ruthless, power-hungry and savage.

We have seen how the DQ-Blue-absolutist system brings us stability, meaning in life and discipline. Alas, it also introduces mindless authoritarian conformity and allows us to justify the most hideous excesses in the name of the Deity, the Movement, the Cause or the System.

The ER-Orange-materialist system substantially improves the quality of our lives. But does it produce heaven-on-earth? Today we pay a high price for life in the fast lane - in our family relationships, our inner spirit and in damage to the environment.

Many have benefitted from the warmth and human understanding experienced within the FS-Green-egalitarian world view. Yet has there not been a disastrous confusion of "equality within the sight of God" or "the essential human dignity of the individual" with lower-order equalities and inequalities? How does the system which purports to heal so often end up romanticising revolutionaries with an entirely different world view and agenda, often supplying them AK-47s and limpet mines? In *The Tears of the White Man*, Pascal Bruckner (who has long personal experience of assisting the Third World) provides a searing indictment of Sixth Level assumptions about "the noble savage", as well as the destructive illusions of sentimental "Third Worldism". Compassion ultimately becomes contempt, and it is the enlightened egalitarians who are the first to disappear in a revolutionary society. America's failure to redress imbalances via the welfare state bears eloquent testimony to the fallacy of this thinking, while many liberal South Africans are aghast at the current political violence in the "Third World" communities they had adopted and romanticised. They feel a sense of betrayal.

Why does the world not work the way it should? Why does "doing more of the same" only make things worse? The steps and stages of change, as described in Chapter 3, provide at least a partial answer. The BETA state attempts to regain the ALPHA conditions that are believed will restore the stability of the old order. The threshold of change necessary for a transformation to the NEW ALPHA has not yet been reached. Lacking, among other things, is insight - a mode of thinking which has the complexity to address the new problems. Perhaps a better question would be: "How" does the world work? But we believe there is a better answer to the question. We have in mind the New Paradigm.

The New Paradigm: Principles, Paradoxes and Processes

What systems of thinking should South Africans use, in this final decade of the 20th century, in addressing levels of complexity to the Power of Seven? What political and economic models should be considered? How can mixed levels of development be managed? What form should a new constitution take? How can major social issues such as violence, education, health care, community

NEW PARADIGM THINKERS

1
Think in Open Systems in Contrast with Fixed, Ideal States.

2
Integrate Natural Differences in an Evolutionary Flow.

3
Connect Everything to Everything Else in Quantum Chunks.

4
Act For the Entire Organism in Creating and Distributing Abundance.

5
See Everything by Holographic Scanning Before Acting.

6
Employ a Full Range of Tailored Problem Resolution Processes.

7
Consist of Resourceful, Fearless, Tough, Competent, Yet Playful People.

development and many others be handled? In turn, what might the South African crucible be forging that could be of practical use to global citizens as they encounter the same problems on a larger scale?

We will respond to these and other questions by: (i) constructing the scaffolding of the New Paradigm around and within South Africa; and (ii) applying its concepts as a developmental template to illustrate practically how the entire society might move out of BETA and GAMMA and through DELTA in the design of the first-ever Seventh World society (NEW ALPHA).

The Table Mountain Summit

For the remainder of the book we will take you to an imaginary meeting of what we call the first Table Mountain Summit. This will be unlike previous summits between the South African government, the ANC and others. Those meetings resulted in such documents as the Pretoria Minute or a series of recommendations on the control of violence and intimidation. Instead we introduce you to the New Paradigm at work. We believe it is the missing link, so far a blind spot in problem resolution. Table Mountain is a commanding vantage point and symbolic of South Africa. It is a place which inspired Smuts the visionary and is a worthy symbol of the drawing together of other South African visionaries, of all groupings, for a Third Trek to new pastures, which will involve all South Africans. Observers from other societies are welcome.

Problem Resolution in the New Paradigm

Each of the individual rings on the Spiral makes decisions in different ways. AN-First Level uses an intuitive, non-linear, holographic sense to detect and solve problems in the natural milieu. BO-Second Level tunes in to the spirit world, convenes a meeting of elders and relies on the chief to determine and announce what he believes to be the consensus (perhaps after consulting the sangoma). At CP-Third Level the Boss makes arbitrary decisions because of the demands of surviving in a hostile jungle. DQ-Fourth Level decision-makers argue from premises already held, rely on those in authority and codify the decisions as laws, regulations and traditions. In the ER-Fifth Level competitive world, decisions are reached via negotiation, deals, leverage, gamesmanship and pressure. In the FS-Sixth Level world of consensual thinking, everybody gets together, shares experiences and viewpoints and makes a decision based on what is fair and equal and caters for the sensitivities of all.

We do not believe any one of these processes - or all of them in combination - has the insight, power or technology to resolve problems to the Power of Seven. Yet each may be selectively utilised in sub-problem resolution, where problems have to be solved at the particular level it represents. The critical importance of selecting the appropriate technology will be described in a later chapter.

The Westernised ER thinking within F.W. de Klerk's cabinet is, for instance, set to play the negotiation game of power-sharing. The negotiating table is decorated in orange. The ANC, on the other hand, believes a transfer of power (Red) to a government-in-waiting (Blue) is in order. These modes of problem resolution are obviously in different frequencies, they produce different outcomes and they will create major conflict when they attempt to function at the same table.

Seventh World Thinking

In this problem resolution process we recognise the reality of Spectrums of Difference (Chapter 2) and Spirals of Change (Chapter 3). We are aware of the uniqueness of the South African situation (Chapters 4 and 5). We have interpreted the South African experience through the use of a new psychological Rosetta Stone (Chapters 6,7, 8 and 9). Now we are ready to put everything together, to lay out a strategy for the entire society over both the short and the long terms. A caution: every reader will interpret and assess this approach through his or her own level of psychological development. He/she may specialise in only one part of the whole, what we have called the elephant. We are now serious about finding a way to manage the whole elephant, to keep it healthy and growing. We call on all for assistance from their own area of expertise. Some will have the perceptual range and emotional freedom to think and act for the entire organism. The input of both categories is essential.

The New Paradigm Pentad

The situation calls for application of the Seventh Level thinking system, which focuses on five essential characteristics: the Law of the Spiral, Multiple Intelligences, Integrative Structures, the Power of the Paradox and Synergistics/Value Management.

The Law of the Spiral

For whatever reason, we as a human species are driven to utilise the genetic capacity within our DNA to reprogramme our minds and collective brain syndicates to deal with emerging complexities in our world. Our personal crucibles forge the new paradigms. That drive toward greater complexity has created the Spiral - the ever-enlarging rings that ascend and descend as our problems of existence ebb and flow. If that is the case, our ultimate objective should be to act in ways to preserve and expand the range and operation of the Spiral. Individual rings (value systems) are assessed not in terms of their relative importance but by whether or not they contribute to the health of the Spiral itself. Each of the human systems - from animistic to global - is treated with respect because each is a type within us that continues to function within complex psychological stacks and mosaics.

The Spiral is neither mechanistic nor symmetrical. It has its own internal logic and is rather like a living organism which is held in place by dynamic tension. Each system is anchored into the First Helix - the problems or conditions of existence within the milieu that brought it to life. When those conditions are steady, it will be steady. When those conditions are in a fluctuating, chaotic state, it will reflect that turbulence. So long as the Young Lions of the townships continue to inhabit moral and social jungles, they will organise in violence-prone gangs. The book (and film) *Lord of the Flies* illustrated how perfectly normal and civilised boys (DQ and ER) could down-shift into survivalist gangs, ridden with superstition, when they were isolated on an island after an aircraft crash.

Secondly, the systems interact on one another, sometimes in conflict, sometimes in congruence. Movement in one will impact on the entire stack, as with falling dominoes. Spiral managers have to be able to see everything at once. They need to think in a holistic fashion and have to be prepared to act - harshly if necessary - on behalf of the entire organism. This can perhaps be construed as "playing God", yet has been the case whenever a more complex system has performed such a role in respect of a less complex system, ever since mankind has inhabited the planet. But in the case of the New Paradigm, the command and control centre is located within GT thinking, in the interlocking holographs and networks. The bottom line is to think and act for the entire Spiral, not a particular part of it. (This in fact replicates the way we understand the functioning of the human brain. Memory is stored holographically and not simply in one mental library. Decisions systems are more like networks that draw information and insight from a number of neurological centres).

Abundance is therefore created and distributed on behalf of the Spiral rather than on behalf of a particular racial category, ethnicity, religion, national preference or sex, or as First World privilege. When the Law of the Spiral is observed, all its contents and value structures appear to flourish. The process of change and flow is facilitated, but not at the expense of stability and order. Movement up and down the existential staircase is a function of natural dynamic tension between vertical levels of development. Different economic, political and social models are not judged in comparison with one another but are laid out on an evolutionary spectrum. They are evaluated in terms of their congruence with different needs all along the Spiral. We will illustrate exactly what we mean by this concept as we deal with the issues germane to South Africa, specifically, and Planet Earth in general. Think of it as Spiralocracy - government of the Spiral, by the Spiral, for the Spiral. Abraham Lincoln put it rather differently in his Gettysburg Address, but then he lived and died in the mid-nineteenth century - a World to the Power of Five - when pluralistic, multi-party, free enterprise capitalism was in the ascendant.

Multiple Intelligences

Thirdly, the Spiral is best managed by the accumulation of multiple intelligences up and down its various rings. Without attempting to enter the realm of the esoteric or metaphysical, we believe the Spiral has a collective intelligence of its own, which governs how it will make decisions. In a sense it is a Spiral DNA. Each value system level has its own unique intelligence, or command and control centre, within its particular paradigm. This intelligence (as with the San Bushmen) is calibrated to its specific terrain on the First Helix. It has little or nothing to do with cleverness. Some of the Young Lions who operate at CP-Red have developed a street cunning which could border on genius. How else does one explain a ten-year-old boy organising an entire township army and being known as a "general"? Consider the intelligences of the Blue-thinking custodians of orthodoxy, who have developed a saintly wisdom in dealing with matters of truth and tradition. But the intelligences remain calibrated to their operating circumstances, and it is in vain that outsiders attempt to "jump-start" people into Orange-thinking entrepreneurial modes. It appears to happen when it wants to happen, not in reaction to artificial stimuli. This explains the failure of so many "black advancement" schemes. Their proponents appear not to have stopped to ask themselves why black society should be expected to produce proportionately more entrepreneurs than white society.

In other words, each system has its own version of cleverness or smartness, and all are essential if the Spiral is to retain its strength and integrity. Each system has its specialists, its individuals who possess that spark which places them above the ordinary, and they are to be found at all stations on the Psychological Map.

The Spiral also produces men and women with the perceptual insight and the "big picture" perceptions necessary if they are to think in terms of the Spiral itself. These generalists perform a function which individual value system specialists - however brilliant in their own right - are unable to fulfil. The late American anthropologist Margaret Mead suggested that crucibles of change (such as South Africa's) often produce "sapient circles" who seem able to step out of any particular dogma, territory or role to act for the whole organism. They command a universal trust and respect because they display a neutral objectivity combined with a capacity to empathise with all positions on an issue. Several such have already emerged to prominence in South Africa, on either side of the racial divide. These are our 21st century Bushmen who are able to enter anybody's "virtual reality". South Africa needs to harness their talents, much as the collective talents of England were harnessed in the "Invisible College", which later developed into the Royal Society. Note the words of Jonas Salk in *The Survival of the Wisest*:

"We must look to those among us who are in closest touch with the unfathomable source of creativity in the human species for an understanding of the workings of Nature and for insight into Nature's 'game', as we enter upon an epoch in which new values are required for choices of immediate need as well as for those with longer-range implications. This is especially important when, as now, the number born in each new generation exceeds the number born in each of the earlier generations. For this reason, the character and quality of the individual which will survive and predominate in our period will have a very profound effect upon the character and quality of human life for a long time to come."

These collective intelligences might reside in the collective wisdom of voting majorities. But if the intelligences necessary to manage the entire Spiral are not reflected in that majority rule, "the people" will bring chaos and destruction to the entire organism. In South Africa's case, the tyranny of the majority would simply replace the tyranny of the minority.

In other cases the intelligences may express themselves in rare and competent individuals who, working alone, produce feats of brilliance that neither collective thinking nor mathematical majorities could match. In other cases these multiple intelligences are sparked off by gatherings of the visionaries, Margaret Mead's "sapient circles", often from different levels of psychological existence on the scaffolding of values, who combine their intelligences within dynamic interactive group settings in a search for solutions to common problems (a good example was the Natal/KwaZulu Indaba). The human brain is unique in that it can function within all three arrangements, provided that leadership observes the Law of the Spiral.

Clearly, the disasters of Africa, the continuing racial conflict in the United States and the volatile eruptions of the Middle East are all of them the result of failure to respect these basic laws of nature. As Jonas Salk warned, we can no longer repeat the mistakes and expect to survive and prosper. "Nature will win out," Salk says.

Integrative Structures

Fourthly, GT-Seventh Level thinking utilises integrative structures in linking up what appear to be conflicting rings within the Spiral. Instead of attempting to weaken, eliminate, ignore or neutralise any of the six systems, integrative thinking links them up in a dynamic and interdependent relationship. When each is healthy, it contributes to the overall well-being of the Spiral. When a system is destructive, it cracks or collapses the Spiral, impairing the health of the entire organism.

The expression of intelligences within the New Paradigm can be compared with the integrative circuitry within computer technology. Imagine a large corporation which, over the years, bought into a number of different computer mainframes and individual personal computers - none of which had the necessary language to communicate with any other system. A Tower of Babel would result. The corporation's business activities would be chaotic. Just so with a political system where the different modes of thinking are unable to communicate effectively.

A magazine advertisement offering open systems computer

technology provides what amounts to a hardware version of GT-Seventh Level "mindware": "The network Application Support Environment for Manufacturing can unite Digital systems, Sunwork stations, IBM and HP machines, PC compatibles, MACs, all the different computers, applications and operating platforms so typical of large manufacturers." We suggest that the Gravesian Seventh Level thinking paradigm - the New Paradigm - has a corresponding power and the versatility to integrate all the positions in the alphabet soup of the South African political environment - ANC, NP, IFP, PAC, AZAPO, CP, AWB, DP, LP - and the rest. Each political grouping believes it speaks for the whole, for the entire elephant mentioned in our Prologue, when in fact it is able to speak for only a small part.

Power of the Paradox

The 19th century German philosopher, Georg Wilhelm Friedrich Hegel, first introduced the concept of a "synthesis of opposites". The Hegelian dialectic consists basically of the juxtaposition of "thesis" and "antithesis" as opposites. From their interaction, "synthesis" energes naturally. Consider then the following South African dialectic:

THE SYSTEM - "thesis"
>The philosophy and order of separation and dominance
>based on race or ethnicity

THE STRUGGLE - "antithesis"
>Moral, economic, political or military attack on
>"the system" in order to liberate and control.

THE SYNTHESIS - "new thesis"
>A higher and richer order that blends and integrates
>the best from both "System" and "Struggle", with new
>insights and discoveries from the changing
>environment.

The dynamic process pushes individuals and society toward greater complexity (synthesis). The "System versus Struggle" engagement is necessary because growth does not occur without it.

Such is the theory. Yet it turns out that various factors can block this process and prevent the dialectic working its magic. One is censorship, which prevents the free interplay of ideas. Another is political intolerance. When the Afrikaner bullyboys of the 1940s and 1950s physically disrupted United Party political gatherings, they were shutting down the healthy dialectical process. When black student bullyboys terrorise speakers on the campuses of the University of the Witwatersrand and the University of Cape Town, they are doing exactly the same thing, they are preventing synthesis. (Totalitarianism comes in many racial and ethnic packages but the results are invariably the same). The shutting off of entire communities from contact with one another, so fundamental to apartheid, has had even more impact in terms of preventing synthesis. And the cultural isolation of South Africa completes the process. All these artificial constraints block a natural evolution through inevitable stages.

It is vitally important that personalities and parties from all along the political spectrum should be encouraged to participate in the free-wheeling process of dialectical engagement. The radical elements of both wings need to be drawn in, as well as church and other leaders (no matter how egocentric), farmers' associations, business and professional organisations and youth groups. All are grist to the mill of socio-political evolution and they contribute value to the process. When the various levels of psychological existence are expressed in their positive ranges, they contribute to the life of the Spiral. But exaggerated lust for power or over-rigid commitment to exclusive ideology become malignant, they destroy the dialectic and the Spiral is endangered. It makes little difference whether such closed systems emanate from the so-called Right or the so-called Left. In fact the conventional conservative versus radical spectrum altogether misses the point. Fanatics can and do exist in both camps. Eric Hoffer, in *The True Believer,* puts it this way:

"Though there are obvious differences between the fanatical Christian, the fanatical Mohammedan, the fanatical nationalist, the fanatical Communist and the fanatical Nazi, it is yet true that the fanaticism which animates them may be viewed and treated as one."

Another way to express the principle of the Hegelian dialectic is to examine the role and function of a paradox. A paradox is when opposite options or alternatives appear at two poles, apparently mutually exclusive. Because the western mindset has taught many of us to think in absolute categories - good/bad, black/white, right/wrong - we are trapped. We are instructed to argue "for or against" positions. The middle ground disappears and to consider both alternatives is seen as feeble. Yet paradoxes can be powerful if approached differently.

Briefly stated, a paradox consists of conflicting options, often expressed as two horns of a dilemma. How can one accept proposition A while at the same time accepting proposition B? On the surface they appear to be contradictory. Our language is full of popular examples of this exclusivist thinking. "You can't have your cake and eat it." Or: "How can you fly like an eagle when you work with turkeys?"

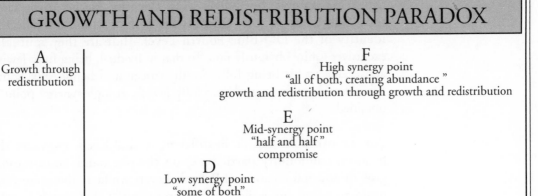

GROWTH AND REDISTRIBUTION PARADOX

A
Growth through
redistribution

F
High synergy point
"all of both, creating abundance "
growth and redistribution through growth and redistribution

E
Mid-synergy point
"half and half "
compromise

D
Low synergy point
"some of both"

C
Negative synergy point
"destruction of both options"

B
Redistribution through growth

Let us consider an example to illustrate this fourth principle of the New Paradigm Pentad. Generally speaking, the ANC's position on the new economic order is expressed as "growth through redistribution". Make that one horn of the dilemma. The traditional response of the business community has been "redistribution through growth". That is the opposing horn. Let us now form these apparently contradictory positions into a paradox.

Instead of seeing issues as "one or the other" or "for or against", thus locking parties into rigid position bargaining, paradox resolution has the potential to produce synergy. Think of the poles as the positive and negative wires in an electrical system. Rub the two together and there will be sparks and loud popping. Rub the two horns of the dilemma together and sparks can fly, creating synergy - new entities that may exceed the sum of the two parts. A sparking of "hard minds" and "soft hearts" could, for instance, produce compassionate pragmatism.

Paradox management allows one to see how "both/and" tends to replace "either/or" as the course of action. It may be useful to have paradox poles as end points in the creation of dynamic tension, a necessary condition for growth and development. In rearing a teenager, the child's "need to be independent as a person" often has to be balanced against the reqirement to "conform to the needs of the family." Obviously both are necessary, but in some kind of ratio. As the child matures and gains in experience and confidence, the tension points slide toward more independence and less conformity.

It can happen that the poles of paradox are located within one value system, as different expressions of competitive content. A person could, for example, be "fully Jewish" (Identity A) and at the same time "fully South African" (Identity B). Both fit within the collective identity of the DQ-Blue-Fourth Level - but are they mutually exclusive? Quite obviously not. To that individual, being fully Jewish adds value to his being fully South African and being fully South African adds value to his being fully Jewish. A high synergy point is obtained.

But the two poles can be in different vertical levels. How can the business community participate, on the one hand, in economic growth and job creation (ER-Fifth Level) while at the same time protecting and preserving the environment (GT-Seventh Level)? Once again, it is by balancing the range of creative tension that a powerful medium is discovered to maintain the overall health and vitality of the Spiral.

Synergistics: Value Management

Synergy literally means "together energy". The aim is to create something new and better instead of simply adding up the sum of the parts. But can this really be achieved when there are so many different and conflicting ideas, agendas, points of view, needs, aspirations and conditions? If negotiation (Level Five) and consensus-finding (Level Six) lack the capacity to resolve problems in a World to the Power of Seven, what can? Is there another and better way to build a just and healthy society out of the chaos of the crucible? Can it be made to work at both local and national levels? How can the Spiral best be managed? What will it take to keep the totality healthy and growing?

The answers to these questions may well be found in what is termed "Value Management". The doyen of this movement is Keith van Heerden, a South African engineer with considerable experience in the mining, construction and mineral industries in this country. He is widely travelled in the United States, Japan, Brazil and Europe. His writings and workshops are punctuated with such names as J.C. Smuts, Edward de Bono, W. Edward Deming, Peter Drucker and other creatively thinking theorists and practitioners. Van Heerden is currently managing director of the South African Value Management Foundation, an organisation supported by several of the country's large business houses.

VM is a highly disciplined decision-making process that utilises creative, scientific, holistic and participative mechanisms in unravelling complex technical and human problems which range from the corporate suite to the coalface. While it developed originally out of Value Engineering - a technology to reduce costs in large projects after they have already been approved - applications in

South Africa have enhanced the process by adapting the VE principles into a VM format. VM is operative before contracts have been concluded, thus significantly enhancing the "value" of the decisions at the front end. Quality is built in at the beginning instead of being frantically rescued at the last minute.

In the socio/political context we are discussing, VM decisions would be made by all involved; all the facts, ideas and possible solutions would put into the mill and then the decision group would put itself through a rigorous and disciplined process of sorting out and implementing specific, practical and workable solutions. Everybody is able to watch while this is happening. Since everybody is involved in the process and has a say, co-operation and ownership are built into the solutions produced. Solutions are not made exclusively by the "experts", the authorities or by counting heads, they are made instead by engaging the minds of effective people who are affected by the solution.

VM is unique among the decision sciences for a number of reasons. It involves contributions from across the spectrum, life cycle or impact range of a particular issue. In the world of business, VM sessions might see the company's customers involved with its production and marketing teams, streamlining their business relationships. If the cleaners are affected by specific problems and possible solutions, they are in the decision-making teams, possibly placed beside the managing director.

Unlike the quality circle programmes typically being used in South Africa, VM cuts across lines of authority, functional unit and status level. It should not be confused with the "feel good" session; the work is rigorous and demanding and difficult, but the rewards can be extraordinary. The step-by-step process often triggers spectacular results unforeseen at the start. VM appears to unlock the latent thinking abilities of the full spectrum of employees, and translates their insights into practical action. Many South African companies produce vision, mission, value and goals statements which never get further than the paper they are written on; the ideas are not implemented in the working environment. VM provides the integrative process which closes gaps between strategy and performance. The people called upon to make reality of the ideas were involved in formulating them.

In a typical VM session the participants identify the objective, isolating and ranking the key functions and creating plans of action. The "big picture" and "practical steps" are integrated. Politics, territorial imperatives and personal agendas are refined out in this decision-making crucible. Little time is wasted on defining problems or studying symptoms.

Dick Stringer, one of the country's several certified Value specialists, uses the term "detoxification" to describe how information is freed from the contamination of emotional or narrow thinking. At some point in the process, he says, a shift into Second Order Change thinking occurs. The collective intelligence of the group is then brought to bear in a creative manner on seemingly insoluble problems. Mental discipline, personal rigour and emotional commitment to the process are needed to spark the quantum leap.

VE and VM have been used by many South African industries to remove huge and unnecessary costs from major capital projects. Other applications have dealt successfully with highly emotional issues in employee and union relationships and hostel management. W.D. Winship, chief executive of Hulett Aluminium has produced a culture of VM within his managerial team, and says the process was invaluable in maintaining morale and production at a time when many of his employees had to pass daily through Pietermaritzburg's worst conflict zones on their way to and from work.

Winship believes that "every company chairman in the country should insist - and for that matter so should the decision-makers in government - that no project proceeds without first having been Value Managed." Gordon Dunningham, former deputy chairman of Barlow Rand, comments: "If only half of what has been demonstrated as achievable is translated in the South African economy, the results would be a staggering R6 billion saving of fixed investment or, putting it another way, an additional R6 billion of capital would be available annually for new capital plans or housing, with the attendant creation of jobs for South Africa."

We have dealt with VM at some length. As we will discuss in a following chapter, it is a technology which could well be the key to handling complex racial, economic, political, social and community issues in South Africa. A civil service imbued with VM disciplines, and a culture of reaching out for the active participation in decision-making of the communities served, would be in a position to resolve a major portion of the country's social frustration. VM could turn out to be the only decision-making mechanism with the capacity to keep the Spiral (the elephant we mentioned in the Prologue) alive and well.

*Ask, and it shall be given you; seek, and ye shall find; knock, and it shall
be opened unto you:*
Matthew 7:7

Common ground, Common Purpose

When American congressmen and senators took their seats in the
cold Capitol building in Washington DC in the winter of 1861, all
were fully aware of the crisis which confronted the country. Wave
after wave of violent unrest had disrupted commerce and alarmed
the churches and those few political figures who sought conciliation.
Inflammatory and polarising rhetoric from both abolitionists and
defenders of the status quo poisoned the atmosphere. Newspaper
headlines shrieked and the sabres rattled in both North and South.

As each politician rose to speak it became clear there was no room
for compromise, no reaching out to find one another, no meeting of
minds. Ill intent was assigned in total to the opposing side.
Diametrically opposite positions were being taken up. What was the
nature of the Negro slave - human being or chattel property? What
was the nature of the Union - contract or compact? These were
adversarial arguments, there was no point of contact from which to
set out on any sort of syllogistic process: "Since we agree that ...
therefore it follows that we should ..." Each side stared at the other
in blank righteousness, believing it alone had The Truth revealed.
We all know what followed. The fighting broke out at Fort Sumter
on April 12, 1861, and a long, bloody, costly and cruel civil war
began.

Without sharing common overarching goals it was impossible for the
senators and congressmen to engage in the art of negotiation. In the
absence of such overarching goals and values, even war was a more
welcome choice than national unity, social stability and life itself.
Every attempt to find such values ended in stalemate, gridlock, a
trapping of all the national elements in isolated and self-serving cul-
de-sacs. All were involved in First Order Change, doing more of the
same in the attempt to return to better times, but it only made
matters worse for everybody. What they needed was to discover some
superordinate goals.

Superordinate goals are comprehensive outcomes, values or
objectives which everybody needs to have realised but no single
group or person working in isolation is able to create or sustain

alone. What are the available superordinate goals for South Africa? What will bind together diverse political, economic, religious and social interests in common cause? Do such goals exist? Can they be created? If so, by whom? Is the prospect of South Africa's descending into the full horror of another Beirut sufficient to cause people to turn back from the abyss? And it is not only political violence which has to be addressed. South Africa is beset by a range of ills, from malnutrition and unbridled population growth to industrial pollution to a water shortage to a crisis in education to a shrinking First World component being called on to carry the impossible burden of an expanding Third World mass which increasingly demands affluent, comfortable niches.

The safest place in any multiple crisis such as this is the hard truth. The hard truth about South Africa is that these problems are likely to get a great deal worse before they get better. And at the same time the areas of common ground and common purpose necessary to address these questions are shaky, unstable and fractured. The purpose of this chapter is to construct a common basis or underpinning for the New South Africa, a necessary step before any attempt at peace-making, negotiation or nation-building can have a hope of success. We will seek out "common ground", superordinate goals in what we have called: Design of the Seventh World; the quest for reconciliation; the creation and distribution of abundance; and the gentle art of nation-building. If we find such ground, common purpose should become possible.

Design of the Seventh World

Time is not like a straight arrow that projects the past and present into the future. Change is chaotic as new life forms are produced in crucibles, which have resulted in new and quite different needs and aspirations. The expected linear flow from "have not" Third World to "have" First World is no longer possible at the level of affluence enjoyed by the developed societies. We have already used up too many of our natural resources. The environment (including the ozone layer) cannot sustain the cost of such extravagance. This is not a voice of doom and gloom, it is rather the forecast of a healthier condition for the species. Less can become more. The overall quality of life in the Seventh World would almost certainly exceed that of the First.

Christopher C. Cowan, of the National Values Centre, Denton, Texas, has published a highly relevant document under the title: *Disparate Synchronicity and the First-World/Third-World interface.* His basic thesis is that "the human parade is not a long, sequential column. Instead it stretches across a broad front.
We march side-by-side toward disparate futures, sharing common

time and the same earth."

Seventh World thinking avoids a massive influx of inappropriate First World solutions on Third World problems. It recognises that the transition out of Third World must pass through the authoritarian and disciplinary conduit of the Second World before the thinking systems of the First World can be realised. The movement must pass along a developmental continuum; it is not an easy hop from have-not to have.

Ignore this law and modern machinery rusts, massive new infrastructures collapse in on themselves and intelligent people experience the rage of inexplicable failure, even though it is no fault of their own. (A good example is in the frustrations following the financial collapse of Share World, a First World initiative in Soweto, launched by emerging Orange-thinking black business leaders. There was poor planning, poor market research, inadequate financing and a frustrated group of investors. Everybody lost). Cowan insists that the attitudes of both First World and Third World thinkers must change, often radically, if the Seventh World is to be designed. Waste, conspicuous consumption and corruption must be significantly reduced. All capital projects should be Value Managed to avoid duplication, overlap, waste and shoddy construction. The myth of the inherent moral superiority of under-developed Third World communities - the "noble savages" of an earlier era - has to be exploded. Different mindsets and operating systems must not be labelled superior or inferior. Politeness and healthy respect in human relationships are perfectly possible without losing sight of certain realities of difference. Dichotomous thinking (us/them, rich/poor, north/south, oppressed/oppressor, system/struggle, black/white) by definition leaves little room for meeting on common ground.

As First World-Orange thinkers flow into Green, Yellow and even Turquoise world views, materialism becomes less important. The entire First World society goes through the equivalent of a human being's mid-life crisis, seeking a more meaningful, slower-paced existence where there is time to smell the roses. By meeting the Fifth Level needs of their children, many First World parents are stunned when their material lifestyle is rejected by those very children, especially after attending liberal institutions such as the University of the Witwatersrand or the University of Cape Town. The rising generation, graduates from an Orange world, are already demanding a more human-centred existence, the World to the Power of Six. Living a more simple life has its intrinsic rewards for those who have already sated themselves on the riches of the upper regions.

Third World leaders, on the other hand, have to show considerable discipline in lowering expectations, insisting on Second World conduits rather than First World, and avoiding the extravagant and ego-serving displays of wealth and status that so often accompany the first flush of affluence. But it is not easy. It is difficult for responsible leadership to balance the pressing needs of "the people" against the spurious demands of political opportunists. It is important that they keep perspective because if they fail to create and maintain that balance, their days in leadership could be numbered and they are likely to be replaced in power by demagogues who promise all (though in the end are also unable to deliver). Corruption is an unacceptable facet of the Third World and it has been tolerated for far too long by the developed donor nations. It is simply not good enough that a generation of African leaders should have been allowed to privately define liberation as freedom to plunder the wealth of their developing societies, often placing the proceeds in numbered Swiss bank accounts to the benefit of themselves and their extended families. Others have profited immensely from the "struggle industry" and white Western guilt. America's Agency for International Development (AID) at one phase of its operations in South Africa channelled money indiscriminately toward anyone who flew the banner of anti-apartheid. In spite of open records laws in the United States, the patterns of those dollar distributions have yet to see the light of day.

The developing nations of the Third World appear to have been sucked into the slipstream of the First, to their great detriment. As Arnold Toynbee wrote, they are hellbent on following the technology of the West "because they feel that unless they get even with us in technology, which means in material power, they will be at our mercy and we shall continue to abuse our power and exploit them." First World technocrats and Third World tyrants could between them be the saboteurs of the Seventh World.

Cowan concludes: "It is abundantly clear that the planet cannot stand hundreds of millions of new Yuppies, thousands of wasteful new industries and dozens of new nation-tribes vying for power, extracting whatever they can from whomever they can to satisfy their lust for material pleasure, and rattling nuclear-tipped biochemical sabres purchased from the guiltless and irresponsible arms industry. Surely Saddam Hussein and Iraq taught us that lesson. A new form of earthling society must emerge - a new place in the sun for everybody. We have no choice. The sooner the better."

The Quest for Reconciliation

To "reconcile" means to return to a previous relationship, to restore a balance, to bring back elements that were once "together" but have now separated, often in anger and bitterness. The violent epochs of South African history, as described in Chapter 4, give reason for doubt whether such a previous happy relationship ever existed between white and black, Zulu and Xhosa, Boer and Briton or capitalist and worker. Why even use the term "reconciliation"? We seek a more profound meaning for the term, one which cries out for an integration, a fusion, a unity, a new synergy, a coming together of the parts of our common humanity which lie fragmented at deeper levels of our conscious selves. In fact this split self haunts the deepest centres within our neurological circuitry and chemistry.

On March 3, 1954, Laurens van der Post addressed a meeting of the Psychological Club of Zurich. His speech and the ensuing question and answer session was published in *The Dark Eye of Africa*. The Mau-Mau uprising was in full spate at the time and many were searching for causes of the African discontent. Van der Post was convinced that "there is no solution for the conflict in Africa, or in the world, unless there is first of all a change in the heart and understanding of man and I do not see how that change of heart can come about until the white man in Africa starts to think about himself in a new way."

He faults the white man for discrediting the way Africans live and deal with the forces of nature through institutions, customs, initiation rites and rituals. It was inevitable, he believed, that sooner of later Africans would reject what we refer to as the BO-Second Level and CP-Third Level world views. They would at least be subsumed to more complex levels of coping. He laments that nothing was put in the place of those world views and values. The materialistic, scientific "left brain" European outshone every aspect of the communal, intuitive "right brain" African, just like the imperialist sun. The two expressions of the human spirit were out of balance, in conflict and alienated from each other. Both European and African were fragmented, each having only one part of the human equation. Should they be reconciled, the whole human being would be together again.

Van der Post's thinking is greatly influenced by the insights and archetypes within C.J. Jung's psychological perspective. He naturally would sense the deep myths and metaphors that shape events on the surface. In his Foreword to *Modern South Africa in Search of a Soul*, Van der Post says that "the only way the Afrikaner can fulfill his historical destiny is to go through a great metamorphosis, to put it symbolically, an alchemical transformation of the base material of history into the transcendent philosopher's stone, really transforming past and present." We call this a crucible. And we suggest that Africans, likewise, must experience such a rebirth, as must all within the species *Homo sapiens*. That is probably the only possible pathway to reconciliation.

However, beware *The Voice from the Casspir*. It is able to block reconciliation. Anybody who has lived in South Africa knows *The Voice*. It emanates with the preliminary squeal of a portable microphone from the great armoured dragon-vessel that prowls the townships on tall wheels, capable of spitting teargas, fire and death. *The Voice* is in turn arrogant, abrasive, condescending, threatening, cajoling, menacing. It speaks sing-song in a guttural, heavily-accented English and it tells people exactly what to do: "You people ... unless you ... we will ...." It is humourless and remorseless. It is Orwellian authority, Big Brother knowing best. It fully reflects the corruption of absolute power held too long.

However, the police armoured vehicle in the township is only one manifestation of the *The Voice*. It is also heard in Pretoria's authoritarian bureaucracy as it mandates exactly what everyone will do. It does not always have an Afrikaans accent. It is heard in the black liberation movements and the trade unions as people are ordered to march, stay at home, go to school, boycott - whatever *The Voice* decrees. It is the identical *Voice from the Casspir*, it subscribes to the same values and would use the same methods to enforce its wishes. *The Voice* often has an American twang these days as the Administration or various congressmen articulate their positions on normalising relationships with South Africa or as certain American blacks do the most absurd things supposedly in support of a "mother continent" which they neither understand nor have very much to offer. This is a sad phenomenon. They find themselves still rootless sojourners in an alien land where racial conciliation is still a long way off. In the end they will probably have to learn from South Africa.

In contrast with the tyranny of *The Voice* is the melody of South Africa, in whatever language. It is heard in the gentle harmonies of Ladysmith Black Mambazo (a name which could have emanated only from South Africa) first conveyed to international audiences in Paul Simon's award-winning *Graceland* album, which synthesised the African and the European. There is surely a strong metaphor here. Sport is also a potent force for reconciliation, the roar of the crowd part of the national melody. The annual Comrades Marathon between Durban and Pietermaritzburg is an affirmation of genuine non-racialism the camaraderie of commonly endured hardship. Sport has played a major role over recent years in breaking down the barriers of apartheid and creating opportunities for common ground and common purpose. Even the most diehard conservative Afrikaner would find it difficult not to cheer the green and gold of his national sports colours, just because some of the skin underneath was black. Sports isolation has, in certain cases, achieved certain short-term objectives in breaking down apartheid. But for too long, now that internal change has been wrought, South Africans have been deprived of the experiences of reconciliation which sport can bring about. (Some maintain that the only unifying force in Ireland is the national rugby team, which is drawn from North and South, Protestant and Catholic).

Johan Heyns, former Moderator of the Dutch Reformed Church, speaks of a symbolic event which he anticipates being staged at Ellis Park stadium, Johannesburg, possibly to be repeated in Durban and Cape Town as well. He sees a colourful procession of the country's various religious groupings, backed by the melody of mixed choirs. Such an event would make a more powerful statement than any political leader could manage. It would have significant power of reconciliation. South Africans in fact need to reach back into the richness of the different African intelligences in their natural form and to fuse them with the best of European experience to form new and exciting alloys. Many Africans seem to have forgotten they were firing up iron smelters long before the Europeans arrived; the depth and richness need to be rediscovered. If South Africans are to successfully put together a Seventh World society on this southern tip of Africa, it will be populated by powerful, balanced whole brains and brain syndicates with which to contemplate the nature of life in the 21st century.

The Creation and Distribution of Abundance

The Cornucopia or Horn of Plenty is, of course, a Spiral. Fruit and vegetables pour out of the opening in the widest and most open ring. The Spiral naturally produces abundance. Managed effectively, the abundance of the Spiral is distributed in a way based on the internal logic of the organism. The health and future of the species *Homo sapiens* is completely wrapped up with the vitality, responsiveness and dynamism of the Spiral itself. When the Spiral thrives and prospers, so does humanity. When it is impaired by primitive thinking in one of its rings or overwhelmed by nature's wild cards (such as floods, drought or epidemic disease) or by attempts to mechanistically manipulate it for selfish gain, it ceases to produce abundance. This book has described the nature of that collective intelligence and has cautioned that such intelligence will not be found exclusively at any one level but is the product of the synergistic intelligences of all of the systems. The majority of people, their interests, the total health of the Spiral, the inherent nature of change and transformation and the anticipation of future needs and aspirations are all factored into decision-making in the Seventh World.

Most discussion of South Africa's future centres on the redistribution of wealth. We believe this is entirely the wrong focus - at this stage at least. People would do better to focus on the questions: How might South Africans, working together, create abundance? How can the size of the collective cake be significantly increased? How can new sources of wealth be identified and maximised? What overseas resources are available? How can savings of an economy of scale be expedited in the administrative systems? What external systems of funding can be tapped? What destructive or counter-productive forces should be reduced or eliminated? How can the new Seventh World be made to flourish in South Africa? Which individuals and groups have special contributions to make for the common good? How can they be mobilised and shaped strategically to integrate into healthy outcomes? How can the Spiral be prepared for a strong evolutionary thrust?

You will note that not one of the questions focuses on redress for past grievances. None resurrects old feuds or attempts to replay and repay the past. None so much as mentions redistribution. When the Spiral is fully understood, the inequities, disparities and historic barriers (GAMMA state) are dealt with in a constructive fashion. The decision-making system is not tilted toward the "white" First World, nor is it overwhelmed by the admittedly pressing needs of the Third World segment. It acts always on behalf of the Spiral in its entirety which, in turn, has the support of the entire population. The needs of people all along the various rings are met more quickly, thoroughly and progressively. Money is not pirated away to show up in private Swiss bank accounts. The rich do not necessarily become richer, but nor are they taxed to death. Welfare is at a minimum. Education, job training and individual accountability are stressed. Yet there are social safety nets and supportive book-ends at the beginning and end of life. Society is neither capitalistic nor socialistic - nor is it "mixed" in some elusive way. Resources are not wasted in bureaucratic bungling and inappropriate administrative structures and procedures. Abundance is created at all positions along the Spiral because people are encouraged to produce at the level where they are able to maximise output and earnings.

This is not Utopia. Life will always be turbulent, full of surprises and subject to sudden collapse. The various value systems and the respective content will be in conflict and competition. But the Spiral offers a better way to handle such perturbations, to "go with the flow", at the same time maintaining the integrity of the systems. There can never be any guarantee.

The Gentle Art of Nation-Building

The Amish of Western Pennsylvania are known for their ability to gather as a community and build a barn for a neighbour in a single day. While neither Rome nor South Africa can expect to be built quite that fast, the achievement of "common ground" requires careful analysis of the next step, which is nation-building. Aggrey Klaaste, editor of the *Sowetan* (South Africa's largest black newspaper) has already adopted this theme.

Nation-building is not to be artificially and arbitrarily forced on people. Attempts to coerce peoples or ethnicities under the same "national" control system are doomed to failure, as we have seen in the countries of Eastern Europe and in the Soviet Union. We have to assume that people are ready and willing to engage in the exercise, with appropriate caution and justified reservations. But we are able to offer some recommendations.

First, the concept of "nation" is viable only in the DQ-Fourth Level and ER-Fifth Level systems. FS-Sixth Level begins to move away from dogma, national boundaries, cultural imperialism and ethnocentrism. Listen carefully to the words in John Lennon's song, *Imagine*, and these sentiments come across clearly. GT-Seventh Level thinkers acknowledge the functional role of nationalism and will recognise when that system within themselves begins to pulsate, should conditions "D" on the Psychological Map return.

In DQ-Fourth Level-Blue thinking, however, national identity is a critical concept which allows an individual to connect with something larger than self, to connect with a cause, principle, piece of territory or belief that gives him purpose and meaning. At that level of psychological development it is an enriching experience, and the Blue belief structure will have plenty of content, whether healthy or malignant. When people shift out of Purple animism and Red exploitation, they are primed to enter a phase of their lives where they may fixate on, and bond to, an absolute order. The commitment might take the form of a fanatical zeal, as in the Crusades or when thousands of Iranian teenagers marched on the Iraqi machineguns to certain death.

The DQ-Fourth Level values container is capable of holding a number of different Blue contents, and here lies the key to understanding how ethnic mosaics might be managed in South Africa - a critical issue. Leadership, present and future, has to understand and accept the legitimacy of an entire kaleidoscope of the most diverse Blue content. These versions of DQ thinking are to be seen in religion (Hindu, Christian, Muslim or Jewish); in ethnic preferences (Xhosa, Afrikaner, Zulu, English, Tswana, Greek etc); and in social and political activities. If any one of these sub-contents were to gain supremacy and dominate the entire belief structure, the others would be pushed aside, even suppressed.

From the perspective of historical hindsight, most people can now see how Afrikaner political ascendancy, with its cultural emphasis on Christian Nationalism, imposed one version of DQ on the rest of the population. Arthur Keppel-Jones (then a senior history lecturer at the University of the Witwatersrand) saw it coming in 1947 when he wrote *When Smuts Goes: A History of South Africa from 1952-2010*. This futurist scenario, designed to shock South Africans into a realisation of what would happen if Smuts were to be defeated in an election, correctly warned that the Nationalists would meddle with the trade unions, set up a propaganda machine against the evils of the "British-Jewish imperialistic system", abolish the representation of "natives", disfranchise the coloured people and firmly entrench themselves in power as a one-party state (the last was not achieved *de jure*, but for many years the country might as well have been a one-party state).

We wonder what Keppel-Jones would write today about the surgings of the liberation movements. Much of their rhetoric, positioning, posturing and actions have a familiar historic ring. The Afrikaners also threatened to nationalise the gold mines if they came to power. Will the 1990s produce a black version of the Afrikaners in the 1950s? Some of the versions of black (or African) nationalism reflected by a segment of the ANC - and virtually the entire spectrum of idealists from the PAC and AZAPO - threaten to repeat the tragic excesses of apartheid. The Afrikaner monolith of 1948 provided no common ground for South Africans in general. There would be as little common ground in the 1990s under a "mass democratic" DQ-Fourth Level system of authoritarianism.

A new South African nationalism, designed for the Seventh World, will have to develop a clean and open-systems expression of DQ content so that all who embrace it are able to maintain their other religious, ethnic, social and even political affiliations. It will be important to preserve the particularisms and traditions of the past in order to provide stable anchors in what is going to be major transformation. As we cautioned in Chapter 3, the flow through the DELTA passage, following the release from GAMMA barriers, can be fraught with difficulty and danger.

Various writers on the side of "the struggle" have, for instance, called for destruction of Afrikaner monuments, such as the Voortrekker monument in Pretoria and the Taal monument at Paarl, in order to eliminate the last vestiges of apartheid. Such primitive vengefulness is unhelpful. (The Nationalists took the relatively mild step of removing the portraits of George VI and Elizabeth from their positions of prominence in parliament when South Africa became a republic - and they left Queen Victoria's statue undisturbed outside). The urge to destroy monuments is a symptom of CP-Red Third Level thinking, infused with a sense of power and destiny but well on the way to becoming fanatical, violent, destructive and barbarous. Civilisation, order and decency have collapsed before under the assault of such thinking and it can happen again. Those who speak for the liberation movements need to keep a tight leash on some of their followers because pointless provocation of this sort only prompts retaliation. South Africa's divided society has lurched often enough in the past into civil war and rebellion without recklessness of this sort to urge it on.

The Khmer Rouge of Cambodia believed they could simply eradicate every vestige of the old order. They sought to impose by force a brand of Marxist purity which would establish a New Order and lead to universal contentedness. The infamous "killing fields" resulted and the ensuing tragedy and chaos plumbed the very depths. The leadership on all sides in South Africa needs to proceed very cautiously in such matters. To quote Ton Vosloo, Managing Director of Nasionale Pers: "It will be an evil day if Afrikaners from all sectors of the political spectrum conclude that they are forced to unite and literally fight for the preservation of their language. Their capacity for destruction will make the IRA's struggle in Northern Ireland, that of the Basques in Spain and that of the ANC in South Africa look like cowboy games in a creche."Vosloo should be heeded. Remember, the Graves technology predicts that human beings can down-shift to value systems which were once held but have been subsumed to more complex versions. The CP-Red Boer commando and the DQ-Blue fighter for the Volk exist still in the hearts and minds of even the most liberalised and Westernised Afrikaners. They can be re-activated if the individuals are threatened by the same thinking systems in the black population. In 1899 the more enlightened and progressive quarters in the Transvaal strongly opposed war with Britain. They went on to produce some of the ablest, most courageous and most tenacious of the Boer fighters, many continuing the struggle long after the others had given up.

The design and acceptance of national symbols, flags, anthems, holidays, memorials and monuments will obviously be a difficult task. Not everything from The System was necessarily bad. Not everything from The Struggle has been necessarily good. The negotiators will have to work within The Synthesis, garnering the best of both and creating something entirely new. But, we emphasise, such symbols are of secondary concern and should not be elevated to the same importance as actually constructing a Seventh World system for South Africa. By sparking the two poles together, the Power of the Paradox could well generate its own new national design.

States are, as it were, born unequal; so much so, indeed, that by comparison the natural inequalities among individuals appear almost marginal. Moreover, to the inequalities that attend the birth of political collectives must be added the unevenness that marks their subsequent development. The age of industrial civilisation has strikingly accentuated this unevenness of development, thereby heightening earlier disparities of power and wealth.
Robert W. Tucker: The Inequality of Nations

Flatlanders and Flowstaters

In his book, *Flatland*, Edwin Abbott, a leading scholar and theologian of the Victorian era, described an entire mythical society existing in only two dimensions. (It was, of course, something of a satire on the self-satisfied age of Queen Victoria). The world of *Flatland* was flat, horizontal and bipolar. Its inhabitants could understand left and right and front and back, but they were blind to ups and downs. They could not detect the vertical currents moving above or below their field of vision. (Small wonder that the 19th century British so misunderstood both Africans and Afrikaners).

Many *Flatlanders* are alive and well and living in South Africa today (and everywhere else also, for that matter). Their language is full of such rigid classifications as black and white, Afrikaner and English, conservative and liberal, free market and Marxist and African and European. Shades and spectrums of difference, levels of complexity or even the possibility of evolutionary stages and phases escape them altogether; they do not appear on their personal radar screens.

Such people honestly believe - because it is what they can see - that once in a category, always so classified. If one inhabits *Flatland*, the senses are unable to detect the third dimension - much less a fourth. *Flatlanders* have to deny that it is possible for people actually to change either in horizontal categories or in vertical levels, living as they do in a two-dimensional plane. A white is always a white and only a white (or European). A black is inherently a black and will always behave according to black (or African) types and traits, claim the *Flatlanders*. It is astonishing how many elements of the AWB, the PAC, the Conservative Party and AZAPO are actually neighbours in *Flatland*.

But what if people should suddenly discover that there are other dimensions, up and down as well as left and right and back and front? The world must surely then take on entirely new and exciting dimensions. It should be possible for both white and black to be able to think and act through Orange values. For Purple, Red, Blue, Orange and Green value systems to pass through a black individual in his lifetime? It becomes possible that whites were in Blue when they devised apartheid but have moved into Orange and Green now they are dismantling it. Why else would they be doing it? If many blacks were in Red during the phase of struggle but have matured into Blue and Orange by the time they sit down at the conference table to design the Seventh World in South Africa, does this not open a new window of opportunity? On the other hand, what would the consequences be if a great number of those blacks remained in Red, if they were trapped in the fanaticism of Blue? Would negotiation then be possible? Would their children and grandchildren one day bless their memory as peacemakers?

To readers who are prepared to abandon *Flatland* to become *Flowstaters*, this chapter will make a great deal of sense. However, we must warn that *Flatlanders* come in many colours, guises and forms. They are everywhere. They will be found as university professors, in various pulpits of religion, in the corridors of power at parliament and in the bureaucracy; as chief executives of major companies and corporations; in the ANC national executive and among its cadres; in the media; and certainly in the police force. They will find this book as confusing and irritating as did Hennie Burger and Ann Thompson in Chapter 9. The reader has to decide between being a *Flatlander* or living in *Flowstate*. We recommend the latter because the world then makes much more sense - and life is more fun.

Indexing and Dating

The language and currency of *Flowstate* expresses an understanding of spectrums of difference and Spirals of change. *Flowstaters* borrow heavily from a list of communication techniques advocated by Alfred Korzybski, who is known as the father of the General Semantics Movement. In his long and complicated book, *Science and Sanity*, Korzybski describes the use of a number of devices designed to clarify, purify and add precision to language and thought. We mention only two - indexing and dating. With indexing one inserts a number following each symbol to indicate to the reader that it is different from the other uses of that same symbol. Thus ANC^1 is not ANC^2 is not ANC^3. As we suggested in Chapter 7, one finds ANC thinking in the Orange, Blue, Red and Purple bands. $Democracy^1$ (of black nationalism) is not $democracy^2$ (of the Scandinavian countries) is not $democracy^3$ (of free market capitalism). Three people with these different definitions in their minds could otherwise engage in the liveliest conversation, thinking they were all discussing the same thing. In fact they would be light years apart and the occasion would be as meaningful as the Mad Hatter's tea party. Different people mean different things with the same words.

Practitioners of Value Management therefore insist on functional, operational definitions of every major concept. If the words "justice for all" are used, the user has to define precisely what he means by the expression. If the term "law and order" has a particular meaning, this has to be clearly spelled out. Expressions such as "power to the people" and "liberation" have to be carefully defined. Decision-makers are in real danger of being misunderstood if they simply assume that others attach identical meanings to the words and symbols they use. A Zulu of the Inkatha Freedom Party will have a different definition of the term "cultural weapon" from that of a Zulu who lives in Soweto and supports the ANC. Cultural weapon[1] is therefore not cultural weapon[2].

Dating works in much the same way. You[1960] are not You[1981] are not You[1990]. The National Party[1948] is not the National Party[1968] is not the National Party[1992]. Joe Slovo, leader of the South African Communist Party, claimed on Republic Day 1991 that "the people who govern the country now are the same as those who governed it in 1961". He was apparently subject to the contrast effect described in Chapter 7. From his ego-involved position it would have been difficult for him to detect shades of difference in the political hues on the spectrum (indexing) or the evolution of the Afrikaner Volk through the value system stages (dating).

After every word, concept, idea, system, person, organisation or even country, an index or date - or both - should be inserted, at least in the mind of the individual considering these matters. Korzybski and other semanticists believe this a necessary process to separate mental wheat from chaff, otherwise we live in an insane world without realising it. We naively accept that people mean what we mean. Meanings are in people, not in words. When one considers the different ways in which the various value systems see the world and interpret events, one is entitled to wonder whether people will ever find one another in this chaotic crucible.

Steps and Stages

Developmental programmes seldom manage to actually develop the target peoples or societies, in spite of the noblest motivation and often massive funding. Why should this be? Two fallacies in thinking dominate the development industry.

The first contends that paternalism works. Initiatives which were faulted from the start have broken down all over South Africa, and not only in the bantustans. Educators, community development professionals and well-meaning religious leaders who inhabit the DQ world of Blue are convinced they are able to deposit "the truth", "the order" or "civilisation" into the minds of the unconverted. When Fourth Level evangelists enter the Fifth Level world of materialism, they become positively Machiavellian in their attempt to induce growth in people through scientific manipulation, using the carrot and stick approach. But their machinations are in vain.

The second fallacy takes the opposite extreme. The doctrine of *laissez faire* is believed to be the answer. There are two expressions of this guiding philosophy. One flows out of the ER world of Orange. If individuals are left entirely alone in a libertarian environment, they will automatically self-develop. They can and will pull themselves up by their own bootstraps. This strategy can be recognised in the claims of the free market advocates. They point to the phenomenon of astonishing growth in the black taxi industry as evidence to support their claims.

Laissez faire also flows from FS-Green-thinking egalitarians. Since everybody is at the same level of development, if only the DQ authoritarians and the ER materialists would back off, "the people" would be empowered to develop "the community". Unhappily this brand of thinking, emanating from Scandinavian, Canadian and American Sixth Level moralists, falsely raised expectations in Africa, only to come crashing down on the heads of innocent people.

This is not to say that the two approaches have failed altogether. Each can point to significant successes. We simply maintain that neither can develop the entire social organism, the whole elephant. They are for the most part designed for *Flatland* - not *Flowstate*.

We believe the key to the riddle of development is to be found within the Law of the Spiral, a dynamic process which incorporates versions of both paternalism and *laissez faire*, but in different configurations, ratios and equations. The quantum-based thinking within the GT-Yellow world view is the basic starting point. This practical approach to development utilises all available resources in sparking the natural, evolutionary shift up and down the existential staircase. For significant development to take place anywhere along the Spiral, the entire Spiral has to ratchet up simultaneously. If the top rings of the Spiral are destroyed or impaired, the bottom rings will likewise wither and die.

In 1983 the Eastern Transvaal experienced the worst drought on record. Worse, most of the country's electric power is generated by Eskom power stations in the region. The level of the Grootdraai Dam, on which these stations depend for cooling, was critically low. The only alternative source of water was 200 km away in the Vaal

Dam - but downstream. The challenge to the Department of Water Affairs and Eskom was to somehow make the water flow 200 kilometers upstream. In a brilliant feat of engineering, seven weirs were built on the Vaal, pumps were installed and water was lifted up successive levels until it reached Grootdraai. Not a single watt in power was lost and a R2 billion loss to the economy was averted.

We find this technological achievement a striking metaphor of the type of thinking which will be necessary to develop South Africans who presently exist at different levels of complexity. Upliftment has to be innovatively engineered, using the Seventh World principles of the Graves technology. A series of psychological weirs will have to be constructed and numerous colour-coded (value system) pumps installed. The individual and collective minds of South Africans will have to be lifted up at various levels. The "water" of growth and development will flow uphill, through CP, DQ, ER, FS and into GT and HU.

We will focus on four specific aspects of the process: appropriate technology, containment of explosive conflict, education and so-called black advancement.

Appropriate Technology

Africa is littered with the wreckage of ambitious schemes which violated the principle of applying appropriate technology. Tractors rust in the fields because spare parts or even petrol were not available when needed. American educational and training manuals gather dust on schoolroom shelves, machinery stands idle in company storehouses. Zambia experienced near-famine in the 1970s when it switched to Eastern Europe for advice on agriculture. The British Labour Party is still haunted by the failure of its massive post-war ground-nuts scheme in East Africa. The First World has a bad habit of dumping left-overs, last year's models and second-hand technology on developing societies in a self-serving pseudo-philanthropy which secures tax advantages, offloads guilt and scores political points at meetings of stockholders.

Barely literate homeland government ministers are driven to their offices over rough, dusty, essentially Third World roads in expensive German limousines. First World housing schemes are imposed on Third World communities who are not particularly grateful and would really prefer the money to be spent on something different. People seem to be very good at telling others what it is they need and want. However, in a Seventh World system a great deal more time and effort would be expended in asking people what it is that they need and sitting down with them for joint planning.

The importance of this simple concept is becoming increasingly apparent to the people of South Africa, but only after other approaches have failed badly and continue to do so. At the same time, there have been some remarkable breakthroughs and innovative developments with implications for the rest of Africa and the world at large. Hundreds of examples could be cited, but a few are sufficient to make our point.

Ian McRae (known throughout the sub-continent as "Mr Electricity") and John Maree are top executives at Eskom, the South African electricity utility which could well develop into a power system for Africa. Eskom is notable for its introduction of appropriate technology and has entered areas where an electricity utility does not normally function. Several years ago Chief Engineer Alec Hamm called for a radical change in thinking about the development of black townships, notably Alexandra on the northern boundaries of Johannesburg where 95 percent of the houses were to be demolished to make way for new ones and Fifth Level white business interests could hardly wait to get started. Many challenged the involvement of an electricity company in town planning, but Hamm's ideas are now being implemented under the leadership of Nic Terblanche, Eskom's Architecture and Civil Engineering Manager. Instead of demolishing existing homes, Hamm and Terblanche insisted on upgrading what already existed, in recognition of "the lifestyle of urban blacks, their strong social orientation, the important role which tradition plays in their lives and the fact that natural associations have been formed between individuals and groups over many decades". (Contrast this with the ideologically-inspired "slum clearance" of District Six in Cape Town, which has left a physical scar in the heart of the Mother City and a scar on the collective psyche of the coloured community). Local labour was trained and used in the rebuilding process in Alexandra, another advantage over the original plan. Eskom has also introduced the "smart card", a pre-paid coupon which buys electricity through the meter and eliminates a number of frustrating First World processes, including meter-reading and collection of payments. Others at Eskom have experimented with setting up local, community-led power co-operatives, which bring the management of the townships closer to the people.

Unidata operates under the chairmanship of Nicholas Frangos as a strategic, global First World player but is at the same time developing unique and relevant technology for the Third World. Unidata engineers have designed an ATM system that allows KwaZulu pensioners access to their money using their thumb print instead of the more sophisticated (and stealable) card. This technology has already saved a considerable sum of money by eliminating fraud while protecting the interests of legitimate pensioners.

Durban inventor Brian Johnson and his son Clinton believe they have found the solution to one of Africa's age-old health problems. They have developed a mobile, battery-operated, solar-charged water purification unit which eliminates ecoli bacteria. One unit is being used by the World Health Organisation in Mozambique where cholera is rampant, while enquiries have come from several South American countries.

The search for affordable low-cost housing has become something of a national passion in South Africa. First World technology and building methods are being adapted fast to Third World needs and preferences. Many schemes use "sweat equity" - owner building - while others stimulate a profitable construction industry among black entrepreneurs in the making. In May 1991, 59 different types of home across a wide price spectrum were displayed at a housing show in Johannesburg. Such an event simply could not have happened a few years earlier.

While Bob Tucker was Managing Director of the Perm - one of South Africa's largest building societies - he was something of a voice in the wilderness. Keenly aware that the future customer of his organisation would be primarily black, he launched a series of initiatives to adapt forms, procedures and requirements to the needs of Third World populations, black or white. This was not another form of paternalism, it was a genuine recognition of the problems many faced in gaining access to First World financial institutions and resources.

The Triple Trust Organisation was launched in Cape Town in 1988 to spawn informal sector job creation. The TTO recognised that training alone was not sufficient to uplift the thousands of people, with little or no education, who sought to enter the employment market. Training had to be followed up with appropriate financial and marketing support for new businessmen. The TTO works through existing community organisations in the black townships, creating jobs and encouraging self-development. The organisation now offers a "Township MBA" - a 40-hour course of specialised training in using a calculator, investigating the market, managing weekly cash flow and other business skills. The TTO was initially inspired, as were many such agencies, by the FS-Green set of beliefs about people. Many sensitive and concerned South Africans, emotionally dismayed by apartheid, played an important role in assisting, rescuing and providing for its victims. Many had the disillusioning experience of finding the kindness of Green to be often exploited by the raw selfishness of Red, and have gone through a new learning curve to shift into a more complex and demanding operating system. At TTO today one finds evidence of the thinking and discipline necessary to function in the Seventh World. Much the same can be said of organisations such as the Urban Foundation, the Small Business Development Corporation, the KwaZulu Finance and Investment Corporation (KFC) and the KwaZulu Training Trust (in spite of the quasi-governmental character of the three last-named), all of which are heavily and creatively involved in building prosperity and a meaningful existence for many thousands, harnessing the dynamics of the free market.

Rural development is a badly neglected area where innovative thinking - the very antithesis of government bureaucracy - has shown itself capable of yielding the most astonishing results. The Institute of Natural Resources (attached to the University of Natal but funded largely by the private sector) has been conducting practical research for almost a decade into converting small-scale subsistence farming to profitable commercial farming. It has shown that the small land allocations of the homelands can be productive and profitable. Zulus at a large pilot scheme are producing dairy products, timber, fruit and vegetables and poultry, which they had never farmed before. The KFC (mentioned above) and the South African Sugar Association have made available the loan finance for a thriving cane growing sector among small black farmers who now supply a significant and increasing tonnage to the sugar mills. These initiatives suggest that a coherent, Value Managed strategy of rural development could transform a presently poverty-stricken rural sector.

These and many other examples of a shift in thinking on the part of South Africans are likely to pay dividends in the decades ahead. They illustrate how First World segments are forming bridges to facilitate major movement among the have-not communities. The goose lays its golden eggs not just for the haves; the Fifth Level-Orange system is mobilising its resources to enhance the quality of life across the whole of society. Of course, if that goose were to be cooked and redistributed in equal pieces to the masses, it would provide a meal or two and then hunger would set in. The South African crucible has unique features which allow it to forge such positive developments. No other society in the world has quite these unique mixtures. The next decade should see the explosion of a number of technological innovations designed to raise standards of living and enrich the quality of life across the whole of society.

Containment of Explosive Conflict

In discussing Spirals of Change in Chapter 3, we described how personal and societal transformations pass through BETA, GAMMA and DELTA when leaving one system (ALPHA) but before reaching the next state, the NEW ALPHA. Minor conflict and lawlessness may appear in BETA but GAMMA is fraught with high levels of turbulence and massive emotional fluctuations. The crime rate as well as personally destructive activity such as alcoholism, drug abuse and suicide always Spirals up to unprecedented heights.

When large numbers of people in any social system are trapped behind the barriers in GAMMA, the pressure on law enforcement systems is extraordinary, and explosive conflict becomes extremely difficult to contain. If Eskom and the Department of Water Affairs had been unable to contain the flow of water in the conduits up to the Grootdraai Dam, they would have been unable to achieve the results they did. Likewise, South Africa is at considerable risk if society is unable to contain explosive conflict.

In Chapter 8 we discussed the problem of violence. It is something systemic and to be expected in a society experiencing a transition and transformation as profound as South Africa's. It will require the most skilled handling, largely by the police force. Yet there have been cases where police action has created even more barriers and frustrations, deepening the GAMMA crisis and the resulting violence. The whole concept of policing needs to be changed in South Africa (and in various other parts of the world as well) so that policemen are seen to be not as an alien, occupying force or the enforcers of unpopular policies or ideologies, but as upholders of the rights and liberties of the communities they serve and a bulwark against crime and intimidation, political or otherwise. They need to be seen to be a part of the new society being created, not an attempt to re-impose the old order.

Unfortunately (and without detracting from the excellent qualities of many thousands of officers and men over the years, their positive achievements or the difficult and dangerous circumstances under which they presently operate), the South African Police (SAP) have a poor public image, among the black communities in particular. For years they had to do apartheid's dirty work - pass law arrests and the especially demeaning enforcement of a law prohibiting sexual intercourse between people of different races. In the days before black trade unionism was legalised and formalised there was a tendency among industrialists to telephone the police at the first stirrings of labour unrest, expecting it to be forcibly suppressed.

Yet there can be no doubt either that a culture of CP-Red and DQ-Blue was allowed (or encouraged) to flourish in the SAP, an aggressive, bullying approach and the sense of a calling to enforce the authoritarian ideology of apartheid. Black South Africans (and very occasionally white English-speaking university students) were on the receiving end. Draconian security legislation which provided for indefinite detention, incommunicado and without recourse to the courts, made abuse inevitable (as it would have been in virtually any police force given such powers). The list of persons who died while in the hands of the security police is probably the most shameful chapter of South Africa's history. Add to this occasions when police have opened fire on crowds - names like Sharpeville, Soweto, Uitenhage and Sebokeng are seared into the political memory of black South Africa - and the capacity of the SAP to credibly enter the current turbulence as a politically neutral peace-keeping force is limited.

Yet the SAP is all South Africa has to maintain order, short of martial law and a calling in of the Defence Force. It seems the SAP will have to remake its image while still holding the line against serious disorder (not to mention its demanding role in crime prevention and detection in areas far removed from political unrest). It is no easy task and can be achieved only by results which, in turn, can be achieved only by thinking in the command structures of the SAP of a higher order than in the past. The SAP will have to shift into ER-Orange thinking, where race and ideology are unimportant but problem resolution and results are sought. ER-Orange policemen would be motivated to achieve law and order, and if this could be accomplished by pragmatism and deals on the ground, rather than baton charges and birdshot, that would be their route. Directed by GT-Yellow Seventh Level thinking in government, with its concern for the well-being of the entire Spiral, a police force with Orange thinking in its command structures would be an efficient and potent force for securing peace. In crowd and unrest control the SAP are already behaving with a restraint amd maturity which was lacking in the past, and this should be encouraged by the infusion of a strong ER-Orange content in training programmes so that policemen will be absolutely clear in their minds as to their proper role - intelligent, non-partisan keeping of the peace, upholding of the law and protection of law-abiding citizens. At the same time police salaries should be considerably increased (at present they are shameful) so that men and women of the highest calibre are attracted, while recruitment needs to be stepped up because the SAP is at present hopelessly undermanned. The last thing South Africa can afford at this critical stage of its development is a police force which is inadequately trained for a highly complex role, or a police force that does not have the manpower to cope, thereby encouraging political gangsterism and adventurism.

It is vital that the police should be community-affiliated and seen to be so. Not only does it make police work easier if individual officers know and understand the community they serve, it is the only way they will get the community's acceptance and co-operation. There have been suggestions that the SAP should be disbanded, making way for regional and local forces which would be "closer" to their communities. The city of Durban already has its own police force (in fact it is the oldest in the country) which operates in conjunction with the SAP. The city has long been a non-racial "equal opportunity" employer and the Durban City Police draw on all population groups and appear to have good morale and a reasonable standing in the community. But in the same region KwaZulu has its own police force, which is the subject of bitter recrimination. The KwaZulu Police are accused by the ANC of being Inkatha in uniform (CP-Red, DQ-Blue - perhaps a shade of BO-Purple as well) and of the most brutal intimidation of their political opponents. Whatever the merit or otherwise of the accusations (they are strongly denied), the lesson is that if policing is to be decentralised it has to be done in such a way that there can be no question of all of local forces becoming the fiefdoms of local political figures. A centralised professional structure (preferably with minimal political control) would be needed to provide training conducive to ER-Orange thinking, to set standards and to monitor performance countrywide.

There have also been suggestions that township "self-defence units" created by the ANC should be incorporated with the SAP, the suggestion coming from none other the Minister of Law and Order. We suggest caution with such a programme, not because ANC supporters should not be taken into the SAP (in fact there are indications of ANC support among serving black policemen) but because the individuals in those township units would almost certainly be at the CP-Red Third Level of thinking in the Gravesian Spiral, which is altogether inappropriate in policemen. Raw projection of power in the CP-Red mode is likely to aggravate conditions in the townships rather than calm them. The SAP already have experience of attempting to absorb such elements. The "kitskonstabels" (instant constables) are an auxilliary force drawn from the township youth and given the most rudimentary training of a few weeks before being returned to the fray, usually armed with shotguns. They are intended to supplement the SAP's severely stretched manpower in areas of unrest. By the Graves definition they are CP-Red and combatants rather than policemen. The kitskonstabels have been a headache for the conventional SAP - ill-disciplined and erratic - and it is difficult to imagine the ANC's township defence units behaving any differently. CP-Red is CP-Red. They could, of course, be shifted by conventional police training into ER-Orange/DQ-Blue values (as could the kitskonstabels) but that is not the same thing as attempting to simply absorb incompatible elements. Far from bringing order to the townships, encouragement of the self-defence units could be a step along the road to the Beirut scenario.

If policing is to become community-based, it would be a major advance if local review boards were to be established, drawn from local communities. These would monitor the performance of the police in their area, make suggestions, register complaints and maintain close liaison. They could operate effectively, whether the SAP continues in its present role nation-wide or whether policing is regionalised and localised. Such review boards would provide a valuable input to any permanent commission on violence (which was being mooted at time of writing), and they could forge the strongest links between police and communities.

However, police cannot be expected to do more than hold the line while the country reforms itself. They cannot be expected to do so indefinitely. Unless society addresses the problems that created GAMMA conditions, neither the police nor the defence force will be able to hold down the lid forever.

Education

South Africa will not realise its potential without a skilled and educated workforce. Sound public education is the mainspring of the successful economies of the Pacific Rim nations, Japan, Taiwan, Hong Kong, South Korea and Singapore. Bantu Education, on the other hand, has stultified the growth of several generations of South African blacks, while turmoil caused by discontentment with this inferior system has ironically produced a "lost generation" of blacks with virtually no education at all. South Africa is paying dearly indeed for Verwoerd's bizarre dreams. Whereas a reasonable system of black education might have developed out of the old mission schools (which produced such leaders as Mandela, Sobukwe and Buthelezi), the mission system was vengefully destroyed. South Africa now has to expend billions, building on the foundations of a discredited and inferior system. Such colossal and expensive cumulative mistakes have been made over the past four decades that the country simply cannot afford more. It might never recover. If ever there were a case where the Code of the Spiral should be respected, it is in education.

The United States severely weakened its system of education because it neither understood nor respected the Code. In almost every category American students are falling further and further behind their counterparts in Japan and Western Europe. The attempt to use forced bussing as a means to achieve the integration of schools and society has produced mixed results. Many today - in the African-American communities especially - are convinced that the experiment failed. South Africa needs to beware of the same trap.

Americans failed to recognise to what extent slavery, racism and segregation had left their ugly mark on society. Many believed that "minority" children, only two or three generations removed from the most grinding poverty and oppression, could easily mix with their

GRAVESIAN LEARNING THEORY

DEEP STRUCTURE	LEARNING SYSTEM	TEACHING SYSTEM	REASON FOR LEARNING
A-N Survival Sense BEIGE	Habituation Instinctive	Physiological (periodic needs) Biological needs	To satiate senses and respond to biological drives
B-O Kin Spirits PURPLE	Conditioned (classical)	Assuring (aperiodic needs) Ritual, repetition	To find safety and carry on folk traditions
C-P Power Gods RED	Conditioned (operant)	Survivalistic (psychological) >Self-image, power	To feel own power and break loose from constraints
D-Q Truth Force BLUE	Avoidant	Structural (security) Order, show meaning	To be told what's right and find approval in truth
E-R Strive Drive ORANGE	Expectancy	Experimental (autonomy) Adequacy, >success	To weigh options and discover how best to prosper
F-S Human Bond GREEN	Observational	Affiliative (acceptance) Love, understanding	To sense harmony and come to peace with self & other
G-T Flex Flow YELLOW	Informational	Integrative (existence) Knowing, being free	To gather data and make choices based in own principles
H-U Global Flux TURQUOISE	Experiential	Holistic (expansiveness) Becoming, rejoining	To participate in the life process and gain insights

more affluent counterparts in the "majority" populations. Thousands did manage to do so and have performed at the same level as the historically more privileged. Yet thousands of others have been left behind. They fail to acquire the necessary education in schools with mixed racial admission (and mixed value systems). Certain black leaders now demand single-race, single-sex schools in an attempt to correct matters. Such demands are in violation of America's Civil Rights legislation - the product of FS-Green thinking - but a separation might become necessary over the short term so that the sub-culture can be jump-started before being allowed back into the American mainstream. Such a course would be anathema to Green egalitarians because it undermines all they adhere to and hold sacred, but to those at the GT-Yellow Seventh Level of complexity it would be just another practical problem where one ring of the Spiral needs attention so that it can be restored to full health, to the benefit of the Spiral as a whole. By contrast, in such cases Green thinking is artificial, impractical and damaging not just to those it seeks to assist but to society as a whole.

Research by the National Values Centre in Texas appears to bear out the concern of black American leaders about the state of education. The Centre has worked for more than six years with the all-black high schools of South Chicago, right in the heart of the ghettos. Graduates of the public high schools have, as a group, shown considerable weakness in two areas, according to the major industries and other employers in the Chicago area. They have been significantly weak in the analytical, logical and mathematics-based thinking skills. Secondly, there was a recognisable lack, according to the research, in what was termed the "work ethic" - the capacity to respond to highly structured, time-centred, purpose-driven thinking patterns. These problems might or might not translate into South Africa since black[USA] is not the same thing as black[RSA]. But it is a disturbing indicator, given the turmoil in so many of South Africa's black schools, of the devastating effect poor schooling can have on young lives.

At the government schools in South Africa which were until very recently used exclusively by whites, Asians or coloured children, the problems artificially created in America seem unlikely to arise. As the effects of the Group Areas Act (now abolished) disappear, black affluence increases and normal, racially-mixed neighbourhoods emerge, the pupils in local schools will have similar value systems and will find the environment stimulating and healthy. (Note how many of the children of black political and religious leaders attend private schools. This supports our thesis that values speak far louder than race or ethnicity).

However, this solves only a tiny sector of the challenge posed by education. Private schools and existing white, coloured and Asian government schools are a drop in the ocean when considering needs as a whole. It is in the sector termed "black" education (which at present falls under a bewildering multiplicity of homeland and other authorities) that the real upliftment is required. And the project is so vast, the amounts of money to be expended so huge that the potential for disaster is great. We recommend Value Management from the start, involving community leaders as well as educationalists.

What kind of schools do blacks need and want? It could well be that, having lived through turmoil since 1976, they yearn for a dose of good, old-fashioned authority and discipline of the sort which FS-Green-thinkers would find archaic and intolerable. The schools which managed to survive and even thrive through Soweto's education-centred violence have been the traditional, structured, "nuns with rulers" authoritarian establishments. So many black South African children have been trapped in the mindless violence of the CP-Red range on the Psychological Map that they possibly yearn for authority and a sense of purpose in life. Yet other children are at the Fifth and Sixth Levels of thinking and will respond favourably to entirely different learning environments. What we are pleading is that equal education - in itself an excellent thing and long overdue - should not mean grey uniformity. South Africa seems to be headed for a single education authority, regionally organised, and seven years' free and compulsory primary school education, much on the model of Singapore. But it is vital that such an expensive and expansive structure should focus on people's real needs and wants; that educationists should be able to recognise the spectrums of difference and the Spirals of change within society and adjust the structure of education accordingly. How tragic if Afrikaner *Flatland* educationists should simply make way for other *Flatlanders* who happen to be black.

The real challenge is to design schools for the Seventh World. It will require innovative and creative mixtures of computers, communication technology - including complex satellite transmissions in multiple languages - and, of course, sensitive, responsive and demanding classroom teachers. Nowhere is the importance of appropriate technology more evident than in education. It is also important that the economy be prepared to absorb school-leavers, artificially fired up if necessary. Zimbabwe has created a major crisis by enhancing school education for all yet following policies which have depressed the economy. Job opportunities simply do not exist in either the private or the public sectors. It is pointless, if not fatal, to educate children for careers which may not exist when they enter the employment market. Such a lack of foresight and planning could trap an entire generation of youth in the GAMMA state.

Black Advancement in Management

It is self-evident that if blacks are to have a stake in the emerging new society, they need to be allowed to develop to their fullest potential, economic and otherwise. And there can be no doubt that they have a great deal of leeway to make up, given the inadequacies of black education and the unquestioned and automatic exclusion of blacks for many years from management structures. Employers therefore need to give special attention to developing the managerial talents of black staff. However, it is unfortunately not just a simple matter of skin pigmentation, where an organisation can set some sort of ratio or quota for black advancement. It is critically important that the individual to be advanced is right for the role. Where an ER-Orange strategic thinker and problem-solver is required, it is pointless, damaging to the company and frustrating for the individual to appoint a DQ-Blue authoritarian.

As we have argued elsewhere in this book, it has little to do with innate intelligence but everything to do with life experience. As we have also argued, people can and do change, so there is no reason why the DQ-Blue authoritarian should not develop into exactly what his company desires in a manager - but only after the appropriate training. There are few short cuts and there is no substitute for experience. Instead of using bells and whistles to announce black advancement programmes, organisations are better advised to construct large, holistic and integrated strategies to develop people all the way up and down the existential staircase. Where capacities for digital, analytical and logic-based thinking are weak, they can be buttressed with intensive saturation learning programmes. When gaps in literacy and numeracy appear, they can be aggressively closed in. The Triple Trust in Cape Town recognised quite correctly that training alone is not enough.

Those concerned with advancing black employees should always think quantum, which means "big chunks" instead of small pieces. They should look for multiple rather than single causes. Think of a stereophonic music system involving a right and a left channel. When the sound is properly balanced it is "heard" in the middle of the head. What white elements might have done or not done for black advancement is only one channel. The other has to be listened to as well. It might give very good reasons for difficulties with a black advancement programme, which have nothing at all to do with the input of white management. To get a balanced understanding of the problem and its solutions, all problems and failings have to be considered. Development is always a two-way street.

The quantum will never be achieved by fragmented, piecemeal approaches. It would be better to redefine the entire nature of management in the Seventh World (which we shall attempt in Chapter 14). There are reasons for believing that the Western bottom-line based short-term focused management model is, anyway, beginning to lose the game against more complex models from Japan and elsewhere. A new Euro-African model might well emerge from South Africa's own crucible. It is probably faulty and futile to attempt to make Europeans of African managers. Yet business and management sophistication is required of anybody functioning at executive level in a large company. It requires years of education and experience to achieve this peak, and the experience of business cultures all over the world has been that there is no substitute for experience at every possible level of the operation before being taken up in executive management. Tokenism in promotions, assignments and placements is inappropriate, counter-productive and the last thing South Africa needs.

We have been highly critical of the Afrikaner Colossus-on-the-veld for its decades of neglect of black South Africans, especially in management and education. But we have to mention also that, in spite of their disadvantaged background, thousands of black managers are beginning to emerge and do rather well. They are products of Bantu Education and they come from the same squalid townships as other blacks, yet they have risen above it. Who can predict or guarantee human excellence? It cannot come from a book or a teacher, it is somewhere inside the individual who accepts a challenge and rises to it. Cometh the New South Africa, cometh the New South Africans? As a taxi driver remarked: "I'll tell you what us blacks need to do. We need to learn and earn and go for the gaps. It's as simple as that." Perhaps it is.

'n Boer Maak 'n Plan

When the British ambassador, Sir Robert Renwick, left his post in South Africa for Washington DC, he did so with some interesting impressions and musings. Asked what he thought of the Conservative Party, he responded: "It's the only party I've never been able to make any real impact with. I understand the anxieties they're reflecting, but the great Afrikaner statement is, 'Ons sal 'n plan maak'. Where is the plan?"

There could be several answers to Sir Robert's question. One might be that the plan was made many years ago when John Vorster's National Party government, of which the CP were then a part, began the process of balkanising South Africa into "independent" ethnic homelands, according to Verwoerd's master plan. But few would believe that today. Pure Verwoerdian apartheid is the preserve of the extreme (and miniscule) Herstigte Nasionale Party. The CP appears to be pre-occupied at present with thoughts of an even more radical partitioning, leaving the whites with a considerably smaller homeland, and it appears to be nowhere near achieving finality. Its fundamental problem is probably that no significant black grouping accepts territorial partitioning as a solution. Other right-wing groups pursue objectives which range from a fortress-like Boerestaat (based on the old Boer republics in the Orange Free State, the Transvaal and Northern Natal) to the (probably more honest) Volkstaat, to be established by a large-scale trek of Afrikaners into the arid wastes of the North-West Cape, where nobody else wants to live and where they would be a majority.

But these secessionist, partitionist, isolationist ideas have an increasingly nebulous quality today. One senses that the CP is a long way off formulating the "plan" asked for by Sir Robert; that it is hastily attempting to cobble together something from a series of broken, half-discarded plans. The victoriously simple, homespun quality of "'n Boer maak 'n plan" is lacking. Partition, one senses, is not an option because South Africa is unavoidably integrated, demographically, economically and (increasingly) socially.

But if the segregationists lack a realistic and credible plan, what of the others? It would be an exaggeration to say they have formulated anything practical and workable. What is President de Klerk's plan? He must have one. The questions buzz about South Africa, over the braaivleis fires, in bar-rooms, vestries, shebeens, shower-rooms, over the sherry of academics. Is de Klerk genuine? How can he step down without surrendering? Can the ANC back down on one man, one vote simple majority rule? Will South Africa be communism's last stand? What about the army? Won't they step in? Is there going to be a fight to the finish once negotiations break down? What about nationalisation, redistribution? How can democracy work here when it's worked nowhere else in Africa?

Is federation the answer? The Democratic Party are the experts on federation - powerful, territorially defined regions; firmly delineated division of authority between central (or more correctly federal) government and the autonomous regions; the rule of law, independent courts, a strong constitution, a justiciable bill of rights. But are such ideas really of Africa?

Or is the centralised system, to which we are accustomed, the only thing that people understand and are prepared to accept? Is strongly centralised social democracy the answer, as propagated by influential circles in the ANC? A strong state, benignly redressing past inequities through its control over the levers of economic and political power?

The Nationalists seem to toy with ideas such as Swiss-style cantonment or some of the proposals of the Natal/KwaZulu Indaba (of which more later). But is South Africa Switzerland? Where does one find the more or less ethnically homogenous communities living, naturally and without coercion, geographically apart? The Indaba might have sounded good in theory, but it never did get anywhere.

What will the underlying economic arrangement be? Free market capitalism? But then how will the poor and disadvantaged ever win what is their due in a system which has been skewed against them historically? A social market? Full socialism? A command economy? How will wealth be redistributed and by whom? Who gains, who loses? These are questions being asked by South Africans in every walk of life.

Where will the final "plan" be discovered? In the wisdom of think tanks from Washington, London or Bonn? Can models from elsewhere be copied: America, Britain, Canada, Belgium, the Soviet Union, Namibia or Zimbabwe? Can their experience have a bearing on the South African position? Can the good offices of third parties be engaged? Should the United Nations play a role? To what extent should events of the past be projected on to the new arrangement? How far do those crafting formulae for today need to see into the future? In short: Wat is die plan?*

*What is the plan?

176

The New Questions

We suggest that "Wat is die plan?" might be a premature question. Preliminary questions need to be asked and appropriate answers found. Consider instead the following:

- How might South Africans decide what the new order should be?

- What is it that makes South Africa unique in comparison with other countries in Africa and overseas?

- Is this uniqueness susceptible to simple, two-dimensional solutions or is something multiple, complex and transitional required?

- Who, or what body, can design, structure and implement an order which serves every level and component of South African society, according it the respect and attention it is due - what we call seeing to the health of the entire Spiral?

- How may such a system be communicated to South Africa's wide and diverse population?

These new questions are important for at least two reasons. The entire theme of this book has been that it is the South African crucible itself which will have to yield the answers. It will have to create new models which, at this stage in human history, exist in no other culture or society for the reason that the ingredients and dynamics of this society are replicated nowhere else.

South Africa is quite obviously no replica of any society in Europe or North America. Nor is it a replica of any African colonial possession on the eve of independence. The governing group is not about to haul down the flag and depart, leaving the country to an "indigenous" elite. In spite of superficial similarities in racial/ethnic composition (which are in a vastly different ratio anyway), it is no replica of Zimbabwe. There is no colonial authority to convene a Lancaster House Conference and there is nothing like the preponderance of numbers among the beneficiaries to ensure adherence to a Lancaster House-type settlement. In spite of other superficial similarities, it is no replica of Namibia either. South Africa has been sovereignly independent since 1931; there is likely to be be minimal international involvement in its transition. It is not a sparsely populated country with its ethnic groups living largely in isolation from one another, it is an industrialised state where people have been drawn in their millions into close daily proximity.

Probably no person or political party has clearly in mind the structure to manage South Africa's complexity. It is simply too much to grapple with. The "plan" or ultimate solution is unlikely to be found in the Union Buildings, Pretoria, in the Freedom Charter, in the highly skilled scenario planning of the large corporations, in overseas consultancies or anywhere else in Africa. Each one of these is certainly able to contribute value to the process of problem resolution, and none should be ignored; but ultimately it is South Africans themselves who will have to engage the process, push the envelope (to borrow an expression from physics), spark the paradoxes then watch carefully to see what nature itself generates in the crucible. People need to stop looking for the complete and final package which will contain the future. No such thing exists, not in anybody's draft constitution or scenario plan. It has to evolve. Tentative solutions have already been forged in early workings of the crucible, and these interesting new alloys will be examined later in the chapter.

Secondly, as suggested in Chapter 10, use of the New Paradigm Pentad offers a fresh and comprehensive approach to problem resolution. The political theatre of press conferences, demagoguery, foreign tours, mass demonstrations, boycotts, walk-outs from parliament and general protest might be emotionally satisfying, but they do little to resolve problems and conflict. Healthy and genuine contributions to this process do not come by way of the toyi-toyi dance, the flaunting of assegais*, inflammatory banners, burnings in effigy or - South Africa's speciality - by threatening and intimidating others with *The Voice from the Casspir* (available to any group and in any ideological mode). We believe the technology of the New Paradigm Pentad could well have the conceptual range and essential discipline to instead mobilise and integrate the thinking of South Africans who take upon themselves the responsibility for discovering appropriate political and economic models. Bearing in mind the preliminary questions posed above, it is time to search for some tentative and likely outlines of The Plan which, of course, has itself not yet been forged in the crucible.

Outline of The Plan

The word constitution is sometimes best considered in its form as a verb: "to constitute". It "constitutes" a managerial system for the society to which it is applied. If the constitution fails to deal with the reality of conditions in that society, its people's levels of development and the prospect of legitimacy and implementation, it is not worth the paper on which it is written. A constitution provides the grammar or operating system for society to function and complexify. Ideally it should produce operating systems which are slightly ahead of the populace in order to engineer and stimulate further growth

*Spears

and development.

Constitutions in sub-Saharan Africa have failed because the formulae and models were imported from elsewhere, designed for radically different values-based psychostructures. They simply did not "constitute" the appropriate managerial system for the realities of the societies to which they were applied.

A model of government which is based either on a monolith or on mass democratic assumptions is doomed to failure if applied to the entire evolutionary Spiral, as exists in South Africa. It will damage the ER-Orange, FS-Green and GT-Yellow rings of the Spiral, which produce strategic thinking, enterprise and prosperity; fairness and justice; and the holistic ability to grasp the entire picture. An economic system based entirely on Western, individualistic, free enterprise thinking would, correspondingly, damage other rings on the Spiral, for which such a system would not be appropriate. Most political and economic models are two-dimensional. They have, alas, been designed in *Flatland* for *Flatlanders*. For the South African system to work it will have to be designed in *Flowstate* for *Flowstaters*. It will require third, fourth and fifth dimensions.

Ten principles for a New South African Order

1. The diversities within the South African value systems mosaic and evolutionary Spiral have to be recognised and accommodated.

2. An interim process, designed to address the long-term and short-term effects of apartheid, and implemented by some sort of "Council of the Wise", has to be initiated and empowered.

3. Any statement of rights, liberties and opportunities should be joined by an affirmation of duties, responsibilities and obligations.

4. Multiple political and economic systems, mixtures, equations and formulae need to be designed for different states of evolutionary development and change.

5. The overall management of South Africa should reflect the thinking within the GT-Yellow-Systemic and HU-Turquoise-Globalist modes of thinking and problem resolution.

6. A multi-tiered governmental structure needs to be designed which would have the capacity to successfully manage different rings, bands and ranges within the developmental Spiral.

7. Change, transition and transformation should be built into the design of social, educational and political structures to facilitate the movement of people along the value systems trajectory.

8. The new political and economic order has to legitimise the healthy versions of all the value systems, and their respective ethnic and cultural variations, so long as the interests of the Spiral as a whole are protected and preserved.

9. The permanent plan will set in motion dynamic tension, liberating flows and interdependent mechanisms designed to naturally spin the Spiral to greater complexity.

10. The integrity of the unique South African Spiral is guaranteed and enhanced by appropriate interactions with forces, resources and elements outside the country's borders.

The New South Africa Means Different Things To Different Systems

To Purple (Level 2)

The New South Africa must protect the tribal ways and rituals, honour the festivals and ceremonies and preserve the sacred and holy places.

To Red (Level 3)

The New South Africa must liberate the individual to do as he wishes by removing restrictions, regulations and barriers that stand in the way of personal empowerment and freedom.

To Blue (Level 4)

The New South Africa must protect and preserve the traditions, standards and cultures of people who do what is right and wish to see their beliefs passed on to their children and grandchildren.

To Orange (Level 5)

The New South Africa must respect individual rights, encourage a sense of enterprise and achievement and reward those persons and groups who show initiative, are willing to take risks and are willing to pay the price to succeed.

To Green (Level 6)

The New South Africa must instil a feeling of community, provide for those less privileged and facilitate the full development of each human being.

To Yellow (Level 7)

The New South Africa must learn to manage itself in a new and constructive fashion by utilising all its resources - natural, human and technological - to enhance the standard of living and quality of life of its citizens both today and in the future.

To Turquoise (Level 8)

The New South Africa must act to protect the fragile environment, be a good global citizen, mandate a respect for healthy systems and be pro-active in resolving planetary problems and concerns.

This chapter will consider three basic concepts. First we will examine the nature of political and economic theory in general and the genesis of particular theories. Then we will display population distributions and needs profiles all along the Psychological Map of South Africa. Finally, we will explore two early outpourings from the hot and explosive South African crucible. One will be the political model produced by the Natal/KwaZulu Indaba. The second will be the experience of Bophuthatswana, a black homeland which opted for "independence" and has produced interesting results.

The Nature of Theory

Economic and political theories are but fleeting, sketched-in symbolic scaffoldings of what we think we see. All theories are ghostly outlines of our perceptions of reality. Churchill once suggested: "We shape our buildings and then our buildings shape us." It could be much the same with the theories we shape, but which then go on to shape us.

Much as with the computer programmes that enhanced the pictures of the planet Jupiter transmitted by spacecraft, we possess mental computers which enable us to fill in the blanks and translate theoretical sketchings into clear, resolute and immutable pictures. We may even die for those images, believing them to be ideal states sanctioned by Divine force. Whenever we move up or down the Spiral, we see the world quite differently and construct theories congruent with the rings on the vertical spine where we happen to be. If each member state of the United Nations were to display its particular political and economic model, the global Spiral would shimmer with a vast array of value system colours. One would see a crazy kaleidoscope of patterns, from authoritarian command systems to versions of *laissez faire* democracy. The differences would be located in the different rings of the developmental Spiral.

When listening to somebody expressing political or economic beliefs, one should search for the basic motivation for those views. One might be hearing a belief structure - the position on the Spiral - or it could be the belief content, the form that belief takes.

The Purple (Animistic), Blue (Absolutist), Green (Egalitarian) and Turquoise (Global) are all of them communal or collective systems. They automatically focus on the needs of the group, not the individual. Versions of African socialism, Marxist collectivism and liberal egalitarianism flow from these structures.

When the Red (Egocentric), Orange (Materialistic) and Yellow (Systemic) structures shape a person's views, one detects a focus on the individual, not the group. From these starting points one is able to detect expressions of elitism, the focus on individual rights and the spectrum of libertarian beliefs.

By "content" we mean the specific beliefs within a structure, corresponding to the type of liquid within a container. A person or an entire society thinking in the DQ-Blue-Absolutist-Fourth Level system will fix on a single "one right way" viewpoint. The DQ belief structure will spawn a specific ideology as its truth-based content. However, the True Believer is capable of embracing positions and causes across the entire spectrum of political and economic possibilities. True Believers can be in the left and right wings of a political continuum, or even in the mid-range. What a person advocates is not as important as his reasons for doing so. To such an individual the impulse to be "right" is of greater importance than the need to be "reasonable".

As millions of South Africans move into the Fourth Level range of thinking (a natural progression from individualistic Red, having earlier shed the tribal Purple), the content of that thinking is likely to be some form of nationalism. It is perfectly natural. It happened with the Afrikaners as they began to find their feet after the national upheaval of the Boer War, and today it is happening among blacks. It gives them order, discipline and purpose in life, just as it once did for the impoverished Afrikaners. But if the newer, black nationalism should be of a threatening nature, it could activate the anti-bodies of Afrikaner nationalism, setting up a dangerous confrontation with all the ingredients of holy war. If, on the other hand, the content of the DQ-Blue system among blacks should turn out to be a non-threatening South African nationalism, it would be a different matter entirely and a potentially destructive confrontation would be avoided. What seems certain is that the emerging Blue system will embrace some form of nationalism. It is the specific content of that nationalism which becomes the issue.

Value system change may occur in two ways. A person changes when he moves from one vertical level to another, either up or down the Spiral. Or the change may take the form of shift from one content to another, staying at the same vertical level. This explains why it is not unusual for a person to move from one extreme on the political and economic continuum to the opposite extreme. The avid Marxist has been known to become a doctrinaire libertarian but his mode of thinking, his values structure, remains the same. It is only the content that has changed.

It is important to understand the value systems that actually drive a particular economic or political position. This invisible scaffolding helps explain the diversity of, and degrees of commitment to, various positions. The position itself might not be as important as the motive that gives it support. Why people believe something is consequently more important than what it is they believe, though political and economic theories which are buttressed by both structure and content motivations will command greater ego involvement and greater personal commitment.

This might well explain the firmness of conviction of both the Conservative Party on the right wing and the Pan Africanist Congress on the left. Their beliefs are clearly mutually exclusive, they could be mortal enemies. But both positions are permeated by DQ-Fourth Level structures. They have that in common. Where they differ profoundly is in the content of those Blue containers. One believes absolutely that God ordained races and nations and intends to keep them apart. The other advocates a separate identity for the African from the European and believes the African continent and Afro-centred culture are sacred. Both think in a "one right way" ideological mode and see little room for compromise. They are alike in structure but radically different in content.

It might not be possible to change either group from the rigidity of the DQ-Blue value system to the pragmatism of the Orange range, still less to the egalitarianism of the Green. Nobody should expect to be able to do so, and any attempt is ill-advised. But it might well be possible to replace their content with another which allows them to co-exist within a South African collectivity. Members of both the CP and the PAC might, for instance, be persuaded to dedicate themselves to rescuing the entire African continent from its awesome problems. The new Afrikaner mission becomes the bringing of technology and stability to Africa. The new PAC role becomes one of working for the day when the continent becomes a single political and economic entity. They might find themselves able to join minds, hearts and hands in this new endeavour, even though they set out from different points of departure. The area of head-on collision is avoided.

Every major political system contains elements of elitism and collectivism. Elitist leaders need collective followers, and vice versa. One cannot study leadership styles without understanding followership needs. Very often elitism and collectivism are deliberately confused. "Power to the people" usually means "power to the elites", self-appointed spokesmen for the people. "In the name of the people" suggests the existence of a pure collective, yet one always discovers elites within it. And from the most doctrinaire libertarian one is always able to extract the grudging admission that without some basic communal or social contract society would be unable to function.

We believe we have established the principle that there can be no universal economic or political system which is ideally suited for all people everywhere. And each ring of the Spiral requires, as its basic political system, a mixture of elite and communal influences in the various colour-coded value systems.
See Plate VI, Colour Section.

Red Elites and Purple Collectives

Certain patterns are observable in the dynamics of gang or warlord behaviour in South Africa's townships. In these feudal systems the leader and his lieutenants (Red) are the privileged ones. The remainder of the gang are subservient and have to obey orders. They are "soldiers" and disposable. Yet the gang will be infested with Purple symbolism - muti*, special clothing and greetings and an elaborate ritual which reaffirms the group's power pecking order and differentiates it from competitive gangs. This is simply a modern version of the Empire model within the Red band of thinking. The Big Boss operates through the Work Bosses, who exploit the weak and helpless.

Red Elites and Blue Collectives

Daniel Ortega campaigned in Nicaragua under the banner of wealth redistribution, saying it should be effected fairly and evenly for all the people. Nicaraguans universally called this *La Pinata*, equating the give-aways and sales at huge discounts with the wild scramble for goodies at a children's party when somebody manages to break open the colourful paper pinata hanging overhead. The poor received tiny plots of public land, on which to build shanties, or they were placed in farm co-operatives. The elites in or near power emerged as owners of hundreds of thousands of acres, luxury homes and cars. In short, Ortega's version of Marxism projected a Blue collective but ruled as a Red elite.

*Magical medicine

THE EVOLUTION OF POLITICAL SYSTEMS

Bands	Tribal Orders	Empires	Authoritarian One Party States	Multi Party Democracies	Social Democracies	Integrative Evolutionary Flows	Global Orders
AN Beige	BO Purple	CP Red	DQ Blue	ER Orange	FS Green	GT Yellow	HU Turquoise

•San Bushmen
•Pygmies
•Street People
•Clans

•Shaka Zulu
•Township Gangs
•Warlords
•African Dictators

•Free Market Economies
•Multi Party Democracies
•USA, UK, Canada, France, emerging in USSR

•Not yet forged but emerging in some 1st World societies

•Historical Animistic
•Societies
•Bonding Groups

•Religious Order
•Afrikaner & African Nationalism
•Left or Right Wing One party States

•Europe -1992
•Scandanavian Societies
•World Council of Churches

•Not yet forged but emerging in elements within the UN and Trilateral Commission and ecological groups.

Much the same is true as the activities come to light of power elites behind the Iron Curtain. It is quite clear that the benefits promised to the collectives were seldom if ever delivered. The elites used the terror of the state police apparatus as their instrument of enforcement, and lived very well under the banner of communism. On paper there was equality, in practice the state apparatus was used to perpetuate the elites' power and privilege. Much the same was true of Marcos' Phillippines, and in such societies elections are rigged and there only for show. Real opposition is not tolerated. Once again, projected Blue collectives are ruled by Red elites.

Orange Elites and Blue Collectives

The historic Puritan work ethic, fused with the emergence of doctrines of free will, spawned the Western model of governance. The blend assumes that Orange elites will avoid the errors of their Red counterparts by leading from within a set of constraints and laws, all designed to protect the interest of the Blue collective. The United States constitution was written to both empower and control the Orange factor through a series of electoral requirements, a bill of rights and a system of checks and balances.

But Orange leadership functions effectively only while the Blue collective maintains its conformity of ideals and principles and continues to behave in a predictable fashion. Parents have to be willing for their sons to be sent to fight foreign wars in the national interest. Citizens have to willingly comply with paying tax. The general public has to be willing to abide by a set of basic rules and regulations and norms. At present the American system is under serious pressure because of some fundamental shifts. The leadership has become obsessed with status, media exposure and questionable deals with a range of interest groups who are perfectly willing to spend vast sums lobbying for legislation and influence. The Orange system of leadership in business, education, health care and the media likewise fails to deal with new problems of existence which confront Americans. New elitist models, around the Yellow-Systemic set of assumptions, are instead beginning to express themselves across the political and economic spectrum.

Over the past few decades Afrikaner political and business leadership elites have blossomed into the Orange range and are presently showing evidence of Green-Collective and Yellow-Systemic thinking processes as well. Yet the P.W. Botha era saw a great deal of behaviour flowing from Red thinking patterns of assertiveness, aggravated by countrywide disturbances and calls for revolution.

Since, with few exceptions, South Africa's black leadership has been in no position to manage political and economic complexities, one is able to do no more than estimate the degree of Red and Orange thinking among the elites in the ANC, Inkatha or any other group. However, attacks on capitalism and the use of images of oppression, exploitation and struggle have historically been the mark of Red elites.

What is this "capitalism" which is attacked and rejected by so many blacks? Is it possible that when the ANC and others reject capitalism and other people argue in its favour they are actually talking about different things? The rejection of capitalism appears to be directed toward what we will call "Randlord capitalism" or RL-C. This features such things as child labour, oppression, exploitation and the grinding inhumanity of Darwin's survival of the fittest. Add to this restrictive cartels, job reservation, neo-colonial attitudes among executives and generally brutal conditions in the workplace and one has a peculiarly unappealing picture of capitalism. Many South African blacks equate capitalism with this version.

Yet when most business leaders speak of "capitalism" they mean Free Market Capitalism (FM-C), with active labour involvement through the trade unions, profit and revenue-sharing schemes, global competitiveness and the opportunity for all to advance according to competence and skills.

RL-C is not FM-C. Both are individualistic, achievist and elitist-based. Both result in the creation of gaps in affluence among people at different levels. RL-C creates the rigid and punitive class system, militant unions and versions of the ghastly world of Dickens. It invites passionate attack from Marxists and from South Africa's contemporary academic neo-Marxists. But FM-C produces a middle class with opportunities for all, regardless of class or ethnic origin, to pursue success and material gain.

At every stage of development every society has a mixture of collective needs and elitist controls. Each has collective intelligences, historical imbalances, ethnic mosaics and a unique blend of value systems. Sterile theories assume a single, horizontal and homogeneous level of development and unfortunately believe the entire world lives within their *Flatland* community. *Flowstaters* know otherwise.

Economics and Politics

Seek first the political kingdom, Kwame Nkrumah of Ghana once promised, and all else will follow. In 1966 he was overthrown in a military coup and youths marched through the streets of Accra with placards proclaiming: "Nkrumah is NOT our messiah!". What went wrong and why?

Nkrumah believed that once political power was won, economic development would soon follow. The same has been true of many blacks in America, where political advancement has not been matched by economic advancement. Franklyn G. Jenifer, President of Howard University, Washington DC, America's premier black university, voiced the dilemma in a column in the *Dallas Times Herald* of June 17, 1991. "Blacks have learned to play the political game and to play it well," he wrote, but "progress in the political game has not been matched by progress in the economic game. To visit any Ghetto USA is often to visit economic devastation. Few jobs. Few legitimate businesses. Little or no hope. The whole dismal litany." While conceding that racism has held back African-Americans from being major economic players, he concludes: "Still, the inability and unwillingness of significant numbers of blacks to play the economic game cannot be blamed solely on racism." Again, what went wrong and why?

Many have credited South Africa's black community with electing to pursue economic power before demanding political control (partly because economic advancement was not totally closed off to them while political advancement was). The hope has been that economic success and greater material abundance would shift the thinking of the "have-nots" away from schemes for politically-inspired redistribution. The emerging black middle class would join with other moderate elements in rejecting Marxism and other forms of socialism in favour of a free market economy. They would look to Africa and see only desolation, despair, false hopes and faded dreams. Liberia, the proud American experiment in Africa, has been torn by civil war; so has Ethiopia, the centuries-old African empire which experienced only the briefest colonial occupation just before the Second World War. Political power has not produced economic well-being.

However, we believe such thinking is flawed and a totally new approach is required. Political and economic progress and sophistication are not separate, isolated processes that can be treated as being independent. They have to occur simultaneously. The necessary competencies and complexities of thinking that impact on one impact on the other also. Both are developmental products of advancement up the Spiral staircase. Note that this is a step-by-step staircase; it is not a fast-moving escalator. Like the deep sea diver who comes up too soon, societies which attempt to move to greater complexity too quickly suffer a psychological version of the bends. That has been the sad history of Africa. If, on the other hand, progress is too slow, the entire culture might implode as it runs out of oxygen.

Development and advancement, both political and economic, have to wind up the Spiral in a systematic, synergistic, interactive and incremental fashion. Elites may, for entirely selfish and self-serving reasons, raise the expectations of the masses that they are about to enter a Utopia led exclusively, of course, by those same elites. And be they white, black, Asian, African or American, those same dishonest and deceitful leaders so often seem to have money in Swiss bank accounts while the people they claim to represent continue to languish in poverty.

The South African Psychological Map

We reject definitions of people and their thinking systems which are based on race, ethnicity, sex, national origin, age or any other artificial demographic category. We do affirm that individuals are at different levels of psychological existence and will consequently embrace contrasting economic and political models of development. Furthermore, the real impact of apartheid, sanctions, racism and "self development" has been to impede the movement of millions on the Psychological Map because of their race or ethnicity. That will be a long-term, residual legacy of the previous system of classification. The evidence for this conclusion is overwhelming. Our own findings, based on 10 years of rigorous research in South Africa, confirm these observations. The primary issue lying ahead will be how to open the systems, promote the development of people, close the gaps and maintain a healthy and dynamic Spiral.

Every person acts in his own best interest. If he believes he will personally gain the most through a collective wealth-sharing scheme, he will fervently support such a collective system. If he feels he will compete successfully within a market-based economy, he will champion free enterprise. Even those who claim selfless altruistic motives and declare the need for an egalitarian system calculate that such a system will serve them best.

We intend in this section to describe the optimal economic and political systems for the entire Spiral, as well as for its individual rings. Unless the Spiral is healthy and expanding, the needs of people and groups all along its evolutionary spine will be sabotaged. Of course, elites will claim otherwise but they, like our observers of the elephant, specialise only in parts.

See Plate VII, Colour Section.

As you will detect from this schematic, the critical mass of thinking of a majority of the South African population is approaching the DQ-Blue-Absolutist position on the Psychological Map. The rhetoric, imagery, perceptions and tones of the core of the ANC, and the totality of the PAC, AZAPO and other groups, fit within this range. This is the centre of gravity of the Mass Democratic Movement. The path to power is via a constituent assembly, majority rule and the imposition of a one-party, authoritarian system. Competing Tribal Orders and Feudal Empires will have to be subdued. The Young Lions within the Red range will require a firm hand. Law and order will have to be maintained. Children will need disciplining. There will be little room for deviation from the norm. The power of the state should be used to impose equality, a redistribution of wealth and conformity to the new order.

Since Third World elites have yet to develop the capacity to compete within the First World free market environment of Orange thinking, they must, if they wish to exercise power, insist on a communal system they can manipulate. This has been the pattern in all Third to Second World systems on the planet. Such a development would be congruent and perfectly natural with this population grouping. This critical mass would not respond well to multi-party democracy, free enterprise conditions or even an FS-Green version of social egalitarianism.

While a majority of people are moving into the Blue range, a majority of interests - cultural, financial, political, educational and religious - are passing through the Orange system. This includes many thousands of blacks whose thinking has switched on to Orange values and Fifth Level technologies. Other elements within South African society have moved into Green, Yellow and even Turquoise.

If the control point of society is maintained in Orange, the needs of the Spiral as a whole will suffer as the personal achiever is not driven to care for the needs of others. The ANC's reluctance to remove economic sanctions stems in part from a justified fear that if resources did return they would end up in the bank accounts, limousines and holiday homes of the successful elite. The have-nots would continue in their second class condition because they would benefit only from a trickling down. But if the creation and distribution of abundance were located in the Yellow-Systemic command and control system, the entire Spiral would benefit.

The South African Process and Plan

South Africa's next politico/economic/social order will have to deal with the realities of the population distribution up and down the Evolutionary Spiral. It should be designed to accomplish two objectives. First, it should meet the needs of people at their respective levels of psychological development - whether Purple, Red, Blue, Orange, Green, Yellow or Turquoise. Second, the new order should open up the channels for change and movement to avoid trapping people and groups in the GAMMA state. Sterile, narrow-gauged, idealistic *Flatlander* theory is both useless and dangerous.

Consider the importance of first developing an interim, short-term process to deal with the inequities and flashpoints of society. After this a more permanent, long-term plan could be devised to set in motion the natural spinning of the Spiral through a formalised and legitimate politico/economic/social dispensation.

A "Council of the Wise" or "Council of Visionaries" (what it is called does not really matter) needs to be established, drawing competent leadership from all sectors of South African society. It would be something like the original "Invisible College", which became the Royal Society of Britain. It would correspond with the "sapient circles" of the late American anthropologist Margaret Mead - created whenever we, as a species, have confronted new and complex problems. Collections of "wise ones" address those issues until the problems are resolved, at which point the "circle" disbands.

Socio-economic development should be apolitical, free of predetermined ideologies and committed to the process of integrative problem resolution. Excellent examples of resourcefulness and skill in mobilising effort and technologies are already to be found in such areas as the provision of housing, notably in the work of Bob Tucker, former managing director of the Perm, who has also contributed greatly in the area of scenario planning. Once again, the powerful technology of Value Management - inclusion of all involved, concentration on the vital issues and achievement of results - is available to provide the decision-making format and regimen necessary to manage large-scale projects where the input will come from a wide range of sources. By their very nature, professional politicans often lack the vision, patience and temperament to stand back and allow the "wise ones" to find real solutions to real problems. Mike Alfred, publisher of *Manpower Brief*, put it even more strongly (*Business Day*, April 20, 1990): "For me potential tragedy lies in politicians perceiving themselves as saviours, such self-assessment carrying with it the aura of arrogant omnipotence. Strong on power needs, low on intellect, conceptualisation and sensitivity, the universe of politics hasn't been assailed by a new thought for 150 years."

Majority rule, moral authority, First World privilege, economic or military strength, historical traditions, grudges or disparities - none of these centres of gravity has the complexity to manage South Africa. Yet South African decision-makers are in the unique position of being able to observe what has happened elsewhere and to learn from those experiences. In a sense South Africa has been trapped in a time warp, isolated from some of the mistakes and false starts suffered elsewhere, and this could well turn out to be a competitive advantage in that the follies of both Western and other African societies need not be repeated.

The following guidelines might be appropriate in successfully managing the South African Spiral. Consider this psychological Rosetta Stone a companion document to the Freedom Charter and F.W. de Klerk's manifesto, as spelled out in parliament.

1. The Process and Plan should be designed for the entire Spiral, not for any particular racial or ethnic group, for any specific number of people, for majority financial interests or for any other selection of elites or collectives. The theme should be government of, by and for the Spiral in its entirety. When the Spiral is robust and dynamic, each of its rings enjoys good health. Different levels of complexity within the Spiral provide other levels with the nutrients and flow of ideas and technology necessary for movement up the existential staircase. The top rings of the Spiral are neither understood, nor can they be managed, by the mid or lower rings. If the majority of people demand that the critical mass be set between the Red and the Blue range with a "mass democratic system", the more complex Orange, Green, Yellow and Turquoise systems will wither and die. If economic blackmail is used to force elitist, libertarian expectations on a developing society, the mass of population seeking upliftment will flounder and become embroiled in rage and frustration.

2. Political and economic mechanisms should facilitate the movement of individuals and groups along the developmental Spiral. Public and private instruments and resources will have to be mixed and calibrated for each stage of development. The essential mixtures at the Red to Blue transition will be different from the ratio necessary from Blue to Orange. The equations

for growth from Orange to Green are different from the formula that works between Green and Yellow. In short, a single, monolithic, idealistic model cannot handle the complexity of South Africa. The framers of the new South African constitution will have to be complex, thinking engineers, capable of rejecting theoretical, self-serving and cosmetic solutions in favour of a long-term, dynamic developmental process. They will have to be able to engineer the appropriate alloys of systems and patterns all along the Spiral. Clearly, the new order should be Value Managed by holistic/systemic thinkers (GT-Yellow) - those who can see the whole elephant - rather than politically negotiated by status-driven (ER-Orange) or power-driven (CP-Red) elites. In early 1991 a four-day conference was convened in Prague by the Interaction Council, a think-tank chaired by former West German Chancellor Helmut Schmidt. "Neither the capitalist market system nor the socialist command economy have proved to be perfect," the conference concluded. "Most economies are mixed systems with a vigorous private sector and a strong, large public sector." If this is true of the East European countries, who occupy rather a narrow range on the Psychological Map, it is even more true of South Africa, the global microcosm.

3. The multiple intelligences of all South Africans should be used systemically and strategically in both the interim process and in the formulation and implementation of the permanent plan. As suggested in Chapter 10, there are two versions of the "Wise Ones". The first are generalists who can think and act for the entire Spiral. The others are specialists who have the necessary expertise and competency at each of the locations on the spine of the Spiral. DQ-Fourth Level thinkers are not equipped to understand and manage the ER-Fifth Level system. FS-Sixth Level egalitarians are prone to commit major errors when they prescribe to the BO-Second Level or CP- Third Level systems. Instead of presuming, for instance, that everybody requires housing in line with First World assumptions, it would surely be more useful to ask people, at the various positions on the Spiral, to express their priorities. Again, every stage on the Spiral should be enhanced by Value Management instead of paternalistic or *laissez faire* mandates.

4. Each issue such as housing, the economy, education, law and order and community development should be analysed independently of any universal government formula. The national economic model might require different mixes of public and private commitment from that of the community development initiative. The system of education might shift toward a voucher system, spawning a myriad of private,

diversified and tailored schools. This would result in a reduction in the role of central government.

5.The First World economic, educational and political component in South Africa should be strengthened and enhanced. What many Africanists perceive as "European" is actually Blue-Orange. (African-Americans make the fatal error of embracing what they call an "Afrocentric" system in place of a "Eurocentred" bias. By doing so they attack the very thinking systems that produce modern health care, transportation, communications and complex technologies which result in the "good life" they are struggling to attain).

Following an analysis of South Africa's economic power in contrast with the wealthiest countries of black Africa, Gerald l'Ange, editor of the Argus Africa News Service, noted: "Thus one of the most precious assets that the new South Africa will inherit will be its large white population (read Blue-Orange), for it is in this population that the skills at present largely reside. This is an asset that no other African country has ever had and its value is immeasurable." It is against this background that the slogan "One settler, one bullet!" is both primitive and self-destructive.

Most will also agree that the greatest number of black Africans who have moved into the Blue and Orange (First World) thinking patterns live in South Africa. These value systems are a rising tide all over the country. The impact of education at the University of South Africa and elsewhere, coupled with a growing sophistication in the informal economic sector and within First World business enterprises, has contributed to this development. Africans who think First World will reject African communal schemes with the same energy they are rejected by white communities.

It is a serious mistake for blacks who think in Red and Blue to deride their Orange-thinking brothers and sisters with labels such as "Uncle Tom" or "sell-out". This critical intolerance typically emanates from individuals who are either envious or have been unable to discover for themselves, and apply, the formulae for success. Under no circumstances should the high-technology, nuclear-based and sophisticated First World system be controlled by elements from the CP-Red and DQ-Blue positions - whether they are white, black, coloured or Asian - because to allow it would be to commit national suicide.

At the same time, the Fifth Level-Orange business community of South Africa has a unique responsibility. Consider the paradox these men confront. On one hand they have to compete on a global scale because their competition is in Taiwan, Tokyo, Europe, Canada,

Australia and elsewhere. They have to be global players. On the other hand they have to participate in the Third to Second to First World transformation stream. They have to be national players as well. It is by sparking the two poles of the paradox that we are able to see how they can do both and do them well.

For many years Charles Stride, deputy chairman of the Altron group, has played Devil's Advocate to visiting American senators and congressmen and their unsuspecting legislative assistants. Such visitors are usually accorded kid glove, non-confrontational treatment. Stride, by contrast, is noted for straight talk, hard challenges and reality-based discussion of the actual impact of trade sanctions on blacks. Not a few Americans have returned to Washington, their ears ringing with a heavy dose of the South African realities. Stride has also been outspoken on the need for the business community to address the same realities through a national business plan. In *Business Day* (March 28, 1991) he cautioned: "South African business, answering calls for nationalisation and redistribution of wealth, needs to do better than say 'it won't work.' It has to demonstrate, through positive action, that it is committed to redistribution of opportunity. So far, its performance has not been very impressive."

Stride derides the investment of pension funds only in white shopping centres, high-rise office blocks and shares on the stock exchange. He criticises the concentration of the country's wealth in the hands of professional managers who are neither entrepreneurs nor comfortable with risk-taking. As result, a huge opportunity gap persists between the haves and the have-nots, producing a fertile field for schemes for nationalisation. He calls for a national business plan, systemically and strategically drawn, that would bridge the gap between the country's First, Second and Third World elements.

Buddy Hawton, chief executive of Safren, amplified this theme in an address to the South African Institute of Chartered Secretaries and Administrators. He suggested that privatisation and deregulation, as economic instruments, could create more problems than they solved. He wondered why certain black leaders, candidates for participation in a future government, still talked nationalisation when it was retreating around the world. He found three reasons. First, these leaders clung to an ideology which had been the backbone of their struggle for years - and had brought them this far. Second, although they had witnessed the failure of command economies, they had already successfully sold the notion to their "masses" and would be unable to change horses in midstream. Finally, they believed centralised economies would provide them (the leaders) with direct control of wealth creation, thus providing jobs for people in parastatals. They would entrench their positions as the Afrikaner nationalists had done for the past four decades.

Hawton recommended adoption of an "in partnership" approach to economic strategy, instead of the "you versus us" mentality. He acknowledged that the real challenge in South Africa was not the redistribution of wealth but the creation of wealth. At the same time, he noted, "We have some other economic and political restructuring to attend to, which requires government intervention, before we reach the stage where natural market forces can propel us forward."

Both Stride and Hawton express the need for developmental bridges, the private sector acting in conjunction with public interests, to close the gaps as quickly as possible so that the entire society can grow and prosper. In short, it might be necessary for the Fifth Level community to reach back and bridge with developing populations while at the same time reaching out in global business initiatives. The concept "live and let live" will not assist in creating what we have called the Seventh World in South Africa. "Strive and help strive" should rather be the theme.

What will the nature be of the more permanent constitutional model that flows naturally from the interim processes of alignment, gap-closing and creation of the Seventh World?

Early Outpourings From the Crucible

The crucible which lies within South Africa will ultimately forge the new model. At this point nobody has a complete picture of its structure, contours, power-sharing features or procedures of conflict resolution. But from our vantage point, and employing the Graves technology, we are able to anticipate certain key features, given a positive outcome to political negotiations and an acceptance on all sides that ideologies and pet schemes have to give way to the overriding need for growth and development.

We anticipate an over-arching central government, democratically elected by proportional representation so that all interest groups are represented. The political system at this level should be structured to make for inclusiveness and coalition rather than be adversarial, so that government is able to draw on the widest range of talents and as many interest groups as possible are involved in decision-making. Central government would, however, have a limited role internally. It is doubtful whether any centralised system in a country as regionally and ethnically diverse as South Africa could satisfactorily address the needs and aspirations of every region and locality. Central government should therefore limit its sphere of operation to macro-management of truly national issues and matters such as international relations.

Regional and local structures should be designed to manage the mosaics of South African society, integrate differences and build bridges, the structure for each region or locality being tailored to local needs. These would be the key organs of government, designed to ensure the vitality of every community, every position on the Spiral. They should be created in response to needs and only after the most thorough regional and local consulation. Those who will be ruled by these structures should be involved in their creation, ensuring legitimacy and durability. No two regions or localities in South Africa are identical, so it seems likely that the form of regional and local government would vary greatly across the country. Monolithic or simple majority rule structures should be avoided as they contain the seeds of favouritism, corruption and eventually dissent and friction. As at the central tier, regional and local government should be democratic and accountable, elected on the principle of proportionality. And at these levels it is probably even more vital that Westminster-style adversarial politics be avoided. The regional and local systems should be inclusive, all elected interest groups being represented, as far as possible, in executive government. It is difficult to imagine a better safeguard against communal breakdown.

Such a system of government would rely heavily on the expertise and technocratic skills of paid officials at every level, as well as a culture of consultation with affected communities and involvement of private sector skills. The officials would be responsible for seeing to the well-being of every ring on the Spiral - ranging from trade and industry to peasant farming - and would need to be specialists or generalists, depending where on the Spiral they operate. Such officials would require an extraordinary degree of competence, flexibility and understanding of the needs, going beyond what could be expected of elected political representatives. They would be charged with sustaining the vitality of each ring of the Spiral falling within their administrative sphere. A highly skilled and committed corps of adinistrators - most of them inevitably blacks - would have to be developed around the Yellow set of assumptions, instead of the traditional Blue version of the bureaucrat who produces red tape, logjams, middle management paralysis and a general hardening of the arteries of government. They would have to be trained in Value Management disciplines.

Such a system would allow the Young Lions of the townships to pass through DQ-Blue-Authoritarian conduits (the discipline and purpose of New Deal-style public service units might be what they need and crave) without being trapped in authoritarian tunnels. Many would move quickly through to ER-Orange systems of thinking. The existing First World segment would be strengthened and able to use its thinking complexity, international networks and personal resources to increase the size of the national economic cake.

What is needed at national, regional and local levels is an understanding of the code and dynamics of the Spiral. Such an evolutionary model could become the common ground of all South Africans. When the Spiral is dynamic and healthy, the children are properly fed and educated, the business sector thrives, the environment is uncontaminated and the needs of people all along its spine are met in a productive fashion. The political figures are barely noticed. The Seventh World could be close to becoming a reality in South Africa. The rest of the world would sit up and take notice.

If the above should appear somewhat idealistic in a harsh continent which has spawned apartheid among many tyrannies, consider the two early outpourings from the crucible of South Africa mentioned at the start of this chapter.

The Natal/KwaZulu Indaba

The Natal/KwaZulu Indaba was a constitutional conference, the first held in South Africa since the National Convention of 1909 when two British colonies and two defeated Boer republics negotiated the formation of the Union of South Africa. As at the 1909 Convention, the Indaba delegations met to explore possibilities, with no commitment at all to achieving agreement.

However, the Indaba (it means pow-wow) was an intra-regional convention aimed at uniting the Province of Natal and the self-governing entity of KwaZulu which (as described in Chapter 4) had been carved out of Natal for ideological reasons.

It had a dual genesis. One impulse was the frustration of the Natal Provincial Administration (in the hands of a locally based political party) and the KwaZulu Government at the overlapping and duplication of services in a geographically intertwined region - not to mention a strong sense among many white Natalians and Zulus of the absurdity of the separation. The other impulse was a deeper one. By 1986 South Africa appeared to be in a political cul-de-sac. Much of the country was aflame with insurrection. The P.W. Botha administration showed itself bereft of ideas and had retreated into a garrison of kragdadigheid*. Yet in Natal and KwaZulu a powerful black political movement controlling an official organ of government was on cordial terms with the whites controlling another official organ of government. If they could only forge something from this, there might be hope.

When the Indaba convened it was ostensibly to devise a constitution for the future democratic government of Natal and KwaZulu as one *Rule by strength.*

197

region. But the deeper impulse was there all along. Natal and KwaZulu were seen as a laboratory test, as evidenced by the intense interest of the rest of South Africa and the outside world. The constitution eventually produced was indeed designed for the Natal/KwaZulu region. But it was also quite clearly a model with national implications - some claim with implications for other divided societies as well, such as Northern Ireland, the Lebanon or Cyprus.

What is critically important from our point of view is that the Indaba was a crucible process. Nobody prescribed to it, the ingredients were simply poured into a crucible which was then heated by debate. The eventual agreement was the outcome of long months in conclave where, by all accounts, the chemical reaction set off by disparate elements at times caused searing temperatures. And most of the delegations who entered negotiations would probably have been shocked if anybody had been able to tell them in advance what they would eventually agree to, then campaign for with such vigour. It was a long way from the starting-out point of any one of them, a new compound altogether.

The Indaba was not just between the Natal Provincial Administration and the KwaZulu Government. A range of political parties, organised business and agriculture, municipalities and other interest groups were invited, all having equal standing. Pre-eminent were the New Republic Party (which controlled the Natal Provincial Council but is now defunct, its support dispersed between the National Party and the Democratic Party); the Progressive Federal Party (now wholly subsumed in the Democratic Party); and Inkatha. Although all were invited, the gathering was not entirely representative. The African National Congress was at that stage a banned organisation committed to revolutionary war. Practicalities apart, it had little interest in a non-revolutionary regional conference, nor did its surrogates. The right-wing parties declined to attend. The National Party sent observers who participated vigorously but (along with surrogates who were full delegates) distanced themselves in the end. The P.W. Botha government made no secret of its displeasure at the Indaba exercise and allowed it to proceed probably only because of the official status of the convening parties and the intense overseas interest.

All the same, in Gravesian terms all the ingredients which will eventually go into the South African crucible were there in the Indaba mini-crucible as well. There was Inkatha with its range of ER-Orange, DQ-Blue, CP-Red and BO-Purple (all of which exist in the ANC); the ER-Orange/DQ-Blue New Republic Party; the ER-Orange/FS-Green Progressive Federal Party; small Indian and coloured parties and religious and cultural groups with a range of values; the ER-Orange business community. On paper they had little in common and various quarters derided the entire exercise. But, by persistence and the power of the paradox, they achieved an agreement which, in spite of its hostility, the P.W. Botha government never did explicitly repudiate. Today the Indaba constitutional proposals are still on the table for negotiation and many detect echoes of them in utterances by F.W. de Klerk.

It is not our intention to analyse the Indaba proposals in detail. They contained certain unwieldy features, as well as others such as a justiciable bill of rights and proportional representation which have since become almost commonplace. They were certainly democratic. But what made them truly unique was the power-sharing formula. All parties elected above a certain strength to the provincial legislature were to be guaranteed representation in the cabinet. No cabinet can operate without consensus, and the parties would be virtually forced to work together. Minorities would not be excluded from the locus of power. The prime minister of the province would most certainly be the leader of the majority party, but he would have to work with others.

The Indaba's power-sharing formula can in a sense be described as a sophistication of the one-party system which has characterised so many African states. Such systems are often unfairly condemned by Westerners who cannot conceive of the potential fractiousness of African societies which have been catapulted into new states often containing a multiplicity of ethnic groups because of artificial colonial boundaries. The one-party state is very often an attempt to draw all into the decision-making process, to regain a version of the benign circle of elders. But one-party systems do lead almost inevitably to corruption and nepotism. The Indaba formula is in this sense an attempt to avoid the pitfalls of one-party rule; a co-operative drawing-in of different parties on the African pattern, so that they may work together but retain their identities and critical faculties in a way which would be impossible from within a single party. The Indaba cabinet would produce useful synergies. There would be a strong disincentive to slothfulness and corruption because every cabinet member would be under the critical scrutiny of persons not of his own group.

The Indaba formula is also widely interpreted as a means to protect the interests of minorities which, in the case of Natal/KwaZulu, would almost certainly translate as racial or ethnic minorities. That might well be the effect, but from our perspective we are less interested in the representation of racial or ethnic minorities than in the fact that the formula would almost certainly mean a role in the cabinet for individuals from the ER-Orange, FS-Green and GT-Yellow range of thinking, the only people at the levels of complexity to manage those rings on the Spiral producing wealth, justice and the integrated, systemic view which seeks the health and vitality of the entire Spiral, ranging from sound rural development to development of the financial/industrial/commercial sector. Without the Indaba's power-sharing formula, Natal/KwaZulu would be governed by a range swamped by BO-Purple, CP-Red and DQ-Blue systems of thinking - a recipe for Third World, or at best Second World, conditions in perpetuity. Under a Westminster dispensation the majority party would be obliged to take into executive government elected party representatives from that range. Far better that the leaders of the majority party should automatically have with them in the cabinet individuals from other groupings (very probably like thinkers), with whom they could synergistically link up in managing the Spiral. Such a system would be likely, in time, to evolve to a stage where like thinkers cut across racial and ethnic lines to form parties of true common interest rather than racial or ethnic identity. It would certainly enhance the quality of government.

The Indaba power-sharing formula projects readily on to the screen of national politics and it would be surprising if power-sharing were not to become central to constitutional negotiations. If so, it is important that its proponents should project it in its positive sense of contributing to the overall health of the Spiral (and therefore the prosperity and well-being of every person in South Africa) rather than as some sort of entrenchment of the position of minorities.

The Indaba's primary objective should not be lost sight of either. It set out to draw up a system of semi-autonomous regional government. It did not deal with local government and it concerned itself with a largely mechanical division of authority between central and regional government. But it did draw outlines for the future. A series of regional indabas could form the basis for the system of strong regional and local government, beneath an over-arching central government, for which we have argued in terms of the Graves technology. It is essential that such a system be built from the bottom upward so that it accords with local and regional realities, which would imply a somewhat drawn-out constitutional process. But South Africa has surely had enough lessons, since the time of Milner, in the futility of solutions imposed from above.

Finally, the Natal/KwaZulu Indaba is an encouraging indication of what can be forged in the crucible. The ingredients which went into the Indaba mini-crucible are essentially the same (in thinking structure if not always in thinking content) as those that are about to go into the national one.

Bophuthatswana

In 1977, the South African homeland of Bophuthatswana ("Gathering of the Tswanas") took "independence" within the grand design of apartheid/separate development. It is often derided for that, especially as its territorial fragmentation scatters it over a wide portion of "white" South Africa, as well as for its casino gambling industry. It is perceived by many to be a bastard child of apartheid and its leader, President Lucas Mangope, has lately become embroiled in controversy for his authoritarian personal style. It is not our intention to go into the merits or otherwise of this assessment, nor to speculate as to what Bophuthatswana's status within the new South Africa is likely to be. We intend treating it rather as a detached laboratory experiment because, in spite of the controversy some interesting things have happened there. How many states in Africa, internationally recognised or not, have an economic growth rate of five percent? How many have the same degree of inter-racial co-operation? And how many are actually succeeding in uplifting their people into a degree of prosperity? Bophuthatswana's system of education is sound and growing. The benefits of modernisation first introduced to the capital, Mmabatho, are now beginning to spread elsewhere, proving that the essential developmental spikes have to form around concentrated First World activity before general, across the board upliftment can be possible. And this progress has been over a period that Bophuthatswana has been subject to exactly the same economic sanctions as South Africa and has been burdened with the "bantustan" label. How has this happened? Why should it have happened in Bophuthatswana when the outcome in the other homelands which opted for "independence" has been the opposite? (In fact all three are now under military rule and virtually bankrupt).

President Mangope has gathered about himself a core of competent people, regardless of race or ethnicity. He realised that success would depend on the creation of sophisticated brain syndicates, in business, education, community development, entertainment and culture and nature conservation.

Secondly, Bophuthatswana is probably unique in Africa for the way in which its society promotes expression of the entire range of value systems. BO-Purple Tswana beliefs and traditions are strongly represented in architecture and communication devices and strategies, as well as in rituals and ceremonies. Unlike Marxist systems which deny the existence of such deep ethnic structures, Bophuthatswana's nurtures and protects them. Bophuthastwana-the-nation is DQ-Blue while Tswana-the-tribe is BO-Purple, with no tension between the two belief systems. The ER-Orange system is now beginning to develop in the thinking of young Tswanas; the most cursory visit to the university campus or the broadcasting station provides clear evidence of this progress up the Spiral.

Thirdly, Bophuthatswana might well have discovered, in its blend of collective and free market systems, the formula for progress on the African continent generally. In 1979 the government launched the Bophuthatswana National Provident Fund (BNPF), designed to provide relief for its unemployed, building a safety net for the future. Instead of redistributing wealth from haves to have-nots, the fund was designed to create wealth from surpluses and redistribute to its members. After initial problems with management, and complaints from the public, the fund was placed under the control of Paul Stone, chief executive officer of the Sefalana Employee Benefits Organisation (SEBO). Investment policies are not subject to government prescription. Each wealth creation project is considered in terms of market conditions and the overall needs of members, in balancing long-term and short-term returns. SEBO's success is the result of a skillful balancing act in which 75 percent of its investments are placed in safe, middle of the road portfolios, while the remaining 25 percent is split between high-return investments and the lower returns of social welfare projects. SEBO operates essentially within a private sector environment in a number of enterprise-motivated development and growth schemes. This is enterprising public financing, unusual and innovative. A compulsory savings scheme (DQ-Blue nationalism) is managed and enhanced by market-driven growth (ER-Orange free market). This is the power of the paradox at work - what appear to be opposites synergise when struck together, and a Seventh World society could be the result. Nothing illustrates this synergy better than the huge shopping mall in Mmabatho, near the parliamentary buildings, which symbolises progress through Second World authoritarianism into an emerging First World society. Bophuthatswana's performance compares more than favourably with that of other homelands which chose "independence".

Bophuthatswana has had its share of turmoil and its achievements have tended lately to be overshadowed by the personal style of President Mangope and a widespread questioning of the legitimacy of his rule. But the underlying economic progress and synthesis of First and Third Worlds should not be ignored. If history should eventually judge President Mangope a failure, it would be because he failed to follow through on his initial promise.

No Simple Answers

In this chapter we have sought to demonstrate how complex a business the construction of a just and durable constitution for South Africa is likely to be. How much simpler and more emotionally satisfying if it were possible to borrow from abroad, incorporating the best the world can offer in terms of electoral methods, checks and balances, bills of rights, legal systems and the rest of the material of constitution-making; and then to establish something noble and immutable to stand for centuries. Unfortunately this would, we believe, contain only the seeds of future turmoil. The realities have to be addressed, the health of the entire social organism has to be nurtured and there has to be provision for evolutionary flow as people shift into different systems of thinking, as they inevitably must. The structure of people's thinking systems cannot be arbitrarily and artificially altered, but the content of those systems certainly can be constructively channelled by the meeting of people's immediate needs and the setting of superordinate goals with which all can identify. We believe the process of the crucible - the National Indaba - can produce the results required.

In following chapters we will examine practical examples of problem resolution in South Africa using the Gravesian Technology, as well as the implications of this approach for Africa and elsewhere.

CHAPTER 14

*For this is the dawn of the Powershift Era. We live at a moment when
the entire structure of power that held the world together is now
disintegrating. A radically different structure of power is taking form.
And this is happening at every level of human society.*
Alvin Toffler: Power Shift

How Should Who Manage Whom?

Organisations in South Africa are microversions of the global
macrocosm, miniature replicas of the whole. Leaders in both the
public and private sectors deal with levels of complexity which
would confound their counterparts in virtually any other country.
The text books for global management are being written in
Johannesburg, not Boston, in Cape Town instead of London, in
Pretoria rather than Tokyo.

South African managers have to deal with all the mindsets to be
found up and down the Spiral and are compelled to do so on a real
time basis. Alvin Toffler's First, Second and Third Waves are flowing
simultaneously through the executive suite, over the shop floor and
through the administrative corridors. Every company confronts the
entire litany of societal problems - race relations, First and Third
World disparities, change dynamics, haves versus have-nots and
inequalities in housing, education, and career potential. At the same
time, executives have to interact and compete with First World
interests in North America, Europe and various parts of the Far East.
South Africans are already experiencing, in the workplace, the World
to the Power of Seven.

This chapter will apply the Graves technology specifically within the
arena of executive and managerial thinking and organisational design
and development, as well as communication, motivation, training,
marketing and customer relations. (Though it obviously also has
great implications for government and administration as well). We
will construct a model for managing people, using the technology of
the New Paradigm - a comprehensive and holistic strategy for
dealing with everything at once. Consider this a short course in
managing within the unique South African Crucible.

South African Megatrends

A global revolution is sweeping over managerial and organisational
thinking, from ivory tower theory-building and research to practical,

coalface applications. Toffler notes:

"Power isn't just shifting at the pinnacle of corporate life. The office manager and the supervisor on the plant floor are both discovering that workers no longer take orders blindly, as many once did. They ask questions and demand answers."

While South African institutions are being buffeted by these major fluctuations, they are also being impacted on by a significant number of local pressures, problems and complexities.

Note the shifts from:
• A production to a marketing focus.
• Government structures to privatised schemes.
• White/European to a cultural pluralism.
• Bureaucracies to meritocracies.
• Formal to informal sector mobilisation.
• A South African focus to global strategies.
• Isolated to integrated functions.
• Privileged to partnership relationships.
• Linear to multi-dimensional thinking.

The funnelling of black activism through the trade union movement has politicised the work environment to the extent that national issues have become more important than local, job-related concerns. Literacy and numeracy deficiencies and gaps are alarming. Skills in scientific problem resolution are scarce and do not appear to be improving. Many organisations are still coloured by paternalist/colonial or authoritarian attitudes and structures.

South Africa's relatively small and fragile First World component is in danger of being swamped by an emergent, demanding yet under-educated Third World mass. American-originated concepts of victimisation, entitlements, affirmative action and equality of results (instead of opportunity) threaten to contaminate the South African milieu. Heightened and altogether unrealistic expectations of affluence for all - a sense of this being just around the corner - are naive and dangerous.

In Chapter 13 we stressed the need for a relevant and tailored national economic and political process and plan. The Code of the Spiral has to be respected. Systemic thinking should impact upon the the decision-making of executives as well as the design of organisations. South Africa simply cannot and will not become a pristine First World society. Nor can or will Planet Earth. Yet this should not be taken to mean that a Third World system has to be embraced, with all its excesses of incompetence and patronage and the pitifully lower standards of living which come with control by political commissars. A Seventh World society is an alternative and is by far the better option. But to introduce it requires New Paradigm thinking.

Universal Paradigms and Processes

The search for practical managerial philosophies and programmes has been long, trendy, cosmetic and fragmented. The list of fads, quick fixes, flavours of the month and Holy Grails seems to stretch to eternity - the Managerial Grid, Management by Objectives, Situational Management, Brain Dominance, Transactional Analysis, One Minute Managing, Systems Thinking and Managing Change, to name but a few. Now that sanctions and boycotts are history, South Africans can brace themselves for a flood of new panaceas from international sources which stayed away during the 1980s to avoid contamination by the "white minority racist regime."

Chapter 2 briefly described the orginal research impulse that led Clare W. Graves to launch a longitudinal study of the formation, maturation and change in deep value systems. He could no longer rationalise teaching the different and conflicting psychological theories without being able to respond to students' queries as to which was "right". He experienced the same frustrations in the practical world of business and sought to create a framework that would explain why different theories emerge, where and when they are appropriate, and to what extent in the future, as we solve old problems and create new ones.

The Three Blind Mice of Management

South African executives, administrators and managers should recognise and avoid three major assumptions regarding personal and organisational performance. These are by-products of the older paradigm and need to be refined out in the fires of the South African Crucible.

"Mirror Management"

First, beware of "mirror management". It is everywhere. Managers assume that employees are "like them" and expect them to respond to identical motivational packages. Salesmen literally pitch to themselves in assuming customers like what they like. Trainers teach the way they learn. In short, we project our own values on to the employee, customer, client or citizen under the false assumption that others are like us.

In fact, so pervasive is mirror management that we suggest the following rule of thumb to professional communicators: "If what you are about to say or do looks and sounds good to you, don't do it!" (Unless, of course, the listeners or readers have the same value systems as you).

"Car Wash Mentality"

Second, avoid the "car wash" mentality. This presumes that others are carbon copies of our own systems, they are all just the same. What works for one must work for all. Like their American counterparts, South African companies often send their human resources managers to conventions and conferences to locate the currently "hottest" product in organisational development or motivation. They return and put all their managers or employees through this newest and most exciting training programme. Everybody gets the same psychological "car wash", whether relevant to the individual's needs and functions or not. Last year's package is put on the shelf to gather dust because this year's version has been discovered. And the process repeats itself next year. While each approach might in itself have considerable merit, such approaches need to be tailored for people and functions in different settings and at relevant levels on the Managerial Spiral.

"Final State Paralysis"

Thirdly, many South African organisations are vulnerable to "final state paralysis" - the belief in an ideal, fixed and permanent pattern of management organisational structure or bottom line motivation. The way we have managed in the past is the way we will always manage. What worked in the past will, without question, work in the future.

Flatlanders are obviously more prone to this illness than *Flowstaters*, since the ideas of change, evolution and spectrums of difference are not on the Flatland radar scopes. Once the ultimate solution is found, no matter what its particular content or its relevance to the whole scheme of things, it will be fixated upon as the "final state" to which every person in the organisation has to subscribe.

"Mirror management", "car wash" and "final state" distortions are rife in organisational life. They are products of the industrial age, of outdated psychological and managerial theories and of rigid, self-serving thinking on the part of many who are intimidated by innovation and change.

What will it take to transform and revitalise South African companies? Do governmental agencies have to be bureaucratic and tied up with red tape? How should communities be managed? What systems should municipalities employ to avoid partisan privilege or destructive adversarial confrontation? Should schools be authoritarian or democratic in their administration?

The answers to these and other questions are found by understanding the Graves technology and appreciating its impact on vision, scenario and mission strategies and the values stream of thinking. Many South African decision-makers and organisations are engaged in just such a pursuit. Some initiatives have been productive, others a waste of time and effort. In spite of genuine attempts to change organisational cultures or redirect corporations on a new path, few have reported much success. A different approach is required - the New Paradigm.

See Plate VIII, Colour Section.

The rest of this chapter will address the key Gravesian managerial question. While the question at first seems simple, when one begins to explore it in greater depth it becomes apparent that it integrates all the important variables within the organisational loop. The question is: "How should Who manage Whom to do What?"

By "how" we mean what type of managerial, personnel or motivational system.

By "who" we suggest the importance of selecting and matching leaders and followers to produce congruence and a natural fit.

By "whom" we mean which employee or follower in terms of value systems and levels of complexity of thinking.

By "what" we refer to the exact and specific job to be done.

One can see in this managerial equation how everything is connected to everything else. Every issue should be addressed to get a complete and holistic portrait of the working environment. This is in striking contrast to managerial thinking that assumes only one or two variables actually matter. Bad performance may be a function of a poor selection system instead of a lack of proper motivation. If we put the wrong person in a specific managerial position, we may end up with an inevitable conflict with the dominant value systems in the people we have placed in specific jobs.

Furthermore, in place of the verb "manage" one can subsititute such functions as "motivate", "teach", "train", "discipline", "influence", "communicate with" or "persuade". In education, therefore, the key question becomes: "How should Who teach Whom to learn or do What?"

The colour *PlateVIII* describes the relationships between the Spiral and various organisational structures, motivational theories and approaches to training and development. None of the approaches which have developed over time is inherently good or bad, effective or ineffective or right or wrong. The key is to know when to do "what", who should do it, for or to whom, and in what form, structure and sequence. Finally, "what" should be the reason, the motive or the bottom line.

Spectrums, Spirals, Systems and Styles

By recognising and understanding Spectrums and Spirals, it becomes possible to design Systems and Styles. By Spectrums we mean the unique and diverse displays of value systems that permeate people, jobs, organisations, communities and entire societies. By Spirals we refer to the dynamic process that constantly calibrates the mixtures of, and change in, value system Spectrums.

By Systems we allude to the organisational processes and structures that should be crafted to fit each Spectrum-Spiral. Natural leadership styles and behaviours should in turn flow from these natural set points to impact on people in their day-to-day relationships with one another and in their respective jobs and professions.

Spectrums and Spirals

The essential message of this book has been that the problems of existence created by competition, interactions and conflict among the first six value systems - Beige, Purple, Red, Blue, Orange and Green - cannot be resolved by thinking exclusively in any of the six colours. The exploitation in Red, authoritarianism in Blue, materialist manipulation in Orange and egalitarian humanness in Green are limited and narrow in their applicability.

The Law of the Spiral dictates - as interpreted through the Seventh Level (Yellow-Systemic thinking) framework - the importance of creating managerial models that can deal with all the other colours both individually and collectively. In an individual sense, New Paradigm thinkers realise each colour has its own motivational code uniquely written for a specific region on the Psychological Map. They will engineer the design and implementation of the specific organisational package for each value system colour.

On the other hand, when called upon to deal simultaneously with all the value system colours within the workplace, New Paradigm thinkers will design structures and processes that naturally accomodate all the colours. The entire Spectrum of motivational differences is described in the table on page 212. In both cases the needs of the Spiral are balanced against the requirements of specific groups. Note these examples within South African organisations.

1. From Purple and Red into Blue

The development of a huge corps of black civil servants will require the regimentation, structure and discipline of a Blue bureaucracy. Ideally, it would be designed and managed out of the Seventh Level system instead of taking a rigid Fourth Level approach, thus ensuring sufficient flexibility and responsiveness in the organisation. Otherwise the hierarchy will be rigid and imposing, people will be treated as numbers and employees will be motivated only by fear and the threat of punishment.

Neither Orange pragmatism nor Green sensitivity will be as important as Blue planning, controlling and performing of function. Procedures have to be followed by the book. Loyalty, quality and high standards should be expected and maintained. Employees should ratchet through length-of-service awards. A work ethic needs to be established and rewarded. These have in large part been the missing features in public administration on the African continent. But, once again, the issue is value systems, not skin colour.

2. From Blue Hierarchies to Orange Enterprises

Both public and private organisations in South Africa are shifting from the DQ-Blue production - centred set of assumptions, where simply getting the job done is important, to the ER-Orange results-orientated approach that rewards individual initiative and merit. One sees evidence of this in Eskom, Transnet, in the SABC, in many of the financial institutions and even in certain areas of medicine and social services.

Larger organisations have broken into smaller business unit profit centres. People were expected to jettison loyalty and dedication to the collective, making way for self-interest and individual reward. In some cases this has been successful. In others it has been less than well received. Many of the older, traditional values and ways of getting things done had been branded as old-fashioned and out of date. Many are now having second thoughts about this attempt at social engineering and are searching for new alternatives and blends. Some are now seeing the danger of "car wash" thinking which assumes that what is good for one must be good for all.

3. From Orange Competitivess and Status to Green Community and Harmony

The stampede to erase generations of racial imbalance has led many corporate leaders to move quickly into a series of small group or company-wide "experiences", designed to reinforce the company value of "family" and "community". Company publications are full of such allusions with pictures of employees in multiracial groupings and with articles written around the theme of "togetherness". Several have developed this communal theme in a series of public newspaper advertisements and colourful television commercials, reinforcing the sense of oneness.

As with many companies in the United States and Europe, the intention is to eliminate the remaining vestiges of Blue rank and Orange status in humanising the workplace. In the place of individual incentives, corporate egalitarianism and humanness are stressed and rewarded.

Such positive and warm-feeling initiatives look and sound good from the outside but are often rejected from the inside because they fail to deal with the real, genuine and often essential differences in people. It would be far better to create realistic developmental steps up the staircase than to cosmetically paint over differences with a false sense of sameness. Furthermore, many entire companies and sub-units deal in Blue, Orange and even Yellow worlds. Such a stress on Green values comes to be seen as either fanciful or downright dishonest.

South Africans need to beware of importing developmental packages from societies which are genuinely and legitimately passing out of Orange and into Green, having already solved the problem of existence in Purple, Red and Blue as well as Orange. For the most part South African organisations are nowhere near that state of psychological development. To indiscriminately impose such "solutions" on South African corporate and governmental infrastructures is both costly and counter-productive.

Because of the fixation in America with racial and ethnic diversity in the workplace, an entire growth industry has developed around the process of managing cultural differences. Every manager now has to be "politically correct" and "racially sensitive", and is made to be so by near-constant exposure to workshops and seminars that define the differences among and between white Anglo-Saxons, African Americans, Hispanic Americans, Native Americans and Asian Americans. This epitomises a system of racist classification and South African consultants and human resource managers should be wary (now the country has finally succeeded in removing racial classifications from the Statute Book) of importing this virus into the bloodstream of an evolving society.

The entire thrust of this book has been that people simply cannot be defined in such simplistic Flatlander categories and stereotypes.

There is no such thing as a universal "black" type - nor a Zulu type nor an Afrikaner type nor, for that matter, any other type. Systems and levels of thinking flow through and develop within us. We are neither types, nor do we have inevitable traits. To reinforce these classifications simply builds in and perpetuates a racial system. South Africa deserves better.

Systems and Styles

Any organisation, whether public or private, large or small, profit-centred or voluntary, religious or secular, long-standing or transitory, should be seen in terms of Systems and Styles. These, in turn, reflect the unique blend of Spectrums and Spirals within those particular organisations and institutions.

The Seventh Level world view on the Gravesian Spiral offers a new perspective and technology in addressing the critical issues in organisational life in the 1990s. Unlike other paradigms or starting points, it possesses the power and capacity to encompass all the essential elements and processes within the organisation and its marketplace. It offers executives wider choices in identifying and actually implementing the key objectives derived from scenario and visioning exercises. Since it deals realistically with underlying values and beliefs, it guides decision-makers and communicators in translating important objectives and mission statements to those deep structures.

Getting the System Right

Both the organisation-as-a-whole and each critical function should be appropriately designed in terms of the flow of systems. This must be accomplished before any discussion of such elements of style as communication, motivation, training or job performance. Getting the system right must precede making the style fit.

These are the essential components of systems design:
• Decide what business you are actually in.
• Establish cultural and values set points.
• Design right structures for right functions.
• Place the right person in the right job at the right time with the right tools.
• Connect every function to every other function.
• Scan the organisation, searching for turbulence and "messages from the future".
• Shift people, technology and resources as the environment realigns itself.

Organisations are organisms that make their way through a series of loose scrums of shifting conditions and conflicting interests. Change should be built into the systems and structures so that it is seen to be both natural and inevitable. In holographic organisations, everybody is in sales, everybody is in accounting, everybody is in safety, everybody is in training and everybody is managing change.

Making the Style Fit

Finally, Graves identified in his in-depth research initiative a common core of interpersonal managerial skills that generate positive responses from all the individual value systems. This involves a three-step process that can be taught to all managers, administrators, teachers, coaches, ministers and police officers - anyone who has to deal with people. Graves named the core elements P ("politeness"), O ("openness"), A ("autocracy").

"Politeness" means civility, basic respect for the person, friendliness, cordiality and acceptance. Opposites would be harshness, rudeness, aloofness, distance, condescension, arrogance and cynicism. Treated with politeness:

Purple feels safe and protected.
Red has less reason to feel alienated.
Blue sees the presence of "good".
Orange does not have to "win".
Green feels it has found a good friend.
Yellow responds to genuine civility.
Turquoise senses a pleasant spirit.

By "openness" we mean acceptance of different viewpoints, responsiveness to what others are saying and expressing and being available for further dialogue. The contrasting elements would be judgementalism, prejudice, bias and being closed off.

Finally, "autocracy" refers to the responsibility of the manager to shift to the appropriate value system, becoming congruent with the person being influenced.

To Purple he becomes a caring parent.
To Red he becomes a more powerful parent.
To Blue he becomes the rightful authority figure.
To Orange he becomes a successful motivator.
To Green he becomes a friendly person.
To Yellow he becomes an information source.
To Turquoise he becomes positive energy.

Conclusion

South African organisations, in all forms and at all levels of sophistication, have their vital role to play in shaping the country's future. Each has to discover its unique way to resolve the basic paradoxes that confront society as a whole. How can First and Third World views and patterns of thinking be integrated? How can African and European mindsets be harmonised? How can communal (collective) and free market (elitist) systems be meshed to the benefit of all? We believe the answers are to be found in what we have called the Seventh World.

Culture	Mission Statement	Approach to Working
Purple	To serve the tribe and honour ancestors.	Ritualised ways where all benefit: follow shaman/chief; fear of magic forces.
Red	To get quick cash and have a good time.	Hands-on, tough; work controlled by firm, respected boss; trials and tests of worth; macho.
Blue	To earn security and follow what is right.	By-the-book conformity; rigid chain-of-command and ranks; sacrifice for future gain.
Orange	To achieve prosperity and win the game.	Competing to gain advantage and make things better; political, status-driven and influence-driven.
Green	To find peace in a sharing community.	Co-operation in common causes where all can contribute and share in mutual benefits.
Yellow	To be free and learn interesting things.	Independent focus on integrative structures; systemic thinking, functional outcomes, focus on competency.
Turquoise	To explore conciousness and humanity.	Blending with holistic global networks to exchange ideas; experiential; seeks global results.

Bottom Lines

Purple	Safety / tribal needs/adherence to ritual / obeying elders and the chief.
Red	Power /action/excitement/proving individual prowess / instant rewards.

Blue   Obedience to authority / stability / orderliness /
            sacrifice for future gain.

Orange   Success/making things better / progress / prosperity
            / status / glitz.

Green   Affiliation / relationships / humanitarianism / love /
            inclusion / sensitivity.

Yellow   Control of one's time and space/variety of choices /
            self-motivation.

Turquoise
            Consciousness / global community / big picture
            views / holistic nets.

CHAPTER 15

At the Coalface

Much of the thrust of this book has been toward the need for open-ended political and constitutional structures tailored to the realities of South Africa's different communities, dispersed as they are along the developmental Spiral, most of them shifting to new levels of complexity. The creation of such structures would be the business of the political parties and interest groups - the leadership elites - meeting about the negotiating table. However, there are already stirrings at a less obvious level. While politicians, cabinet ministers, churchmen, sports personalities and industrial magnates make newspaper headlines with their ideas for the future, the country is quietly awash with unsung heroes who are already getting on with reform. Much of this is emanates from the workplace and the interaction between management and workforce, and in a country whose already rapid rate of industrialisation and urbanisation is likely to accelerate in the future, it is both appropriate and significant. The unsung reformers are to be found in all kinds of occupations, at all levels; they are in all population and cultural groupings, in every nook and cranny.

It is as if ordinary South Africans have decided to take the future in their own hands. Whatever the political leaders might be doing and whatever a tangle of the politics of yesterday some of them might be achieving, these ordinary citizens appreciate intuitively that something new is being forged in the crucible of South Africa and they are getting on with it. Imaginative and courageous reformers are building new bridges, expanding their minds with creative models, establishing fresh and additive relationships and encouraging realistic hopes and dreams. It is as if they realise time is short and that it is make or break for the country. They realise - white and black - what terrible mistakes have been made elsewhere in Africa (in white-ruled Rhodesia just as much as in Angola or Mozambique) and they are resolved that the same blunders will not be committed south of the Limpopo. Most of these people have nowhere else to go, they do not have dual nationality. They fully appreciate what is at stake. John Kane-Berman, executive director of the Institute of Race Relations, has called these quiet initiatives "the silent revolution". It is a revolution which could end up with the "leaders" being led by the people.

This chapter will describe some of the accomplishments of a tiny selection of these silent revolutionaries. Any sort of representative listing would be impossible because examples are to be found all over the country. We merely mention a few to illustrate the power of New Paradigm thinking when applied at the coalface. While much of this book might read like a theoretical text, perhaps even as a philosophical treatise on the nature of the human species, the content in fact has practical application and has already been applied, to good effect, by real people in the South Africa of today.

Readers will be introduced to a conservative Afrikaner industrial town in the Eastern Transvaal where leaders have established a positive working relationship with the Comrades of the adjacent township. They will be introduced to a remarkable, middle-aged white woman who has lived through the most extraordinary times and has successfully meshed European and African modes of thinking in problem resolution on the mines, in townships and elsewhere. They will encounter a mine manager who has an ability to detect "gold" in the human beings he works with. These are examples of the silent revolution, where the experiences and insights of individuals who have taken the trouble suggest that there are practical alternatives to the methods and outcomes offered by conventional thinking and a range of ideologies. Such people have vaulted in their thinking to that octave higher, mentioned in Chapter 10. They have developed an intuitive understanding of their environment and a capacity for holographic thinking. In their interaction with the individuals and communities about them, they have developed the capacity to enter "virtual reality", to appreciate and anticipate - and respect - the thinking and reasoning processes of others. These are the San Bushmen of the 21st century who have a sure instinct for survival, and they have emerged in South Africa and so far nowhere else.

The Miracle of Middelburg

"Something so unusual is happening at the Eastern Transvaal home of South Africa's stainless steel industry that Archbishop Desmond Tutu cannot believe his eyes," declared the *Saturday Star* (December 15, 1990). "Middelburg today is virtually a hotbed of aggressive peace," Dennis Beckett, editor of *Frontline*, wrote the very next day. "It is so peaceful that yesterday an AWB march through the town proceeded not only without an incident but also with the complete support of the local Comrades."

Why should a place as unpromising as Middelburg - a parliamentary constituency and town council controlled by the Conservative Party - produce such results? The answer would be found by attending a meeting of the Middelburg Informal Regional Planning Forum, which is a spin-off of the enlightened management philosophy of the town's major industry, Middelburg Steel and Alloys. MS&A's super-hot furnaces produce alloys and other metal products; its creative executive and human resources teams have been just as effective in forging, in dynamic human crucibles, unique solutions to social problems within the Middelburg community. They could well have developed a model for managing the whole of South African society.

MS&A has a long history of involving people in decision-making on critical issues, both in the company and within its customer base. In the late 1970s and 1980s the company, through the leadership of managing director John Hall, operations director W.D. Winship and director of manpower Alan Tonkin, implemented an open systems management philosophy. Value Management principles and processes were employed in everything from the design of large-scale capital projects to resolving intricate human relations, manpower or marketing problems. Everybody who would be affected by a decision, or who had unique skills and competencies to add value to that decision, was engaged in the discipline and regimentation of Value Management. If a gathering of MS&A managers from all functions - marketing, production, research and development, human resources or administration - were asked the question: "Which of you is in sales?" all would raise their hands. For many years Keith Luyt, manager of the steel mill, wore a hard hat emblazoned with the slogan: "I am a salesman!" He organised his employees as "The A-Team".

Before it became fashionable to do so, MS&A launched a long-term initiative to uplift the standard of living of its black employees. Tonkin developed an innovative approach to communication on everything from rules and discipline to pensions and compensation, using colourful cartoons and videos with soccer as a metaphor. MS&A became a symbolic reality. Attention and resources were focused on the design and construction of Chromeville, a black housing development in Mhluzi, the black township outside Middelburg. Chromeville was to be a real place for real people, not temporary quarters for transitional employees.

The company's leadership structure changed in the late 1980s, but the philosophy and culture and open systems management remained in place. (In the mid-1980s Tonkin had spearheaded an innovative MS&A 2000 initiative, encompassing vision, mission, goals and strategies. Such initiatives are commonplace today but this was possibly the first in South Africa.) By 1988 John Gomersall became managing director. Keith Luyt now headed the Stainless division, Paddy Probert headed Chrome and Brian Wegerle was human resources director. When social upheaval threatened the town of Middelburg as well as MS&A, the open systems process was extended to include representatives of the community as well: religious leaders, law enforcement officers and political leaders - the

Comrades, the civic associations and other interests as well. The entire community was to be Value Managed.

In May 1990 a Cosatu-backed group of the town's unemployed issued a chilling ultimatum to the company's black personnel officers living in Mhluzi: "Unless we have jobs by four o'clock on Monday, you've had it!" After a tense meeting in the football stadium and a series of highly charged confrontations, an extensive bargaining process began in which Wegerle had to move back and forth between conflicting groups because they refused to meet in the same room. There were boycotts of electricity accounts and counter-responses from the town council. There was a bloody night in Mhluzi in which three people died, 30 were injured and vehicles and houses were burned - the familiar South African pattern. But the Forum persevered, earning trust the hard way. There were setbacks, especially when outside political interests put pressure on their local representatives to participate in national or regional strikes or stayaways. Many lost hope, but always something brought them together again. Communication gaps began to close. Common purpose began to evolve. Middelburg's human crucible slowly began forging a new social system. Only time would tell whether this was to be a false hope, another futile initiative. Much of the credit belongs with Wegerle and his team of professionals, but Comrades such as Doctor Selala, Oupa Mashego and others put their reputations on the line by seeking negotiated rather than revolutionary solutions.

The Middelburg Forum developed into a problem-solving team with the mission "to create a better Middelburg for all its people, around and within existing structures, resources and services." The Forum has members representing all interested organisations and meets both on a regular and on a called basis.

The Forum has five watchwords:
- Is it the truth - am I being honest?
- Am I contributing to the solution or adding to the problem?
- Am I respecting the dignity of others?
- Am I seeking a practical solution?
- Am I seeking the highest solution?

Under Wegerle's leadership, the Forum has adopted an interactive planning process, a way of approaching difficult problems in a systematic, creative and additive fashion. The basic idea is to add value to the ideas of others instead of rejecting them out of hand or wasting time deciding who is right. The process is the key. It is open-ended, devoid of final state thinking and responsive to the search for common ground and common purpose.

John Gomersall captured the importance of this creative process at a function for Middelburg's leading citizens in which he sketched out two scenarios for Middelburg and Mhluzi, which are yoked together in a common destiny. One was of a wealthy town and township - prosperous, peaceful and safe. The second was of poverty, division, violence, pollution and depression. His points were given added impact by two dummy wrap-around front pages to the local newspaper, which were organised by Mark Drewel of MS&A public affairs and distributed at the function. One was headlined: "5 000 Jobs go" and contained an advertisement for houses whose value had dropped from R140 000 to R80 000. The other was headlined: "MS&A - No. 1 supplier in the world!" In this an estate agency had a three-bedroom home for sale at R180 000. Gomersall concluded with the admonition: "We are now at the crossroads at which we must choose the road which leads to a better Middelburg for us all or the road to instability, fear and insecurity." The speech and the dummy newspaper pages caused a stir among those present. Many believe this was the turning point at which the people of Middelburg realised the world was changing for them as much as for anyone else, and it was for them to decide whether they would take charge of the process themselves or be the victims of events beyond their control.

The values profiles of Middelburg and Mhluzi reflect First and Third World differences. As the effects of the Group Areas Act dissolve and racial mixing becomes more commonplace, communities such as Middelburg are searching for ways to integrate the various societies in a way to preserve First World standards, at the same time promoting racial harmony and understanding. The bridge between Mhluzi and Middelburg is not an even walk. It is rather a values-based evolutionary staircase. Until Mhluzi is stabilised around the Fourth Level system of Blue thinking (instead of Third Level-Red), the issues surrounding crime, sanitation, good schools and safe neighbourhoods will not be resolved. It is significant that at a recent meeting of the Forum, several Comrades asked for the institution of a disciplined, para-military Kibbutz-style structure, since they realised they had missed the key stage of order and purpose in their own development.

It is clearly in the interests of the Middelburg Town Council to participate in projects that stabilise and improve conditions in Mhluzi; to share technology, reward individual and community initiatives and work together with the people of Mhluzi to solve common problems. It is in the interests of the people of Mhluzi to learn new skills, gain access to new technologies and work to develop the youth for a more substantial role in the new South Africa. The gap between the two cultures has to be closed in a systematic, step-by-step, evolutionary fashion. Otherwise suspicions will grow, hostilities will increase and decay will set in.

The Middelburg Forum was a bold and courageous undertaking by all involved in its design and functioning. None of the participants claims to have discovered a panacea. All recognised from the start how vulnerable the process was (and it still is) to circumstances and events beyond their control. Yet, to a person, they realised that their futures were bound together. They were in a search for common ground and common purpose. The Forum process works in three stages:

Stage 1:
Define the current reality (The mess)

In this stage each person gives his or her understanding of the issue(s) at hand in Middelburg. As each person expresses perceptions, it becomes clear that each sees the world in quite a different way. These expressions reflect their relative positions within the Spiral. All are legitimate, reality-based and critical. Each person experiences a different version of the elephant mentioned in our Prologue. The task of the Forum is not to determine which reality is "the real one". Instead it seeks a way to integrate these differences in the direction of progress and development.

Stage 2:
The desired future (Short, medium and long-term)

The search is for the "highest solution" available. This future may be short-term and immediate in that a specific crisis has to be resolved. Or it may be of a long-term, permanent nature to establish a new system that can improve the standard of living and quality of life for all living in the Middelburg area.

Stage 3:
Set action plans (Practical, measurable and achievable)

These are the steps necessary to move from "the mess" to "the desired future". To facilitate these steps the Forum organised itself into a series of Working Groups (job creation, education, housing, health and welfare, security liaison and integrated systems). To assist these Working Groups, the Forum established a Foundation to provide the resources necessary to actually implement the groups' decisions. The Foundation's main objective was "to promote the welfare and upliftment of the under-developed and relatively less privileged communities in the Middelburg region and to facilitate the creation of a better Middelburg for all its people". For example, Rod Southey heads up a project known as "Compots" (Comrades' Pots), which is a joint venture between the Highveld Unemployed Workers Consultative Committee of Mhluzi and MS&A. The idea is to design stainless steel pots for use in Africa but provide, in doing so, an opportunity for the unemployed to gain, through "sweat equity" (work), ownership in this commercial enterprise.

The Forum has done more than just talk; it has produced results. There is a better understanding of the legitimacy of diverse perspectives. The unfranchised now have access to the system. Leaders from Middelburg and Mhluzi know one another on a personal basis. New job-creation initiatives have been launched. There is greater stability in the various companies of the region. The Forum has spawned collective support for community action and projects. In fact, ANC and Cosatu-related groups often reject the call for collective action in order to show respect for the integrity of the local Forum.

The evolutionary Spiral provides the insight and incremental process to move from "the mess" to "the desired future". As the population of Mhluzi moves in its collective thinking along the Psychological Map, the various neigbourhoods are likely to be transformed into proper, tree-lined South African communities. Blacks who can afford to buy homes in the until recently exclusively white areas will have moved into the Fifth Level-Orange system and will have more in common with their neighbours there than with many in the black community of Mhluzi. Instead of integrating school populations using the American formula of racial mixing, the entire system of education should be based on the levels of psychological development as described in the Graves technology.

The schools of Mhluzi should be cast within the Blue authoritarian structure with a focus on uniforms, discipline, demerit-based learning and technical training. Pupils who show evidence of conceptual thinking skills should be identified and placed in special learning environments. The schools in Middelburg should begin with the Blue base but shift more into Orange strategic and simulated learning experiences. Black pupils would begin to mix with whites in these schools, sharing the common values of Blue basics but seeking new skills within the Orange band of education.

Wegerle has moved on to a similar role with the Nedbank group. The concept of the Middelburg Forum is now being copied all over the country. Unfortunately, however, many who attempt to implement it will fail, not for lack of good intentions but because they have not experienced the open, systemic and scientific thinking process that the disciplines of Value Management provide. For a whole decade the MS&A corporate culture had been exposed to spectrum and spiral thinking from the Graves technology. If vertical levels of development are not understood, there is the danger that well-meant initiatives will flounder in the rhetoric of equality, liberation, cultural purity and guilt. Beware well-intentioned Green egalitarian thinkers. They will insist that everybody is at the same level of psychological development. In doing so they destroy the delicate bridge-building process, failing to understand the need for a spiral staircase of development.

Conditions in the township of Mhluzi and the town of Middelburg are still turbulent. The bridge between the two is far from steady and dependable. Either end is anchored in unsettled psychology which could result in serious vibrations, if not complete collapse of the structure. But at least, at time of writing, there had been significant progress. Nobody can predict what would happen if Red Third Level thinking systems were to gain the ascendancy on either side, or if national conflicts and crises should overwhelm "the Middelburg miracle". But to quote Godfrey Maseko, of the Middelburg Civic Association: "I feel this forum presents a real alternative for the new South Africa. The ANC and the government do not have the solution yet, but we the people at grassroots are working to find one for them"

He could well be right. The new South Africa could emerge on the factory floors, in the dusty dorps and in the dusty townships before it is seen in Pretoria, Cape Town or Bloemfontein.

Puseletso - "The One Who Comes in After Trouble"

Loraine Laubscher does not look like a trouble-shooter. She is a middle-aged white South African woman without formal university training, widow of a mine manager. Yet her personal library is more eclectic and deeper than that of many a university professor. She also has the gift of a grasp of the vernacular tongues and the rare ability to enter other people's value systems, to understand and empathise with them without being paternalistic - then translate back into the more complex thinking systems of management without losing the trust of those to whom she has been speaking. She is a familiar figure at mines and factories, in the most obscure townships, almost always after there has been "trouble" - hence her Sotho name. She enters the Purple and Red value systems so easily, and functions there so naturally, that the Africans with whom she is dealing instantly recognise her genuineness and communicate with her in that world. She has developed a reputation of near-mystical skill in resolving the most difficult problems. Her name, "Puseletso", was bestowed as a mark of affection and respect. She is one of those rare South Africans able to work in the creases, gaps and cusps between First and Third World environments, African and European mindsets and the so-called white and black perspectives. She goes to places, and achieves results, where First Worlders rightly fear to tread.

After the death of her husband in 1973, Laubscher began work at

Elna, demonstrating the use of sewing machines. In 1975 she encountered, for the first time, the Value Management process through the work of Keith van Heerden, then of South African Value Engineers. She soon adapted some of the sophisticated problem resolution techniques discussed in Chapter 10 into a process known as "Value Circles". Even before the Japanese "Quality Circle" movement had become popular in South Africa, she was training under-educated (if not wholly illiterate) blacks, many of them migrant workers, in productive and relevant decision-making skills. The list of the projects in which she has involved herself is astonishing. They include: the design and implementation of a communication centre at a mine; the design of a church for all religious persuasions; the design of a shopping centre; the creation of township leadership structures; accommodation for visiting wives at a hostel; and an entirely new information system which removes race from job-related categories. Her work has been at the coalface.

Laubscher is at her most effective as a trouble-shooter. She quickly senses the value system conflicts between emerging black leaders who show evidence of Red or Orange thinking. She is adept at translating between these elites-in-the-raw and the Blue, Fourth Level-focused minds which flourish at middle management levels and within manpower management functions. She unravels such problems by running three to five-day workshops or mediating between the conflicting rings on the Spiral. Feelings run high, raw nerves are exposed, but the disciplined thinking inherent in the Value Management process, coupled with Laubscher's ability to read and interpret the deep value structures at play, often results in the forging of new and imaginative solutions which none of the groups or parties would have believed possible. Since this essentially democratic process builds in both compliance and support, the solution agreed on usually works. Whether the issue is the quality of hostel food, inter-group work relationships or even the question of peace and harmony in the wider community, the technology appears to be highly effective.

Laubscher appreciates better than most the unique and powerful intelligences within the Purple and Red thinking patterns. While many Westerners are shut off from these systems, Laubscher affords them the fullest respect and enhances them by introduction to digital, step-by-step, measurement-based strategic skills packages. She has occasionally been accused (by outsiders) of being another white female who treats blacks in a paternalistic and patronising fashion. The accusers are invariably humbled.

The Mine Manager Who "Sees Gold" in People

Over recent years Laubscher has worked closely with Dick Solms, now manager of Anglo-American's President Steyn gold mine in the Orange Free State. President Steyn was the scene of considerable violence in 1989 and 1990, and it was no surprise when Solms was assigned there. The Anglo executives know that Solms is cut from a special kind of cloth.

If you work for Solms, you have to produce. With him the politics of the old boy network and favouritism do not apply. He is a proponent of Value Management and uses it constantly, most recently in his sinking of the shaft at Western Deep Levels South. (Once again, Keith van Heerden was involved). Not everybody is able to cope with the responsibilities of open systems management and the demand for personal competency in place of the protective security of seniority. With Solms it matters nothing whether you are white or black, Afrikaans or English-speaking. What matters is that you are willing to learn and to perform.

He is yet another South African who has moved beyond the colonial and authoritarian style of management into a version which fits well within the Fifth and Seventh Level systems on Graves' managerial map. Closed systems middle managers who hunker down in their jobs soon find themselves packing for other assignments. Young, ambitious trade union shop stewards who attempt to make their mark by issuing demands soon find, to their consternation, that they are confronted with the challenge of actually fixing the problems they brought to Solms' attention. They learn humility, as well as respect for the realities of operating a gold mine. Solms has also earned himself a reputation as something of a prospector, in the tradition of the old gold panning days. When he spots the gleam of a worthwhile nugget he grabs it - except that these are human nuggets. The trade unions complain bitterly that he snatches some of their brightest people by taking them into management. Solms is adept at taking the raw but unfocused energy to be found in the emerging Third Level-Red system in black employees and fashioning it into a constructive version of Fifth Level-Orange. He is engaged in identifying and developing black mine management potential for the next generation. Blacks are being advanced, but there is no need to call this "affirmative action" or "black advancement". Solms has set up a micro-crucible which forges human alloys quite naturally. It is no coincidence that the turbulence at President Steyn has settled considerably.

Soweto's Architect of Nation Building

Aggrey Klaaste is editor of *The Sowetan*, South Africa's largest daily newspaper, which happens also to be black-produced and black-read. He has for some years now advocated a Nation Building programme which focuses on rebuilding black communities instead of fanning the flames for the next explosion. As his marketing director, Eric Mani, explains: "We know there are problems, but we say to communities to spend more time uplifting themselves. We need to be ready spiritually, emotionally, and with a good family base, to help prepare people for that era when black people will be in government."

Nation Building takes the form of sponsoring festivals, cultural celebrations, workshops, educational activities and other initiatives which foster pride in the community. Klaaste believes blacks have been seriously damaged by apartheid and must "heal" and "find themselves" before significant progress can be made. He is especially troubled by the escalating crime rate and the terrible plight of children who have been caught in the wind shear between "the system" and "the struggle".

It is interesting that many African-American leaders are now beginning to appreciate the same problem. Yet others continue to play the old game of racial or plantation politics and place the blame for all their problems on "whites" and "institutionalised racism". There are more blacks of college age in prison than in college in America. Racism has, of course, had its impact but "non-racism" does not solve the problem. Many of America's black leaders see the world through the Third Level-Red system of values. This always finds the causes of its problems outside of itself. It cannot internalise fault, guilt or blame. Yet African-American intellectuals such as Thomas Sowell, Walter Williams, Tony Brown and Shelby Steele see quite clearly where much of the fault lies. For this they are labelled Uncle Toms by radical critics, largely because they threaten those critics' income, popularity and status by shifting the focus from the "white" enemy to "black" responsibilities. As discussed in Chapter 9, the primary issues concern values, not race.

Klaaste is in no danger whatever of being similarly labelled an Uncle Tom. He has been in the forefront, over the years, in denouncing apartheid for its injustices and its ravaging of the black community. But he is one of the more prominent among many black South Africans who urge creative self-upliftment so that blacks may achieve self-respect and their rightful place in the land of their birth.

New Paradigm Thinkers

Laubscher, Solms and Klaaste fit with the personal characteristics of the New Paradigm thinker, as described in Chapter 2: "... resourceful, fearless, tough, competent yet playful people." One is an obscure middle-aged white woman, one a mine manager, the third a black newspaper editor. They are but examples of what is emerging in South Africa.

To quote Shaun Johnson, political editor of *The Star* (July 25, 1991):

"There are fascinating developments in sport, the environment, education, entertainment and culture, business and many other areas of South African life. Already one begins to see, in outline, those individuals and institutions which will survive the transition and probably flourish under the new order. Blacks and whites - particularly among the younger generation - are re-assessing themselves, even reshaping themselves, in their image of the new world they will soon inhabit. Many politicians and activists are considering with glee the prospect of eventually getting out of politics and developing other talents. There is fluidity all over the country: it is uneven, uncertain, serious, funny, vibrant and - above all - exciting."

The Bushmen of the 21st century are about to come into their own.

PART V

Doubtless every era seems chaotic to the people who live through it. And the last decades of the 20th century are no exception. It is as if Spaceship Earth daily encounters squalls, downdraughts and wind shears as it careens into changing and uncharted realms of experience. Sometimes the evidence is furiously evident as thunderclouds of war gather or the lightning of a crisis streaks across the global sky; but often the turbulence is of a clear-air kind, the havoc it wreaks unrecognized until after its challenges have been met or its damage done.
James N. Rosenau: Turbulence in World Politics

Forging the Future

The first 15 chapters have described a new and comprehensive way of thinking about everything at once. We have presented a complex framework for understanding the struggle of a single mind to cope with its problems of existence, as well as they way in which large scale systems (societies) adapt to changing conditions in their respective environs.

We have relied heavily in this analysis of individual and social change on the seminal contributions of the late Professor Clare W. Graves within his "Emergent, Cyclical, Double Helix Model of Adult Biopsychosocial Systems" approach. We believe his name will eventually be included in the pantheon of great psychological theorists, along with those of Freud, Watson, Skinner and Maslow. We have also illustrated the practical application of that technology over an entire decade in South Africa. This is not just another theory which looks good on paper. It has been applied in a myriad of settings by South Africans dealing with real problems at the coalface.

Every South African is experiencing the trauma of sudden leaps and bounds in the complexity of the problems and challenges of existence. Many cultural shocks have been felt over the past decade; many are still to come. The National Party has moved from a pro-apartheid to an anti-apartheid position. The African National Congress was a mass revolutionary movement of armed struggle but is presently reshaping itself into a political party. Many of the very problems confronted on a daily basis in South Africa also reverberate across the entire planet, but in a more diffused form.

In response, human and societal crucibles in South Africa are forging new and powerful models uniquely calibrated to address and deal with those exponential shifts. We alter our human nature and coping systems in a profound manner as conditions call for radical changes in the way we live. Whenever new and strange viruses enter our bodies our immune system adapts its defences against these foreign interventions. In the same way, when new problems of existence explode on the scene the human mind shifts its resources, activates new equipment, suppresses older priorities and ultimately produces the paradigm that fits. Survival is not to the strongest but to those who are able to fit into the specific and more complex niches.

The innovative and adaptive thinking patterns and psychological packages that are emerging in the 1990s are called the New Paradigm. We have tracked the appearance of this complex system in South Africa, from cabinet level strategies to implementation at community level. We have evidence that something new and exciting is indeed evolving in the South African crucible.

Code of the Spiral

The intent of this book has been to explain, document and illustrate how and why that process of change occurs within our neurological processing systems. The evidence is now gathering that the DNA contains the codes and other genetically-based tool kits to provide instructions for literal reprogramming of the mind's priority-driven systems. We are neither "types" nor do we possess inevitable or permanent "traits". We are destined to generate new paradigms when the older ones no longer meet our needs. We are eloquent processors of systems and, because we are of the species *Homo sapiens*, possess the capacity to suppress older, obsolete systems while creating new ones. We call this dynamic process the Code of the Spiral. It is presently at work in a dramatic manner in South Africa. Older codes are being subsumed to new ones. In the psychological sense South Africans are doing what the leopard cannot do - they are changing their spots.

But why do some people change while others do not? What holds the closed system-thinking Afrikaner in the Voortrekker mindset while others are exploring new conceptual worlds, embarking on new Treks? What keeps the African continent in such a state of turmoil, with such untold suffering inflicted on innocents? A Conservative Party member of long standing asked one of us at an informal meeting with the caucus during a session of parliament: "We've tried to educate these people (blacks) for 300 years but have failed miserably. And we still fail. Why?" We believe the Code of the Spiral (and the consistent failure of the education authorities to provide real and appropriate education for black advancement) supplies an answer.

Relief workers in Ethiopia are shocked to discover that the father eats first in a starving family, even if it means children will die. But the idea of "women and children first in the lifeboats" does not hold true at the AN-Beige First Level of human society. The weaker children are designated by the family to be the first to starve. It is a system the mind already knows and the verdict is accepted.

One encounters the same law of survivalist behaviour among the Inuit (Eskimo) people of the far north in the Canadian arctic. When the band's food is scarce the grandparents will voluntarily get on to an ice floe and vanish.

Consider the reasons for these sacrificial patterns, so alien to Western thinking. In both cases the survival of the band is paramount. If the father dies in the Ethiopian desert, the family is lost anyway. If the older ones survive on the tundra but the young are sacrificed, life cannot continue. There is an internal logic to the First Level form of human existence. These survivalists see no other way to live.

The Law of the Purple ring (BO-Animistic) specifies control systems based on the spirits, the powerful chief and responsibilities to clan or tribe. Communalism is dominant.

The Law of the Red ring (CP-Exploitative) dictates such expressions of value as "take what you can", "kill or be killed", "damn the torpedoes, full speed ahead!" and "survival of the strongest or swiftest". The law of the jungle prevails.

The Law of the Blue ring (DQ-Saintly) prescribes seeking the highest good, finding true meaning in life, doing what is right and living in accordance with the requirements of the plan, the movement, the order, the cause or the system. One sacrifices now to obtain later - on retirement, in the afterlife or at the Day of Judgment. The Code of Righteous Conduct is held sacred.

The Law of the Orange ring (ER-Progressive) contends that to be successful one must be resourceful, pragmatic, expedient, energetic and competitive. The good life here and now is the goal. Achievement of status and personal recognition is the pay-off. The "Game" is the game. People can be bought off.

The Law of the Green ring (FS-Egalitarian) demands equality and justice for all in the human drama. Dogma and materialism are both rejected in favour of sensitivity and inner peace. The human community is valued above conflict, competition and elitism. Humanitarianism is the highest virtue.

The Law of the Yellow ring (GT-Systemic) acknowledges the legitimacy of all the operating systems, insisting they be expressed in their healthy versions, and integrates them on behalf of the Spiral. Individual uniqueness is the focus, but expressed in a non-destructive manner. The Law of Nature predominates.

The Law of the Turquoise ring (HU-Globalist) lays down the rules for the planet, the requirements for macro-managing global people and their organisational forms and structures. It prescribes the frequencies necessary to tune into the sounds and rhythms of the Life Force. The Law of Planetary (or large scale systems) Survival is paramount.

Human Central Processing Units

The CPU, or central processing unit, in a computer integrates, links up, meshes and makes sense out of the vast assemblages of information, hardware and softwear contained within that machine. In a similar fashion the human mind possesses a "CPU" that not only instructs the brain when to create new programmes but prioritises the pre-existing systems with their respective laws of operation.

The healthy person is able to up or down-shift to the appropriate system. A "closed" person, in any of the systems, lacks that flexibility. Hard-core criminals may be biologically, if not functionally, in closed systems of value. If specific individuals or groupings are centred within the Second, Third and Fourth Levels of development, the Fifth, Sixth, Seventh and Eighth Levels will make no sense to them. (This book has admittedly been written for people who have access to the Fifth and Seventh Level thinking capacities.)

Consider how the same human CPU works within the brain syndicate of a business, in South Africa especially. One operating system - Orange-ER-Progressive - is designed to make money, score well on the stock exchange and grow and expand. Adherence to the Orange laws and principles makes that possible. Yet the need for social responsibility (Green-FS-Sixth Level) also has to be considered because "profit should not come before, or at the expense of, people". Also, the Yellow-GT-Ecological current introduces a new dimension to the decision-making calculus. The needs of the environment, both present and future, demand attention.

Executives therefore have to find ways to integrate, balance off and respond to these three systems. The demands of trade unions often add a CP-Red element of instant gratification. Conformity to a government-imposed set of rules and regulations introduces DQ-Blue to the matrix. The way in which various sub-groups form into

BO-Purple clans when threatened expands still further the complexity of management in the 1990s.

Finally, since a community or entire society is a collective survivalist enterprise it likewise needs an intelligent, well-informed and responsive CPU to manage all the rings of the Spiral while facilitating its natural growth and evolution. To do so it needs the seismographic equipment to detect the presence, strength, mixtures and movement within the psychological geology lying beneath the surface. These deep structures are hidden from view but impact upon every political, religious or social movement, upon the media, academic debate or societal conflict.

When deep Purple and Red are in the substructure, rigid Blue is also produced with its paternalistic and punitive features. The Northern Transvaal and Natal have a high degree of black/Purple and consciousness-raising black/Red in the rural areas. This produces a white/Blue reaction, with Afrikaner content in the interior and English content at the coast. White inhabitants of the former Transvaal Republic and the province often known as the "Last Outpost of the British Empire" tend to have such a traditionalist and often absolutist value structure in common.

Black/Red and black/Orange in Soweto will contribute to the huge peak of white/Orange rising on the Witwatersrand, especially over Johannesburg, the City of Gold. The Red, Blue and emerging Orange systems within mixed race populations in the Cape Province make possible the elevation of Green and Yellow spikes over Cape Town, the Mother City. But when squatter populations arrive to threaten the lifestyle and security of white suburban communities such as at Hout Bay, Blue and Red thinking systems suddenly appear in Yuppies who had wrongly believed Transvalers were the only real racists. The Orange Free State is more Blue than Orange but is quickly shifting into a value system which justifies its name. The University of the Orange Free State has made a large contribution to the process, as have responsible civic and business leaders.

South Africa is far from being a single-coloured monolith. Every manager of a company with branches nation-wide will testify to how different the company is on the Witwatersrand, in the Cape or in Natal. Many of these differences are caused by the unique clusterings and mixtures of racial and ethnic groupings with their different levels of development. Transkei, Ciskei and Venda are strikingly different from Bophuthatswana (all four took "independence" under the grand apartheid formula) - not just in the content of their tribal (Purple) backgrounds, but in the mix of systems that comprise their development. We have described Bophuthatswana as "the best-kept secret in Africa" because of the way in which its value systems have emerged. It should be carefully studied by the architects of the new South Africa and encouraged to grow and develop since it is well on the way to producing a healthy environment in that region. To place it under the iron fist of a centralised monolith would tragically and unforgivably destroy many worthwhile achievements.

Chapter 16 will describe a total systems approach to dealing with South Africa's underlying psychological geology. The theme will be: "Quo vadimus - where are we going?" Chapter 17 will search for the same underlying structures, veins and pipes internationally and will focus on the implications of the Gravesian technology for management beyond the Limpopo.

Sometimes you have to die before you can live again. You've got to get yourself ready for the future even if it means burning bridges with the past. That's a painful choice to make because friendships are so sacred. The world is changing. We've got to move on ... too much is at stake. We must all be South Africans.
Deputy Minister Abe Williams
(On leaving the "anti-apartheid" coloured Labour Party to join the previously "apartheid" National Party, June 1991)

Quo Vadimus

Imagine falling into a time tunnel in the early 1990s, to appear - at your current age and with your present memory and knowledge - in the late 1940s. You know what damage apartheid, the anti-apartheid struggle and sanctions have caused. You are invited to speak to the Afrikaner architects of the grand apartheid scheme. What would you say to them? Could or would they believe you? Or would they be so caught up in their certitudes that they would be unable to listen? Would they be able to resist riding the powerful, nationalistic surge of Afrikaner zeal and arrogance, the urge for Utopia, for glory and splendour. Would they feel too much pressure from their have-not masses, the poor, peasant Afrikaners who had suffered so much at the hands of the British? Would you be able to convince them that ethnic differences are not as important as they imagine; that their Covenant with God at Blood River did not really mean what they believed it did?

Similarly, if a person were to fall into a time tunnel in the year 2040 and show up in the early 1990s to tell Nelson Mandela and the ANC executive of the consequences of their policies if they gained power in a winner takes all transformational manner, as the Afrikaners had four decades earlier - would they listen?

Several South Africans who made the initial contacts with the ANC in the late 1980s reported that many of the key leaders had a mystical belief in the black majority as if there were a powerful force guiding their destiny. Other observers noted, as recently as the Pretoria Minute, that many in the ANC believed de Klerk was about to hand over power, lock, stock and barrel. They had suffered greatly at the hands of the whites. The international community supported the rightness and moral purity of the black, non-racial majority against the evil "white, minority racist regime". The black nationalists were simply a government-in-waiting.

It was a simple equation - as simple as the equation of the 1940s by which Afrikaners were to wrest control from British South Africans, entrench themselves in perpetuity against competition from black South Africans and redistribute the country's resources to a wronged Volk. The Afrikaner nationalists of the 1940s and the African nationalists of the 1990s have much in common. In their rhetoric and their published papers, both describe the transformational world from CP-Red to DQ-Blue - struggle to ideology - with a growing awareness of pressure from the growing aspirations of ER-Orange supporters.

Apartheid is not in itself the problem. If it were, the solution would be relatively simple. Apartheid is rather the outcome of the faulty diagnosis and correspondingly inappropriate treatment of a deeper-seated problem. It was designed, as described in Chapter 6, as a response to conditions in the 1940s which nobody clearly understood or - anywhere in the world community - had any idea about managing. Almost the whole of Africa was under paternalist authoritarian colonial control at the time. Black Americans were nowhere near real emancipation.

With apartheid, Afrikaner nationalists sought to intensify, codify and enshrine in law the informal segregationist practices which had existed for centuries; to roll back the tide of black urbanisation and economic integration which had reached a peak during World War II; and, in doing so, to secure the position - political, economic and social - of the Afrikaner. As post-war African nationalism and anti-colonialism gathered force, apartheid was adapted to meet the challenge by providing a philosophical and moral basis for racial separation. The ideology attempted to harness the forces of African nationalism to its own ends, to portray the Afrikaners as Africa's first anti-colonialists, who had achieved their own freedom and were now ready to free the subject peoples of the black homelands or bantustans. But its essential underlying motivation - continued Afrikaner hegemony - did not change and if any were persuaded as to the programme's moral content or practicality, they were probably confined to the apartheid ideologues themselves and certain client elites in the homelands.

Apartheid was self-serving and short-sighted. It uplifted the Afrikaner in the material sense through affirmative action, by concentrating resources on such areas as education, sheltered employment in the unproductive public sector and soft agricultural loans. The resources were siphoned from the largely English language private sector and were withheld from the needy black sector. Apartheid was based on an essentially redistributive philosophy. It arrested the development of Afrikaner intelligences, locking thousands of people into positions where they benefitted from patronage which they could not afford to forego. The administration of apartheid became in itself a major source of employment for Afrikaners, who grew altogether too comfortable governing from Pretoria and altogether too dependent on the perquisites of political power. The Afrikaner had moved a long way from the robust individualism of his origins.

The anti-apartheid movement has unfortunately (though perhaps inevitably) become a mirror image of the system it struggled to bring down. Afrikaner nationalism set out in pursuit of freedom and justice but created a monolith which brought to the country ugly repression and the values which are echoed in *The Voice from the Casspir*. We can find no reason why a mass democratic monolith should be any less destructive of society and the evolutionary Spiral on which its health and progress depends.

Our point is that apartheid was based on a mis-diagnosis. Races, ethnic groups and tribes are not the irreducible components of humanity, on which political and social structures have to be built. Equally, those who espouse mass democracy as a panacea also make a mis-diagnosis. The evils and injustices of minority rule are not automatically eliminated by an artificial non-racial majority because there is nothing about such a majority to invest it with superior skills, insights or morality. It is simply a numerical majority, a statistic. And if it ignores the needs of the Spiral, in all their subtleties and sensitives, as apartheid did, it is likely to cause quite as much damage

A New Paradigm, a New Pathway

In this chapter we will describe a new pathway for South Africans in the 1990s. The technology of the New Paradigm was not available to the Afrikaner nationalists of the 1940s when they swept into power (nor indeed to their United Party predecessors, with their mixture of liberalism and traditional conservatism). This integrative, evolutionary thinking process emerged only when the GT-Yellow-Seventh Level paradigm began to be produced in the crucible of the 1960s and 1970s. History can be neither replayed nor repaid. However, the future need not repeat the mistakes of the past. It is time to rather open our conceptual windows and let in the future. The black nationalists of the 1990s have the benefit of hindsight. Information is available on how societies can change naturally and healthily. Technology is able to play a powerful role in speeding up social change. The financial resources are available today, and in greater diversity. The disasters elsewhere in Africa, where Blue monoliths and Red elites "liberated" the black masses from white colonialism, are common knowledge. The question is whether people will be prepared to make use of today's knowledge and the new technologies - black nationalists, Afrikaner nationalists, the business communities, the churches, readers of this book. Will they utilise the new means available to avoid repetition of the mistakes of the past?

We intend describing a possible future for South Africa from a perspective we have termed the Seventh World - a world interpreted from the integrated, systemic GT-Yellow Seventh Level on the Gravesian Spiral. And, harsh as it might seem to say it, from this perspective all South Africa's political parties - white and black - are part and parcel of an age which has already passed. Many have fought valiant and principled battles and campaigns, but those now belong with history. The parties should consider dissolving and regrouping over coming years so that new political structures are able to emerge around natural value system-based alliances. The present political structures are all of them tainted and carry dangerous viruses from the past. The Nationalists "cannot be trusted". The Democrats "represent only big business". The ANC are "bloodthirsty terrorists". Inkatha are "tribal and aggressive". These are perceptions rooted in very recent history and will not be easily erased while groupings cling to their present banners.

Parties which organise exclusively around racial or ethnic collectives are potentially virulent. Those based on "system" or "struggle" rhetoric - or which carry dominant First World or Third World flavours - will likewise contaminate the new political process. The feeding frenzy in sections of the press, local and international, during mid-1991 over the issue of the South African government's secret funding of Inkatha (improper and ill-advised as it certainly was) is evidence of the difficulty the most informed and cultivated sectors have in adjusting from the paradigm of System versus Struggle to the new realities. Those involved in the frenzy appeared to miss the fact that the funding occurred in an era which had already passed; that the disclosures came at a time when all parties were approaching consensus on the management of political violence. (It is significant that the ANC itself reacted in fairly muted terms.) The rhetoric and politics of System versus Struggle is no longer relevant, just as simple, first-past-the-post, Westminster-style majority rule should no longer be a sacred principle because it is not sustainable in a society where the largest group of voters would be concentrated at only a narrow range on the Spiral. The survival and health of the entire Spiral should rather be the concern of all well-meaning citizens, as well as of international observers and critics.

South Africa's quest should be to discover who in the different political parties and movements, parliamentary and extra-parliamentary, have developed to the levels of complexity in their thinking where they are equipped to work jointly in problem-solving groups; to engineer rather than negotiate (in the horse-trading sense) a Seventh World system to serve the country in the 21st century. Every group of significance in South Africa has such people, but they are not all of them conventional politicians. South Africans have to engineer an entirely new model, much as the framers of the American Constitution had to. South Africans are in a new and different environment, they confront challenges never before posed to *Homo sapiens*. They need to preserve the best from the past, integrate it with the needs of the present, then create a dynamic system tailored to the needs of the future.

Humanity is passing through extraordinary turbulence, right across the planet. Most futurists and cutting-edge thinkers believe we are at a profound breaking point in global development. We are shifting from a state-centred control system to one that is shaped by multiple interests, all connecting up in vast political, economic, social, religious and cultural networks. Instant communication and rapid international travel have shrunk the world in terms of time and proximity. British and American two-party adversarial systems of problem resolution are being seriously questioned. Contests between liberals and conservatives, Tories and Labour or Republicans and Democrats no longer make a lot of sense in a complex and multi-faceted world. As Africa contemplates multi-party democracy, the West might well be searching for entirely different models. The Age of Aquarius has indeed been in the ascendant over recent decades. But, as the millenium approaches, it is also certain to set. What will the new age be? South Africans could well experience it first.

The South African (and Global) Mess

South Africa is plagued by the Seven Gs - gaps, greed, guilt, gulfs, grudges, games and glitches. There are too many developmental gaps, too many historic grudges, too much guilt and greed and a huge gulf in skills which separates black from white, African from European and First World from Third World. The dominant value systems are expressed in their negative versions. The Purple system sells war muti to the warriors of Natal and the Transvaal townships. The Red system is engaged in rape, pillage and murder. The Blue system has regressed into punitive, self-righteous orthodoxy. True Believers and faithful followers contemplate holy war or righteous crusade for national liberation. Orange is robbing the country bare in endemic dishonesty and corruption. Green has regressed into piety, unctiousness and naivete. In all cases, doing more of the same only makes things worse.

This is the South African mess. It is an image in miniature of global insanity. Explosive ethnic tension is just beneath the surface, ready to repeat the violence of Liberia, Sri Lanka, Yugoslavia and Halifax,

Canada. Promises of violence by the two radical wings are more than just a passing threat. The population is increasing dramatically, mainly among the poor. The environment is fragile and threatened. The AIDS pandemic is frightening. Slush fund scandals - government dishonesty - capture the newspaper headlines. Many political figures, recklessly aided and abetted by a media with the shortest of short-term ambitions, are playing a destructive game of political pinball. The silver ball of apartheid is put into play and the country is entranced by the flashing lights and clangings as the game progresses. Everybody keeps score, even though the chalking up of political points has not the faintest bearing on securing the future. Isolated and sometimes innocent events suddenly twist and churn as the country goes into another feeding frenzy and people exploit the situation for personal or political advantage. Leadership is often comparable with thousands of ants riding a log down the rapids, each one believing he is in charge and in control. In fact nobody is. The dying throes of the old paradigm present a melancholy spectacle. The Seventh World will dawn not before time.

The Desired Future: A Healthy South Africa

The next South Africa should be built around the Spiral-generated developmental track instead of a single political or economic theory, retributive schemes for redistribution, transformational or emotional rhetoric or racially or ethnically-based ideas. But what should the final product be? What should characterise the new South Africa? What does "healthy" mean?

A healthy and dynamic South Africa would focus on meeting the needs of people at different developmental levels, on the protection of a fragile and threatened environment, on the containment of dangerous diseases and on the mobilisation and channeling of resources to save the whole of Africa. South Africans would value personal accountability and collective responsibility as highly as they do individual rights and freedom of choice. The unique intelligences of South Africans, from every group and from every walk of life, would be recognised, enhanced and brought to bear on the challenges that confront society at large. Problem identification and resolution capacities would be infused into the population at all levels of sophistication, as would skills in conflict resolution.

The Action: Plans and Steps

The converse of apartheid is not necessarily progress. The majority are capable of as much tyranny as the minority. "Liberation" by no means guarantees houses, jobs or good schools. (First World thinkers seldom appreciate the real needs and aspirations of those struggling out of a Third World existence.) Yet virtually everybody is able to subscribe to a basic set of superordinate goals designed to create a healthy society.

To get from "the mess" to "the desired future" we suggest the processes listed below. We recommend that the 1990s become adopted as "The decade of South African Development". The country is simply too fragile, too explosive, too mistrustful and too gap-ridden to make possible the design and implementation of a permanent constitutional order. That will become possible only when a fragmented society has become reasonably stabilised and fear and mistrust have been addressed and a series of constructive initiatives have had the time to build the physical, social, economic and political infrastructure from the ground upward as well as from the top down. In other words, transitional arrangements might have to last considerably longer than many of the players seem to anticipate at present. Transition would not be a short holding process while a new constitution was devised and a new goverment elected, it would be a longer process while the country was made secure for democracy.

Stabilisation

In Chapter 13 we suggested an alternative answer to the question: "What is the plan?" We advised the appointment of a "Council of the Wise" to initiate the process of healing the country's wounds and closing the gaps before a permanent "plan" is negotiated by a constitutional forum of some kind. Such a Council should not be dominated by partisan political interests, it should be selected on a basis of competency rather than affiliation or patronage. It should be a Senate (in the Roman sense of competence and integrity, not as the upper chamber in a Westminster or American-style constitution) permeated by New Paradigm thinking. It should be a distillation of the talent available in the sciences, the arts, the world of business, religion and the law. In much the same way that business and religious leaders mediated in a peace initiative in 1991, so the Council should mobilise resources, second executive talent from inside South Africa and elsewhere and macro-manage development.

Since everything would be interconnected, massive savings could be effected by economies of scale in such a comprehensive and holistic enterprise. Decisions would be taken by GT-Yellow-Systemic elites, who value competency and functionality, rather than by ER-Orange-Progressive elites, who value material success and status, or by CP-Red-Exploitative elites who seek power and instant gratification.

Stabilisation would bring decency and order into the present, to increase positive options for the future. Eight major issues need to be addressed, and these would have a multiplier or synergistic effect on future progress and development. Both stabilisation and reconstruction should be seen to be the superordinate goals necessary for the development and health of society. A constitution is neither feasible nor possible until the country has been stabilised and effective construction projects are well under way.

The Big Eight Stabilisers

These are listed not necessarily in their order of relative importance. However, they need to be addressed all at one time if the momentum is to be created for the developmental quantum leaps which will be necessary during this decade. It is essential that society be provided with foundations which meet the needs of people at all levels of development. No single political group or economic persuasion will be able to deal with these complex issues in isolation.

1. *Nutrition*
Proper nutrition for all South Africans, especially infants and developing children, should be provided through massive feeding programmes in the homelands, in townships and in urban centres.

2. *Public safety*
Effective public safety and the dispensing of criminal justice should be ensured by the establishment of well-managed law enforcement agencies and the development of an informed and supportive public. Justice for all has to be rapid and sure.

3. *Health*
The general health and well-being of all South Africans should be enhanced by the provision of greatly expanded services to provide preventive medicine, care and the containment of diseases - especially the AIDS virus.

4. *Housing*
A national housing initiative should be launched, making available an entire range of options from low-cost "sweat equity" operations to more elaborate public sector and private sector-sponsored projects.

5. *Education*
A national education strategy needs to be designed and implemented - a strategy which mobilises all the country's resources, human, technologcal and financial, so that the intelligences of all the country's citizens are increased, both now and for the future.

6. *The environment*
The protection and preservation of the country's environment and its ecological balances should be aggressively pursued through responsible business practices, the fostering of a well-informed

public, an awareness of the issues at the various layers of government and an underpinning of appropriate legislation.

7. *Employment*

Employment opportunities should be created in both public and private sectors by the mobilisation of all available resources, employment to be based on competency and accountability and reflecting the different developmental rings on the South African Spiral.

8. *Population control*

South Africa has to find an effective method to communicate a sense of family and communal responsibility in the area of population planning and control.

The Construction of South Africa

Apartheid and economic sanctions have between them left behind too many layers, too many differences and yawning gaps in respect of standard of living and quality of life among South Africans. The removal of apartheid will not of its own remove these First, Second, Third and Fourth World imbalances. Like a wound that has to be kept open at the surface so that it can heal from the inside outward, South African development has to move up the staircase of existential values, passing systematically through the different levels of complexity.

Physical Construction

The country's physical infrastructure needs to be carefully assessed and strategically upgraded. The entire country needs to be electrified as quickly as possible, partly to provide the presently disadvantaged with the cheapest and cleanest form of energy available, partly to release rural black women from the unproductive (and environment damaging) daily drudgery of gathering firewood and partly to stimulate small manufacturing enterprises. Patterns of community development, urban planning and development of the transportation network should be the business of a national planning corps charged with deriving optimal advantage from the country's resources.

Social Construction

Clear evolutionary patterns are detectable in people's development of social preferences and social groupings. Neighbourhoods need to be protected, allowed to preserve their characteristics, in order to facilitate a natural progression from smaller to larger houses, from modest to more affluent environments and from lower to higher socio-economic strata. Any open systems environment naturally fosters this stair step effect. As resources and opportunities become available, black communities follow the same developmental tracks as their white counterparts. The African communal lifestyle and code of "ubuntu" is not the product of African genetic material or of an inborn sense of social responsibility, it is a function of Purple thinking. Africans become Red, Orange and Yellow elites, just as Europeans do. These evolutionary patterns have to be left undisturbed, allowed to develop naturally. The repeal of the Group Areas Act and the Land Acts is a beginning.

Economic Construction

South African business operates within a First World economic system where decisions nevertheless impact upon - and are in turn themselves influenced by - repercussions through the Second World and Third World sectors of the population. Charles Stride, deputy chairman of Altron, makes the point that, unlike in true First World societies, when South Africans manipulate the currency to control inflation, people are retrenched without having an economic safety net of unemployment relief. The resulting turbulence in the townships impacts on foreign trade and investment, cancelling out the benefit of the anti-inflation moves. "Everything has to work together," Stride says, "in constructing economic bridges over the First World and Third World differences to insulate the country from these after-effects. Sure, we are a First World economy but we have to learn to function within our Third World milieu."

The vicious circle continues to repeat itself because of the way the economy is managed. It happens on a global scale also as the industrialised First World countries make economic decisions which create disaster in the Third World while their own populations are relatively insulated.

South Africa has to develop the capacity to manage its economy in such a way that the Third World sector of the population is not continually shaken and buffeted but instead develops a sense of participation and continuity. This rules out the *laissez faire* free market as an option. At the same time, the Third World sector is likely to be best absorbed into the First World sector by sustained economic growth, which - on the basis of performance world-wide - would rule out the centralised command economy. A very delicate balance has to be achieved.

Political Construction

South Africans who have until now been shut out of the political process should learn participation from the ground upward, not from the top down. A start has to be made with participation at the level of local or community councils, participants being made aware that their actions have direct impact on their lives. Even at local level the pace cannot be forced. Decades of authoritarian administration by the organs of apartheid have had a deeply corrosive effect.

Representative democracy is the ideal, yet certain realities have to be faced. Given the level of political violence in the country, it is difficult, at time of writing, to imagine a national election campaign producing anything other than a frightening intensification (especially if it were to elect a winner-takes-all Westminster-style parliament).

We suggest inclusion of all parties in government, but gradualism as democracy is introduced a step at a time. Middelburg-style forums, local and regional indabas, should be established during the "Decade of Development" to work out the formulae for political representation which are appropriate to each particular community and region. The new system should be built from the bottom upward rather than from the top down.

To again take the example of Middelburg: before Greater Middelburg has a common voters roll and a one man one vote system in operation, the township of Mhluzi should be given the experience of a series of legitimate voting exercises and the experience of responsible and representative government, providing politicians and administrators with the opportunity to develop their skills in the art of statecraft. This is in no way to argue for continued fragmentation. There should be the closest relationship between Mhluzi and Middelburg itself and it has to be made clear that every step is toward an inclusive system for a Greater Middelburg, the target placed within a specified time frame, otherwise the majority would legitimately suspect that their progress is being stalled. Above all, the involvement and co-operation of those affected by the process are necessary if it is to succeed. They would have to experience tangible progress toward the ideal of full democracy at local level. Given the realities of South Africa and the legitimate anxieties of minorities, we believe such a process would avoid the trauma and likely turmoil of an abrupt transfer of power to a majority whom apartheid has denied the experience of participation in government.

A Constitution for South Africa

South Africa has waited almost three and a half centuries for inclusive, representative democracy. We believe it would be folly, now that such a system is in sight, to rush into it with old and inappropriate constitutional models which have failed in South Africa as much as elsewhere in Africa. We believe a target date for a permanent system of government should be set - say the year 2000, start of the third millenium - and the intervening period used to build the most solid foundations, which simply do not exist in any form at present. It follows that the drafting and implementation of a new constitution could not be the outcome of a once-off convention or all-party conference. It would have the be the result of a painstaking and continuous process which adjusted itself to new and unexpected practicalities as they emerged and as the country went through a process of orderly consolidation and construction. Transitional government (in which all significant groupings would have to be major players) could turn out to be a more drawn-out process than many anticipate. How that transitional government should be constituted and legitimised is not our concern here; it would be the business of multi-party negotiations. Our concern is for an orderly and evolutionary process leading inexorably and unarguably to the target of an inclusive democracy which serves South Africa's peoples at all levels of development without threatening any particular level, without shutting off any level from progress (as apartheid assuredly did) and without damaging the economy which will have to underpin the new South Africa.

We believe this final decade of the 20th century should be devoted in South Africa to a sequence of the three Cs: Consolidation / Construction / Constitution. This would without question be the most effective way of actually meeting the needs of people all the way along the developmental Spiral. Instead of pitting have-nots against haves, capitalists against communalists or the advantaged against the disadvantaged, the strategy could enlist the full co-operation and support of the elements and resources of the entire Spiral.

The anxieties of South Africans in all parties and positions would be addressed - of minorities who have seen turmoil elsewhere in Africa; of the disadvantaged majority who despair of ever being given a legitimate share in their birthright. People would be able to see and experience what was happening as the decade unfolded. The pressure would be taken off everybody as the synthesis and integration of a presently divided society continued in a positive manner.

Every individual and grouping would be able to add value to the process, even those who at present distance themselves from it. We believe, for instance, that the Conservative Party has a major contribution to make. It represents a large sector of the white community who have genuine concerns about future standards in their communities and in the country as a whole. Given the course of events elsewhere in Africa over 30 years, and in parts of this country as well, those concerns are perfectly understandable. They have to be systematically addressed. Conservatives have to be shown that initiatives which encourage and promote the movement of blacks from Beige, Purple and Red, up the developmental Spiral into Blue, Orange, Green and Yellow are not threatening to their values, in fact will serve to bolster them. They need to be encouraged to become involved. The responsibility for facilitating such movement has to be shared by all - not least black South Africans themselves.

The strongest criticism of this sequence of the Three Cs is likely to come from those who demand redistribution, sometimes out of ideological conviction, sometimes out of a desire for retribution and revenge. The impatience of the disadvantaged and dispossessed is understandable, yet the stark fact is that the economy has to grow if the disadvantaged are to improve their lot and redistribution would have the opposite effect. The CCC sequence would involve the bulk of South Africa's peoples moving into the healthy version of the DQ-Blue Absolutist mode, in which they accept the rules of the process of transition. DQ-Blue would inevitably be attacked by those still in the CP-Red Exploitative system which believes instinctively that the "establishment" has amassed wealth on the backs of the working class and still has it hidden away to share. Yet redistributive schemes are invariably designed to benefit those who promote and organise them rather than the people in whose name they are promoted.

There is also the fundamental question of whether redistribution is compatible with the free and open society we advocate. P.T. Bauer put it very clearly in *Equality, the Third World and Economic Delusion:*

"In an open and free society, political action which deliberately aimed to minimise, or even remove, economic differences (ie differences in income and wealth) would entail such extensive coercion that the society would cease to be open and free. The successful pursuit of the unholy grail of economic equality would exchange the promised reduction or removal of differences in income and wealth for much greater inequality of power between rulers and subjects. There is an underlying contradiction in egalitarianism in open societies."

Any "system" of the DQ-Blue Puritan work ethic coupled with ER-Orange strategic and analytical thinking also comes under attack by FS-Green egalitarianism. "Liberation" movements therefore tend to contain the very strange bedfellows of Red and Green, who really have nothing in common. Should Red take power under the banner of "power to the people", it is the Green thinkers - usually, in South Africa's case, affluent white liberals - who are the first to be brushed aside.

The bulk of the South African population have to move through the conduit of Blue and Orange before Seventh World systems can actually emerge. However, as we have argued, this can be achieved surprisingly quickly as people are in a state of continuous evolutionary development and they would react to the stimuli of a purposeful developmental programme. It is if the keepers of the orthodoxy in Blue and the possessors of wealth in Orange shut the door on the aspirations of the disadvantaged and block their passage along this route that revolution is invited. Societies that experience revolutions generally deserve them - and they generally deserve the kind of revolution they get.

We are under no illusion as to the hostility with which our proposals for a managed, calibrated, incremental and (let us be perfectly honest) prosaic process of evolution within a fixed time frame will be received in certain quarters, especially at a time of heightened expectation. However, we invite readers to consider whether they really believe South Africa as it exists today could withstand the shock of an overnight transformation; whether a new and unprepared government - whoever controlled it - would have the means to come anywhere near meeting the expectations of the masses; whether it would not be a great deal safer to reduce the pent-up frustrations, while achieving a balance and an understanding between the country's different power groupings, before proceeding.

Finally, a caution. The country is precariously balanced. Any attempt to gain advantage by upsetting that balance invites disaster. If the Zulus are weakened, they will form impis. If the Afrikaner Volk are threatened, they will laager.* If urban blacks are dismayed, they will close down the economy. If the business community are denied a climate conducive to their operations, they will leave. Each one of those groupings has it in its power to pull the plug on the new South Africa. We believe that unless the process of building a new society is carefully and jointly managed by all of them, the potential for a pulling of one or several plugs is enormous.

*Defensive formation of wagons in a circle.

We now live in a world where the tensions are more likely to be North-South, white-nonwhite, rich-poor, developed-underdeveloped, educated-undereducated. We grew up fearing the power of a strong Russia; how then do we adjust to a world in which a greater threat to our stability comes from a weak Mexico?
David Alberstam: The Next Century

Beyond the Limpopo

Gather all the social, economic and political conflicts South Africa has. Transpose these on to a mental colour slide. Project this mental slide on to a curved, three-dimensional, holographic screen representing the world as a whole. The holographs of South African conflict are projected as a world image - and this accords with reality.

A First World minority leads a privileged existence within a sea of Third World poverty. The First World minority is for the most part racially Caucasian, the Third World majority mainly non-Caucasian. The minority is overwelmingly dominant, militarily and technologically. The minority has static or declining population growth. The majority is experiencing a population explosion which far outstrips resources. The majority challenges the legitimacy of the existing order and clamours for a new one, for a redistribution of wealth and opportunity. The minority acknowledges the disparity but disputes the legitimacy of the demand for redistribution.

It does not really matter whether one is considering South Africa or the world at large. The issues are the same. And it surely follows that a resolution of South Africa's problems would be the forerunner to the resolution of global problems. The way South Africans resolve the First World-Third World impasse will surely instruct the global architects in the technology necessary when dealing with the tensions of North versus South, white versus non-white, rich versus poor or developed versus under-developed. The South African crucible is forging models for the evolution of global society.

James N. Rosenau, from the University of Southern California, has documented in his book, *Turbulence in World Politics*, a major shift from a state-centric world of international politics to an autonomous multi-centric one. In this new world order, racial, ethnic, social, religious and political sub-groupings are weakening the long-standing structures of national and international authority. Such mosaics (as also identified by Toffler) are operative within the South

African microcosm, just as they are within the global macrocosm. (The pressure on apartheid is a product of the focusing of these sub-groupings on Pretoria, rather than conventional pressure from national states). Rosenau maintains there is clear evidence of a major paradigm shift (he calls such phenomena breakpoints). "Global life," he says, " may have entered a period of turbulence the likes of which it has not known for three hundred years and the outcomes of which are still far from clear."

The problems we confront as global citizens are new, demanding and complex. The shift from a world order based on state independence and sovereignty to one dominated by a myriad of expanding and contracting interest groups and mosaics is a primary cause of global turbulence. To deal with this chaos, Rosenau contends, "theorizing must begin anew, and present premises and understandings of history's dynamics must be treated as conceptual jails from which an escape can be engineered only by allowing for the possibility that a breakpoint in human affairs is imminent, if not upon us, as the twentieth century comes to an end".

Likewise, "theorizing must begin anew" with regard to the quality of thinking necessary to resolve the global-in-miniature issues and turbulence south of the Limpopo. We believe the Graves technology offers such a conceptual jailbreak. Many are still trapped in the cells and jail yards of the thinking patterns described in this book as AN-Beige, BO-Purple, CP-Red, DQ-Blue, ER-Orange and FS-Green. Break-out is in the colours Yellow and Turquoise.

The End of History?

The Cold War was, at base, a conflict between two DQ-Blue and ER-Orange monoliths (with a strong CP-Red power urge also present in the Soviet one). It was Western ideology and materialism pitted against a Marxist-Leninist version (content) of the same two belief structures. Karl Marx was a secular theologian who replaced a belief in the hereafter with a soaring faith in the ultimate and inevitable victory of the proletariat. The major global struggle since World War II has been between a substance and its shadow, between a thesis and an antithesis, between mutually exclusive "truths" within the same ring of the Spiral.

Why did the West's content of Blue and Orange ultimately outlive and dominate the Soviet version? There is obviously more than one reason. Perhaps the Judaeo-Christian version of ideological Blue inspired more hope and devotion than atheistic materialism, with its promise only of a heaven on earth. America's vast breadbasket out-produced anything the Soviet Union, China or any of their client states could offer. The impact of the Russian climate and the country's lack of access to the world's sea lanes also has to be taken into account. Meanwhile, America's lack of encumbrance from the past gave it advantage. European cultures - in both the East and the West - are built on Purple, Red and Blue ethnic memories and historical grudges. America had a freshness, a willingness to take on challenges and an orientation toward the future rather than the past.

For whatever reason, the Western version of DQ-Blue and ER-Orange was more open and dynamic. Personal freedom was more highly valued. The expression of these two systems was more complex and healthy. The success in Orange materialism was disseminated throughout the middle class instead of being the prerogative of the power elite. The resulting technological advantage out-spent and out-gunned the Soviet military machine. Finally, Western societies had the motivation and resources to launch explorations into the complexities of the FS-Green and GT-Yellow conceptual worlds. The Law of the Spiral holds that the more complex systems, if properly understood, supported and maintained, will always outmanoeuvre and dominate the less complex.

Francis Fukuyama, a State Department analyst, startled the world by declaring that the cessation of the Cold War was not just the end of a particular phase of post-war history but "the end of history as such: that is, the end point of mankind's ideological evolution and the universalization of Western liberal democracy as the final form of human government." We maintain that (unless the world is about to end abruptly) he could not be more wrong. He is guilty of "final state" thinking as flawed as that of his Marxist opponents who contend that history ends with the attainment of communism. What happened in fact was that the Cold War temporarily froze the Spiral by imposing a two-valued (capitalism versus communism) bipolarity on a complex, multivalued world, blocking and distorting the natural evolutionary process. The entire planet is now being reorganised around the Spiral. Western liberal democracy has yet to be experienced by the vast majority of the world's population. It might be argued that this is a beginning of an epoch in history - it is certainly not the end. What we are witnessing is the emergence of a New Paradigm.

We hope to support this thesis by focusing on various applications of Gravesian analysis in areas "beyond the Limpopo". We will examine the experience of post-colonial Africa itself. Then we will consider the action of the Spiral in the United States, Europe, the Pacific Rim, the Middle East and elsewhere.

Once Again Darkness: The Death of Africa

Sub-Saharan Africa (leaving South Africa out of the equation) has been one of the great disappointments of the period since World War II in which the great European-centred colonial empires were dismantled. Whereas other parts of the Third World have produced such brutal episodes as Cambodia under the Khmers Rouge, they have also produced such successes as Singapore, Taiwan and South Korea. In Africa, the picture has been almost universally catastrophic: a succession of military coups since the independence process began in the early 1960s; major civil wars in Zaire (then known as the Congo), Nigeria, Angola, Uganda, Ethiopia, Sudan, Mali, Mozambique and Liberia; near-genocidal ethnic strife in such countries as Ruanda and Burundi; especially brutal despotisms in Uganda, the Central African Republic and Ethiopia; authoritarian one-party rule almost everywhere; nepotism, mismanagement, corruption and a siphoning off of overseas financial assistance into the Swiss bank accounts of ruling elites; calamitous neglect of natural resources. Within three decades Africa, which embarked on independence with such optimism and the goodwill and generous assistance of the developed world, has become a debt-ridden derelict, its people stalked by famine and disease in ever-expanding deserts. Its record has served the arguments of racial theorists (in the "white" south especially) and causes misgivings among the most well-disposed of non-Africans.

Why should Africa have collapsed in this way? To ignore the more crass and primitive racial theories, there are explanations such as the precipitate departure of the colonial powers, leaving each country to the rule of a tiny, ill-equipped elite; the imposition of sophisticated democratic systems rooted in the historical experience of Western Europe, which bore no relation whatever to that of Africa; the colonial division of Africa, cutting across tribal and ethnic settlement patterns, guaranteeing the artificiality of each new state and the existence in almost all of them of various competing ethnicities; grandiose attempts to implant First World industry and infrastructure instead of developing peasant agriculture for food production. There are more sinister theories of neo-colonialism, manipulation of raw material prices to keep the former colonies in thrall; of the continent becoming the cockpit of cynical competition by surrogacy between the United States and the Soviet Union, neither of them with a colonial history in Africa or a real understanding of its needs. As Kenyatta put it: "When elephants fight, the grass is trampled."

We would not necessarily disagree with any of the above. However, we believe the Graves technology provides more meaningful insights to the disasters which have befallen Africa.

When the European powers began seriously colonising the continent during the 19th century (the initial, and only partial, penetration had been by European slavers on the West Coast and the Indian Ocean Arab slavers of the East Coast), they encountered communities who had been existing in isolation, and in largely healthy equilibrium, at the levels on the Gravesian Spiral of AN-Beige survivalism and BO-Purple animist tribalism. Third Level CP-Red empire had begun to show itself in various regions such as in the Ashanti kingdom of present-day Ghana and the Buganda kingdom in Uganda. A fully-fledged CP-Red empire in Ethiopia (then known as Abyssinia) dated back to biblical times. Ethiopia retained its independence, surrendering it only temporarily and briefly to the Italian fascists just before World War II; the flickerings of CP-Red independent statehood were otherwise either crushed by the colonial intruders (for example, Britain's Ashanti War) or, more usually, co-opted into the colonial scheme of things by the system of indirect rule. Traditional kings and chieftains were absorbed into the colonial administrations as agents of the colonising power, leaving their traditional powers and lifestyles largely intact. This was probably most effectively achieved in British West Africa.

The bulk of the colonial populations were left undisturbed in a way they were not in Southern Africa where there had been heavy and permanent European settlement over centuries. Even in a country such as Kenya, where there was a significant settlement of British colonials engaged mainly in agriculture and commerce, it was made clear at an early stage that this would be limited; the interests of the indigenous inhabitants would be paramount. The Pygmies of the rain forests therefore remained at First Level AN-Beige; the Masai of Kenya continued to roam the plains as their forefathers had at BO-Purple.

The ethos of empire was DQ-Blue authoritarian, the code of the colonial administrators. Taxes were collected, medical services maintained, veterinary and other regulations enforced, accounts properly kept. Government functioned, the trains ran on time. Everything operated according to the book. But (apart from irritation at irksome rules and regulations) all this had little to do with the indigenous inhabitants; the colonial codes were expressed and enforced in French, English and Portuguese by colonial servants who were only temporarily in the colonies and looked to retirement in the metropoles. The sense of dedication and mission, the discipline of DQ-Blue thinking, the commitment to "doing things the right way" had little impact on the thought patterns of the subject peoples as very few were exposed to it, and those largely at the more humble clerical levels.

Similarly, the very limited manifestations of ER-Orange materialist and achievist thinking in the colonies was confined almost entirely to expatriate commercial agents and traders, whose presence was as temporary as that of the administrators, and (in East Africa) a narrow stratum of Asian traders. Exploitative CP-Red on the part of colonists was generally discouraged in Sub-Saharan Africa north of the Limpopo (though with notable exceptions among the Belgians and the Portuguese).

The Gravesian Spiral consequently existed in a most attenuated form in colonial Africa. The rings of AN-Beige and BO-Purple flourished. Incipient CP-Red - the drive for power and control - was crushed and suppressed by the colonial authorities (for example, the Mau Mau rebellion in Kenya), while DQ-Blue and ER-Orange were the domain of outsiders who were eventually to depart. FS-Green egalitarianism was virtually unheard of and unconsidered in the period up to World War II.

The colonial era in Africa lasted a remarkably short time. The Conference of Berlin had fixed the final colonial boundaries in 1885. By the 1960s, the colonial powers were (with the exception of the Portuguese) hauling down the flag and departing. We do not intend exploring the reasons, involving as they do such factors as post-war national finances, hostility to colonialism by both the Soviet Union and the United States - the pre-eminent post-war powers - and the generally weakened international position of the colonial nations. However, it is interesting to note that a new paradigm emerged internationally after World War II, in which moral considerations made it impossible to justify colonialism. This coincided with an upsurge in Europe and elsewhere of FS-Green egalitarian thinking which was also imported to the colonies themselves by African students returning from overseas studies, churchmen, a new and younger generation of colonial administrators and even returned colonial soldiers who had experienced a wider world.

The colonies were headed inexorably for independence though few, if any, were equipped for modern statehood. The vast majority of their populations were at the levels of AN-Beige and BO-Purple on the Gravesian Spiral. Migration to the seaports and cities established by the colonials had produced the succeeding ring on the Spiral of CP-Red - power-hungry exploiters - previously suppressed but now free to pursue their ambitions as urban elites. The discipline and dedication of healthy DQ-Blue was almost wholly absent. This thinking pattern, so basic to the functioning of any effective government bureaucracy, departed with the colonial servants. ER-Orange remained the preserve largely of expatriate managers whose real interests and loyalties lay elsewhere, as well as of increasingly nervous Asian traders whose material success was widely resented by the less advantaged CP-Reds. The Spiral was decidedly out of kilter and unhealthy to begin with.

On to it was grafted one or other version of a democratic European constitution - DQ-Blue and ER-Orange, in Gravesian terms, with influences of FS-Green. These functioned well in their home environments. DQ-Blue reflected the basic and universal belief in the system by the inhabitants of those countries, providing the milieu within which a professional bureaucracy could give expression to those beliefs, providing continuity. ER-Orange reflected the quality of political gamesmanship within those constitutions, the capacity for politicians to make deals the way businessmen make deals, to seek advantage and move in and out of power in terms of the rules of the game. FS-Green reflected the drive toward distributive justice and fairness. These constitutions worked well in their home environments because the populations they governed were largely at the Blue, Orange and Green levels of thinking.

Yet in Africa these essentially DQ-Blue and ER-Orange constitutions were applied to populations where CP-Red competed (often voicing the slogans of FS-Green) for the support of people who were either themselves at CP-Red and eager for a share of the spoils or at AN-Beige or BO-Purple. As we have noted, DQ-Blue did not exist - nobody really believed in the system. Nor did ER-Orange exist. For elites at CP-Red this was no game where one sat in the opposition benches for a spell, waiting one's turn. Power was the urge, and immediate power - there would be no second chance. In such a contest, which would be decided by votes, is it surprising that CP-Red elites should have turned to their tribal origins at BO-Purple for unquestioning mass support? That those supporters should have been rewarded, to the disadvantage of other tribal groups? Is it at all surprising that public administration should have collapsed when the bureaucracies were staffed not by individuals in the DQ-Blue range (who were not at hand anyway) but by political supporters in CP-Red? As noted in Chapter 2, every level of thinking along the Gravesian Spiral has its positive and its negative qualities. In a struggle for power, the negative is rampant, hence the drive among those CP-Reds for self-enrichment and - for those near the top of the heap - the prospect of amassing funds abroad. And, in such a struggle for raw power, is it at all surprising that competing Red elites should (sometimes for the most moral reasons, let it be said) intervene via the armed forces to topple the incumbents who have made life intolerable and cannot be removed by constitutional means? Hence the sorry record of coups d'etat, civil war, corruption and collapse.

The constitutions foisted on the African colonies were doomed to failure because they were designed for versions of the Spiral which simply had not been given the opportunity to develop in Africa. It is facile to attempt to attribute these collapses to defects in the African character or intelligence. Failure was built into the political systems.

And white South Africans who might be tempted to sneer at the rest of Africa need only examine the record of the presently governing Afrikaner nationalists. Having won an election in the CP-Red mode of sectional struggle, they proceeded to pack the civil service and the military with their CP-Red supporters and tamper with the courts and the constitution to secure themselves in power, seemingly in perpetuity. Their current apparent readiness to share power is due to pressures other than constitutional. Westminster indeed has much to answer for.

Africa is vibrant today with talk of democratic renewal. The International Monetary Fund makes its loans conditional on the recipients' applying sound, market-orientated economic policies. With the collapse of socialism in the Eastern Bloc, there is a readiness to abandon the versions of socialism adopted in many African countries. With the burgeoning of democracy in much of Eastern Europe, there is a rising and healthy clamour for multi-party democracy in Africa as well. However, and with the greatest regret, we counsel caution in any such course. What makes Africa today different from Africa in 1960? The main difference, we suggest, is that its people are considerably worse off materially than they were then and the infrastructure which existed then has been all but destroyed.

Why should multi-party democracy work any better now than it did then? The rings of the Gravesian Spiral which have developed are still AN-Beige survivalist (though, tragically, today's survivalists are often the inhabitants of famine relief camps); BO-Purple tribalist; and CP-Red power demons. We are aware that, over the decades, a burgeoning African intelligentsia has developed that was not there before in anything like the numbers. We are aware also that those intellectuals suffer agonies of frustration at the misrule and corruption they have to witness. But are they there in numbers and influence sufficient to lead and dominate ER-Orange multi-party democracy? And can the leap be made without society being taken through the purposeful and stabilising experience of healthy DQ-Blue? The Law of the Spiral dictates otherwise.

We would be the last to advocate a propping up of the corrupt and inept dictatorships that characterise so much of Africa. We would deny the people of Africa a meaningful vote and voice in the way they are governed as little as we would deny the people of any country. But we are wary of that term "multi-party democracy". It sounds very much like what failed so badly before. The democracies which appear to be emerging in Eastern Europe are being constructed on societies either with a historic memory of such systems which were disrupted by events (in other words, the full range of the Gravesian Spiral still exists or can be repaired), or on societies at least with the experience of shifting through DQ-Blue, even if it was an unhealthy communist version of DQ-Blue. The transition to ER-Orange and the ranges beyond is feasible.

This is simply not true of Africa at present. It would be futile and tragic, we believe, to attribute its past failures to the failure of individual leaders, to evil dictators or to the corrosive effects of the Soviet-American power struggle, now ended. To attempt to apply once again the Blue-Orange democratic models of the West to societies still essentially in Purple-Red would be to invite a repetition of the past. We would urge the African intelligentsia, and outside agencies which involve themselves, to focus their energies instead on developing the DQ-Blue level on the Spiral. This would make for purpose, honesty and efficiency in government and confidence in the system. It would counteract the power urges of CP-Red. It would open the way for a natural evolutionary flow along the Spiral to levels of greater complexity. This is not to argue against democratic elections or accountability in government. These are wholly desirable. But we argue for something different from the competitive, adversarial ER-Orange system, for something inclusive rather than divisive. South Africa is in search of very much the same formula. Whatever is forged in South Africa could well have an application throughout the continent.

The American Experience

American culture has in it a strong strain of DQ-Blue Fourth Level Puritanism: a work ethic, a sense of morality and rightness and the acceptance of "mission", a duty to "save" the world. Such values are deep and pervasive. The American constitution is based on the assumptions within the ER-Orange Fifth Level system of checks and balances, competitive advantage and the guarantee to every citizen of "life, liberty and the pursuit of happiness". American society is based on a culture of elites, not on collectivities. Individual rights are supreme. Group rights flow indirectly from the freedom of individuals to associate with whomever they please, unless the collective is a conspiratorial one which threatens to overthrow the government by force. Virtually anything else is tolerated - in theory anyway.

This historic Blue-Orange traditionalist Yankee hegemony is presently under assault from two sides, which has repercussions all over the world. The surge of have-nots - victims of slavery, racism or male chauvinism - out of Purple and Red and restricted versions of Blue and Orange threatens to undermine the Caucasian male domination of society. Fourth and Fifth Level thinking is a huge, imposing edifice which stands between the underclass and the affluent. But there are attempts to undermine it. The canons of

Western civilisation are constantly being challenged by groups who demand the inclusion of the literature of the oppressed in American university curricula.

Blue and Orange are also under assault from the FS-Green egalitarian set of assumptions at the Sixth Level. Blue dogma separates and punishes. Orange elitism divides and confers the benefits of materialism on the successful. (Losers simply have to accept their fate in this Darwinian world of survival of the fittest. They have to be content with less, with roaming the streets or fantasising the good life by watching televsion). But Green demands not only that all should have equal rights, they should share equally in the American dream as well. The American political process is weighed down by single-interest groups demanding equal results, not just equal opportunities. Americans are becoming obsessed with equality. If the population ratios of white, black or Hispanic are not reflected in various occupations or functions, the institutions are labelled "racist".

Yet, paradoxically, minority cultures such as African-American or Hispanic, are themselves moving through a version of Blue nationalism which produces exclusivity, partition and inverted racism. African-American leaders in Dallas, Texas, demand group rights, protections and quotas which resemble the arguments of South Africa's Conservative Party on the need for racial purity and separateness. America is being balkanised by the emergence of new racial and ethnic divides. The African-American and Hispanic cultures appear to be on a collision course as they emphasise their separate identities and compete for increasingly fewer valued niches in employment, housing and education.

Another anomaly of American society is the cohabitation of CP-Red Third Level and FS-Green Sixth Level thinking systems. They are strange bedfellows because they have nothing in common but their rejection of Fourth and Fifth Level thinking and their focus on the needs of people here and now. The more liberal (FS-Green) elements in American churches, educational institutions and government do not hesitate to lend moral and financial support to the "struggle" of those in CP-Red who seek to escape domination by the majority. The anti-apartheid movement therefore acquired huge momentum once launched in America. It was able to ride the crest of these powerful waves of change in American society. The curious Red-Green alliance has also had its effect on mainstream American politics, to the huge detriment of the Democratic Party. While the Republicans are still clearly centred in the Blue-Orange spectrum, the Red-Green alliance has so influenced the positioning and rhetoric of the Democratic Party that its traditional mass support in the South has evaporated. (Interestingly enough, traces of the Red-

Green mesalliance are also to be found in South Africa's Democratic Party).

A new political persuasion is likely to eventually form around the Seventh Level GT-Yellow world view. At first it will appear to be "conservative" rather than "liberal" (to use the word in its American sense) because Seventh Level thinking is individualist rather than collectivist. Such a new movement would reject a role for Washington DC and federal government in local affairs. It would instead press the primacy of cities and communities, multi-centric values and interests and the sovereignty of social mosaics of all types, hues and beliefs. America is likely to develop into an integrative, evolutionary network with expanding global connections. But it would quickly down-shift once again to Blue patriotism if threatened, since that sub-system is likely to remain strong until well into the 21st century.

Here is how we would colour-code the dominant thinking patterns in current and past American presidents:

George Bush	Orange strategic with Yellow systemic views.
Ronald Reagan	Orange materialism with Blue patriotism.
Jimmy Carter	Green/Orange with heavy moralistic Blue.
Gerald Ford	Orange/Blue traditional Republicanism.
Richard Nixon	Orange/Blue with a strong Red (power urge) sub-system.
Lyndon Johnson	Power-driven Red with Blue (of the John Wayne shade).

Here is how we would colour-code various African-American personalities (real and mythical):

Purple:	Aunt Jemima and Uncle Remus.
Red:	Big, bad Leroy Brown and Super Fly.
Blue:	Booker T. Washington, Martin Luther King (Sr and Jr).
Orange:	Jesse Jackson, Andrew Young, members of the Black Caucus.
Green:	Ralph Bunche and Stevie Wonder.
Yellow:	Bill Cosby and Professor Shelby Steele.

Europe - 1992

The 12 European countries that will come together in a new collective in 1992 will be governed by a European Parliament that is already cast within a strongly FS-Green structure. (Even the Europe 1992 logo is a circle of equals). The European Community is moving into a competitive collective designed to benefit all. The sanctity of national boundaries, traditions, currencies and values will be inexorably eroded. Hence strong, instinctive resistance to the process by figures such as Margaret Thatcher (who has a strong DQ-Blue sub-system of "Rule Britannia!"). The French are also expressing concerns about the future purity of their language, not to mention the fate of their cuisine. Several countries experience spasmodic right-wing protest as sub-groups in the different countries, who have experienced Orange affluence, feel threatened by the prospect of current European have-nots doing better than they.

Many in the former West Germany have been shocked and disappointed by the difficulties experienced in uniting with the former East Germany. Yet it should not be surprising. They speak the same language, eat the same food, have the same traditions and historical myths and are of the same Germanic stock - but their value systems are entirely different. To the East Germans, affluence and their country being a centre of culture and learning is as distant a memory as the Kaiser. The collective memory is of the economic collapse and despair of the Weimar Republic; insane Nazi tyranny; catastrophic military defeat and invasion; and the imposition for more than 40 years of brutal Stalinism. They have been through one of the unhealthiest versions imaginable of DQ-Blue, dominated by a grasping CP-Red elite. By contrast, the West Germans have been through Marshall Aid, the wirtschaftwunder, affluence and deliberately fostered liberal democracy. They are in the healthiest versions of DQ-Blue, ER-Orange and FS-Green. They have an entirely different world view, an entirely different response to the challenges of life. Robert Leicht, deputy editor of the weekly, Die Zeit, says bluntly: "Integration doesn't work. You see a lot of differences in mentalities. If those were the Germans we thought they would be, you would see an enormous push of initiatives." He maintains further: "If you put an East and West German together, you will find they are more different than a German is from a British person ... the traditions and habits of these people are impregnated more than they realise."

The two Germanies provide a perfect illustration of the Gravesian thesis that individual and social behaviour is governed by evolutionary progress through the different levels of complexity in thinking. No people could be more homogeneous in terms of history, culture, language - even genetics - than the East and the West Germans. Yet West Germans feel more at home with Britons because they share the same values. Forty-six years are barely a scratch on the face of history, yet they were enough - given a sustained (and largely successful) programme in subverting Western values - to make the East Germans into a different people who have to struggle into the ER-Orange system while their fellow-countrymen are already experiencing the satisfactions of FS-Green and GT-Yellow world views.

The Soviet Union

The Soviet empire was held together by sheer force. The inner core of "European" Russia insulated itself from danger by gathering about it a protective cordon of ethnic republics. The spoils of World War II provided yet another cordon in Eastern Europe, further protection against what was analysed perfectly seriously as Western imperialism and expansionism. Russians tend to interpret history, from Tsarist times, as a series of assaults launched from the West; and - given Bonaparte and Hitler - this is understandable. But the disparate Soviet Union required a uniting ideology. This was provided by the secular religion of Marxism-Leninism. The ruling elite convinced the masses that they were under threat; communism would nevertheless protect them and time was on their side, victory inevitable. A final, ideal state was almost within reach. Once achieved, justice and happiness would prevail.

The Soviet command and control system operated out of the Red to Blue range. Only the materialism within Orange was utilised. The strategic thinking component of Orange and the need to uplift the middle classes were ignored, not even understood. Five-year plans were drawn up and implemented (after a fashion) by grey, unimaginative bureaucrats in conformist DQ-Blue. With benefit of hindsight, it was impossible, given the greater complexity of thinking in the competitive West, for the Soviet Union to have succeeded in its contest with the countries now known as the Group of Seven - the United States, Canada, Britain, Germany, France, Italy and Japan.

If Gorbachev had not launched Glasnost and Perestroika, somebody else would have emerged to do so. The Soviets had attempted to correct matters for so long using First Order Change (as described in Chapter 3) that they reached the point of social, economic and political collapse. The Law of the Spiral is often as unforgiving as it is certain. Second Order Change was attempted in the face of staggering difficulties. Gorbachev failed because of a simplistic approach and the abortive putsch of August 1991 represented a perfectly futile attempt to return to First Order Change

Thinking at ER-Orange Fifth Level is not switched on or off like a light. It has to pass through a healthy version of DQ-Blue if it is to establish itself, a version in which the population is provided a vision of the future and is motivated to work toward that future in an orderly and disciplined way. This would entail altering the content of DQ-Blue thinking in the Soviet Union from its mindlessly hidebound and demotivating values to a new version in which progress toward the attainment of a free market was set as the ideal and society was motivated toward achieving it. But instead Gorbachev and those about him appeared to believe it was possible to simply grasp at the entrancing wealth and opulence of the West (ER-Orange values) without first embracing the DQ-Blue work ethic and discipline which produced it. The Law of the Spiral dictates that a transition to ER-Orange from CP-Red power play and an unhealthy version of DQ-Blue authoritarianism is simply not possible. Gorbachev was unable to produce the economic results which might otherwise have underpinned his reforms because he did not have the self-disciplined workforce to do so. His reforms also produced glimmerings of FS-Green - freedom and justice for all - and the Soviet Union found itself in the exhilarating, yet unstable and precarious state of DELTA (described in Chapter 3) as regions and nationalities demanded liberation from centralised control by the Communist Party and its apparatus.

Soviet Lessons for South Africa

What might South Africans learn from the extraordinary events in the Soviet Union which suddenly exploded on CNN news as if made to order for television?

Firstly, revolutions do not cause change; change rather sparks revolutionary movements. These manifestations merely confirm, like surface level earthquakes, profound change which has already occurred within the deep fissures of thinking. Once that happens, the genie cannot be put back in the bottle, no matter how many tanks are lined up. The American longshoreman philosopher Eric Hoffer noted in *The Ordeal of Change:* "Revolutions are not set in motion to realise drastic change; drastic change sets the stage for revolution."

Soviet mind shifts have been deep and pervasive. The tyranny of the Marxist monolith had trapped and punished the naturally evolving value systems for generations, both in the inner sanctuary of "European" Russia and in the republics. Only now has the hammer and sickle, with all its ideological and authoritarian connotations, been replaced by a new federalist banner, the traditional Russian tricolour. The old, grey apparatchiks will pass into history and power will shift from the centre to the outer regions. Cultural and ethnic mosaics are likely to bubble to the surface. Empire will struggle to translate itself to enterprise. The after-shocks are likely to continue reverberating for some time. At time of writing the fall harvest was lean, foreign debt was massive and the infrastructure was in disarray. Only vodka was plentiful.

Federalist Russian president Boris Yeltsin represents a next stage in the Soviet Union's evolution. He is likely to transform where Gorbachev could only reform. He bailed out Gorbachev, rallied the people against the military and will be seen as the architect of the new order. Gorbachev is likely to be seen (as P.W. Botha was in South Africa) as the first stage of a rocket. Yeltsin, like F.W. de Klerk, will be recognised as the second stage, calibrated to put the system into a proper orbit.

The Gorbachev tremor was the initial shock but it attempted to reform by simply liberalising the Communist Party, taking it out of CP-Red and DQ-Blue into versions of ER-Orange and even FS-Green. This contradicted the Law of the Spiral. Without a new system (a healthy version of DQ-Blue), a fresh paradigm, the initiative was doomed to failure. The food queues grew longer. The same apparatchiks were seen to be in control. The Gang of Eight attempted to steady matters with First Order Change (more of the same) but were crude and inept, trapped in the oppressive thinking of the 1950s and 1960s. These were individuals chosen by Gorbachev and they believed in change - but not if it threatened their own hegemony and privileges.

Secondly, the West needs to concede that it is not possible to impose its version of democracy and freedom (DQ-Blue/ER-Orange/FS-Green) on societies that are only now escaping authoritarianism of either the left or the right. The infrastructures of thinking that underpin free market, pluralistic democracies are long in coming. (As we have noted, West Germans find more in common with the British than with their fellow-countrymen in East Germany).

The West should concentrate instead on ratcheting economies in transformation through a series of developmental stages. Basic survival needs have to be guaranteed. Entrepreneurial seed beds should be developed and provided the appropriate economic nutrition. Second World to First World transitional bridges need to be constructed. Joint ventures should be created. The Spirals of development have to be nurtured.

The lessons for South Africa are clear. The entire world is wired for sound and sight - CNN television is everywhere, facsimile transmission machines make censorship impossible. A right-wing coup d'etat would be brought into the cabinet rooms and living rooms of the world and would appear just as primitive as the Soviet one did. The new world network of instant information would expose any heavy-handed totalitarian elements just as effectively and damagingly.

And intimidatory monolithic thinking certainly is discernible in the relentless attack from certain quarters in the ANC on competitive black groupings and systems elsewhere, such as in KwaZulu or Bophuthatswana. The best indicator of what a party will do in power is what it does in the process of gaining that power. Promises mean nothing. The positive experience of all groups should rather be sought so that all are able to add value to the long and complex process of nation-building. The establishment of a permanent peace commission could diminish the intolerance of those who thirst for power, privilege and patronage at any price. They come in all colours, in terms of skin pigmentation. In terms of the Graves technology they come in CP-Red.

The deep value systems that lie in South Africa's political geology bear some resemblance to those which spawned the Soviet Union's stages of change. Like the Soviet republics, South Africa consists of sensitive and potentially explosive ethnic mosaics. Neither monolithic ideologies nor mass democratic majorities are capable of managing such diversity.

The West should avoid demanding too much change too quickly by forcing its view of democracy and freedom on a developing society, especially not on one as complex as South Africa's. The psychological viruses introduced to the social bloodstream could otherwise destroy what is targeted for liberation. Americans in particular make the mistake of attempting to micro-manage complex systems abroad in order to ease internal racial or political pressures. South Africans have a better collective sense of what they should do. Once the mechanisms are created for straight talk, visionary thinking and strategic planning - in short, Value Management - they are likely to achieve results at an astonishing rate.

As with the Russians, South Africans will be able to celebrate a birth of freedom when the evolutionary models and structures are discovered within which all segments and groups can feel secure. That day could dawn sooner than many think. The models and structures will have been forged in the South African crucible, nowhere else, on South African terms and within a South African timescale. This is the real message of events in Moscow.

Yugoslavia

The violence and suffering in Yugoslavia is a message from the future as well as from the past. The imposition of a DQ-Blue command system without the consent of the ethnicities so governed will end in an eruption as soon as the authoritarian structures and leadership begin to crack. Tito might have been more skillful and successful than his successors in managing the ethnic tensions of his country, but he relied in the last resort on force, not persuasion.

Pockets of ethnic conflict, and potential conflict, are spread all over the planet. But once the Spiral is understood it is possible to approach these explosive configurations in a new and positive manner and defuse them. The means of doing so could well develop in the South African crucible.

The Pacific Rim

Japan's immense success since the mid-1950s is attributable to the country's singleness of purpose, the manner in which its value systems are focused in the same direction and the country's motivation to rise like a Phoenix from the ashes of World War II (quite literally in the case of Hiroshima and Nagasaki) to a position of world dominance. The British Isles led the advance of capitalism and imperialism in the early version of ER-Orange during the 19th century. The Japanese islands are now the leading force in global materialism, reflecting the maturity of the ER-Orange Fifth Level system at the end of the 20th century.

Japan is a collective society with heavy pulsations of Purple and Blue in families, education, corporate culture and national purpose. The Emperor no longer occupies the mystical place (Purple) he once did in Japanese society. Corporate Japan is now "the god". The Samurai warrior (Red) lurks as an archetype in the Japanese strategist (Orange). Willingness to sacrifice for the greater good (Blue) keeps the system focused on quality instead of profits, long-term rather than short-term benefits and communal rather than elitist benefits. The crowding together of so many people in limited space makes individual rights and assertiveness difficult to satisfy. Because Japanese society is totally dependent on the rest of the world for raw materials and other resources, everything has to be carefully planned and synchronised.

What will Japanese success produce? As increasing numbers of workers achieve high levels of affluence, will they work as hard? Now that Japan has proved itself globally, will it be motivated to continue striving to dominate? Will the youth continue with self-discipline in the highly competitive and unforgiving school system, or will they exchange their uniforms for the trappings of punk, their shushi for hamburgers, their traditional music for American pop? The Law of the Spiral predicts that the Japanese should be headed for versions of FS-Green and GT-Yellow. In that case the Koreans, Taiwanese and other surrounding societies might take the place of the Japanese working and entrepreneurial classes in the DQ-Blue and ER-Orange ranges. The Japanese would have the time and the resources to become global citizens. But would they do so? It could be that the Shinto religion is too strong, the cultural constraints too tight and national fervour too restricting to allow this to happen.

Singapore: A Society That Works

An appropriate model for the next South Africa could well be Singapore. Lee Kuan Yew, Singapore's leader at the time of independence and now an elder statesman, created for this former British colony a DQ-Blue developmental conduit through which the multi-ethnic society could progress, joining hands in a national movement while preserving unique customs and beliefs. He inserted a new Singapore Blue command system (content) into ethnic Blue structures - then built an ER-Orange layer on top of it. Singapore is disciplined, orderly and functional. Each ethnic group gets two national holidays a year. Everybody learns at least two languages, while English is the medium of commerce.

Any visitor to Singapore is impressed by the display of discipline and affluence. Yet the country's accomplishments have produced new problems. FS-Green is beginning to appear on the horizon. Many ask why the Chinese are so much more successful than the Malayan communities. Many of the younger generation chafe under tight restrictions and regulations; they explore the option of emigrating to more open environments. Singapore now faces the challenge of keeping the conduit in place while finding ways to respond to the new aspirations of youth. It will be a difficult transition because of the fragile nature of Singapore's economy and its dependence on Japan and the other Pacific Rim societies.

The Middle East

Jerusalem both benefits by, and suffers from, being the Holy City of three DQ-Blue world religions - Judaism, Christianity and Islam. The turbulence is due in part to conflict within the Blue belief structure, all three claiming exclusive Truth and Divine sanction. There are also other factors such as a complexity of historical forces and experiences. Beneath the DQ-Blue religious orthodoxies of the Middle East is a complex and rumbling geology of Purple, Red and other Blue cultures.

Of these religious systems, the one which manifests itself politically and geographically as Israel has successfully meshed the conservatism and orthodoxy of Blue with scientific, strategic and materialistic Orange. (Christian societies have done the same, of course, but they are located mainly in Europe and the Americas, not the Middle East). Contributions in money, technology and political influence from the Jewish communities of the Diaspora have played a major role, but Israel's development of the ER-Orange complexities of thinking, as well as a DQ-Blue ethos of national survival (as distinct from the DQ-Blue of Judaism) has allowed it to successfully assert itself in the face of hostility from Arab neighbours who are largely at

CP-Red (feudal) and BO-Purple (tribal) levels of complexity. The Rev. Jesse Jackson commented in 1988 that the best way to bring peace to that region would be for Israel to develop into the Hong Kong of the Middle East. He is probably correct. As long as Israel's very existence is threatened, it will respond with Blue patriotism and exploitative CP-Red in its suppression of Arab communities within its borders. As far as the status of Jerusalem is concerned, this is unlikely to be resolved at current levels of thinking in the Middle East. It will require a shift through FS-Green (justice for all) into GT-Yellow (systemic overview) for the city to be made freely accessible to all who regard it as holy. Some sort of international status suggests itself, and this could well be the outcome of GT-Yellow systemic influence (as personified by President Bush) in any international conference on the Middle East.

Arab societies still suffer in varying degree from strong Purple and Red factors in their cultural underpinnings. Their strict moralistic code, for women especially, will stay in place so long as the CP-Red value system remains as strong as it is in Arab men. In fact highly punitive authoritarianism in individuals and collectives is a by-product of a fear of the Red-egocentric factor. Attempts to liberalise such customs will fail unless the Red ring on the Spiral weakens while the Orange ring correspondingly grows in strength. The guiltless Red-exploitative system is not difficult to detect in a Middle Eastern personality such as Saddam Hussein. It is also detectable in the tendency of Arab military units to collapse under strong attack because sacrificial thinking is not part of the CP-Red system. (Contrast this with the fanatical DQ-Blue of Iranian youths who did not waver under Iraqi machinegun fire, or the entirely different, disciplined DQ-Blue of British forces in recapturing the Falkland Islands against heavy odds).

There are, however, signs of movement. Hussein's inability to mobilise a Jihad during the Gulf War was due in part to the extent to which Arabs have been influenced by modern Western (ER-Orange) values. A decade ago, an Arab leader who landed missiles on Israeli cities might have been guaranteed all-round support. But during the Gulf War other Arab leaders perceived perfectly clearly that Hussein was a secular, not a religious, figure and that they themselves would be on his agenda for conquest if he were to lead any kind of pan-Arabic nationalist movement. This was a function of ER-Orange strategic thinking and is grounds for optimism about securing a stable and lasting peace in the Middle East.

The Developing Countries

In June 1991 the United Nations released a report containing a "human freedom index" which ranked 88 countries according to the degree of freedom enjoyed by their citizens. Sweden ranked as the world's freest country with 38 out of a possible 40 points. Iraq scored zero. There was a high overall correllation between human development and human freedom. The world's poorest countries are also its least free.

Spokesmen for the Third World bloc at the United Nations protested against the report and its release. Some drafted a resolution which would have banned the further publication of human freedom indices. The attitude is not suprising. As demonstrated in this book, Third World cultures are spread between the Purple and early Blue ranges on the Psychological Map. They have yet to reach the stage (Orange) where individual rights are valued above collective mandates or power elite commands. Passage through the Blue conduit of Second World thinking requires a willingness to sacrifice now in order to gain later.

The non-aligned, developing "have-not" societies of the international order are located between the Third and the Fourth Levels of existence on the Gravesian map. They advocate a New International Economic Order, they are nationalists rather than globalists and they are emotionally united in their opposition to apartheid. By sheer weight of numbers they dominate the United Nations General Assembly and various other bodies such as the United Nations Economic and Social Commission and the World Health Organisation. In the undoubted qualities of Nelson Mandela they see a leader they wish they had. In turn, both Nelson and Winnie Mandela appear more comfortable in the Second World environments of Cuba, Mexico, Brazil and Libya than they do in Washington , Paris or London.

And this brings us to the nub of South Africa's dilemma. Does it want to become another Cuba, Mexico, Brazil or Libya? Is that any way to put food into the mouths of millions; to provide accommodation, shelter, clothing, medical services and education; to provide people with the creature comforts and dignity which is their due as human beings? We argue otherwise.

Conclusion

South Africa will be saved only by thinking in the New Paradigm. That is the thrust of this entire book. First Order Change - more of the same - as advocated by groupings such as the Conservative Party will hasten South Africa's collapse as surely as it did the collapse of the Soviet Union. More of the same, as advocated by confused liberals who are trapped in the paradigm of majoritarian Westminster democracy, will lead at best to outcomes such as those of Zambia, Tanzania and other authoritarian and bankrupt states.

More of the same, as advocated by ideologically inspired radicals who take Angola, Mozambique or Ethiopia as their models ("This time it simply will work!") will lead to outcomes of desolation and tragedy on a scale difficult to imagine.

We doubt whether the international community has any enthusiasm at all for South Africa following such courses. The world recoils at the prospect of a racial war in Southern Africa. It recoils equally at the prospect of a modern industrial economy and a large, modern military machine, with the capacity to manufacture and deliver nuclear weapons, falling into the hands of a potentially unstable Second World or Third World regime. Iraq gave the world a very bad scare.

We believe there are other options. Something entirely different, yet just and democratic, is waiting to be discovered. We have called it a Seventh World system in which the social mosaics work together for the common good. It has to be discovered by the people of South Africa themselves, forged in the crucible of the realities about them and managed by levels of thinking which are of a higher order than those of the past. We have attempted in these pages to provide some outlines, as well as the innovative cutting edge technology by which such outcomes can be achieved. All South Africa's leadership elites - black nationalists as much as white nationalists - have to gather themselves for a conceptual quantum leap if the country is to develop in a positive and meaningful way.

The six have assembled to discuss the thing they encountered in the dark place.

The Beige Man: "A piece of rope? What luck! I can sell it for wine, like all I find on the rubbish tips."

The Purple Man: "The spirits of the ancients have come to me. They have annointed me to interpret the strange meanings of this sacred fire hose. Be careful and obey what I say."

The Red Man (brandishing a sword): "I felt that spear and it spells danger. I will protect you. And you will all obey me!"

The Blue Man: "I have heard the word of God. This is the tree of the people. It is my duty to decide for them on what to do with it."

The Orange Man: "This leather curtain has commercial value. Leave it to me, I'm the one to clinch a deal."

The Green Man: "Look, we've all got to share this wall, there's enough for everyone. Let's sit down and talk about it."

A seventh joins them.

Chorus: "Who are you?"

The Yellow Man: "Nobody really. But I've got a strong torch and I've been looking at that thing you found in the dark. You'd be surprised, the possibilities..."

Chapter 1
Crucible of Chaos

Ilya Prigogine and Isabelle Stengers observe in *Order out of Chaos: Man's New Dialogue with Nature* (New York: Bantam Books, 1984): "In the past few decades something very dramatic has been happening in science, something as unexpected as the birth of geometry or the grand vision of the cosmos as expressed in Newton's work. We are becoming more and more conscious of the fact that on all levels, from elementary particles to cosmology ... our vision of nature is undergoing a radical change toward the multiple, the temporal and the complex." Lee Cullum, leader page editor of the *Dallas Times Herald*, suggested in her weekly column that "modern science is posing new challenges to philosophical thought. Dr Ilya Prigogine, director of the Centre for Studies in Statistical Mechanics and Complex Systems of the University of Texas at Austin and winner of the 1977 Nobel Prize in Chemistry (imagine the road from simple chemistry to statistical mechanics and complex systems), has put the ancient question in terms of 'reality as timeless or reality in time.' 'The 19th century's ideal,' wrote Prigogine, 'the Victorian idea, was one of stability, of a timeless hierarchical society. It was also the period of timeless laws of basic physics. The dramatic changes which are going on today affect the problem of values.' Today's science, Prigogine pointed out, is 'an effort to transcend the classical oppositions between what is in time and what is out of time, between eternal truths and time-oriented evolution.' Then he added: 'We have to look for the stable element in the changing universe.'"

We do not claim that more complexity is better than less; that less simplicity is better than more. We are simply reporting on the apparent transformation to greater complexity that appears to characterise the human experience. We find five essential characteristics of greater complexity:

1. The number of individual actors, entities or collectives.

2. The extent of dissimilarity or variety among the actors.

3. The degree of actor interdependency and action consequences.

4. The intensity of actor dynamism, emotional commitment and ego involvement.

5. The conditions of existence in the milieu.
For an analysis of the current shift in thinking in the direction of chaos theory, see James Gleick - *Chaos: Making of a New Science* (New York: Viking, 1987). See also Pierre Berge, Yves Pomeau and Christian Vidal - *Order within Chaos: Towards a Deterministic Approach to Turbulence* (New York: John Wiley, 1984).

The classic statement on paradigm change is in Thomas Kuhn - *The Structures of Scientific Revolutions* (Chicago: University of Chicago Press, 1962). See also Fritjof Capra - *"Paradigms and Paradigm Shifts"*, presentations and discussions from a symposium sponsored by the Elmwood Institute, Big Sur, California, November 29 - December 4, 1985, reprinted in Revision Vol. 9, No. 1, spring 1986, p. 11). Capra's books, *The Turning Point* (New York: Simon & Schuster, 1982) and *The Tao of Physics* (Berkeley: Shambala, 1975) are also useful.

The best summary of the interaction between turbulence and paradigm formation, especially in the area of political theory and development, is in Peter A. Corning - *The Synergism Hypothesis: A Theory of Progressive Evolution* (New York: McGraw-Hill, 1983).

Chapter 2
Paradigms Lost, Paradigms Gained: the Quest for Order

The unique ability of the human mind to rewire and reprogramme itself is attributed to what University of Syracuse (New York) physicist Erich Harth calls "The Promethean gene". (See *Dawn Of A Millennium: Beyond Evolution And Culture,* New York: Penguin Books, 1991.) Harth notes: "We might as well assume that there existed in the brain of prehistoric man, like the invisible images on an under-developed film, the latent abilities to carry out functions that would not find expression for many thousands of years. By what strange principle of evolution did they get there?

The best analysis of evolutionary theories from a sociology perspective is in Stephen K. Sanderson - *Social Evolutionism: A Critical History* (Cambridge: Basil Blackwell, 1980). See also Gerhard Lenski - *Human Societies: An introduction to macrosociology* (New York: McGraw-Hill, 1987). From an anthropological perspective, see Marvin Harris - *Cultural Materialism: The Struggle for a Science of Culture* (New York: Random House, 1979).

This presentation of the work of Clare W. Graves is essentially a popularisation designed specifically for the South African context. The Graves technology is described in considerable depth in a number of publications, dissertations, research documents, theoretical summaries, videos and monographs, available through the National Values Centre, Box 797 Denton, Texas 76202-797, USA. For an up-to-date bibliography, fax 817-382-4597 (Texas). Because of health problems Graves was unable to complete his book, *Up the Existential Staircase*. The National Values Centre is a repository of his original research papers and other documents. NVC worked closely with Graves during the final decade of his life. He participated fully in the design of this South African initiative, from 1980 until his death in February of 1986.

Graves referred to his concept as "The Emergent, Cyclical, Double Helix Model of Adult Biopsychosocial Systems Development." He would often chuckle as people attempted to process in their minds what all this meant. Graves fits within the systemic school of thought, along with Piaget, O.J. Harvey, Laurence Kohlberg, Jane Loevinger and many others.

By "emergent" he meant that the systems have arisen in our species over time as we acquired greater complexity in our thinking/coping mechanisms. Actually the systems can ebb and flow as conditions get better or worse. As a result they are not permanent states, types or traits.

By "cyclical" he suggested the pendulum swinging back and forth between "express self" and "sacrifice self", moving against nature and moving in harmony with nature, and between elitism and collectivism. The swing is not triggered by any mechanistic or predetermined signal, but by the problems created by excesses at each of the end points of the swing. Thus the "me decade" will ultimately produce, because of its inherent selfishness, a swing back toward the "us decade". In turn, the blind conformity required in collective sacrifice will ignite a movement in the direction of individual rights and freedom - creating a new sense of "me" instead of "us". The odd-numbered systems - 1, 3, 5, 7 and eventually 9 - are "me"-focused as values are expressed from the inside out. The even-numbered systems - 2, 4, 6, 8 - are "us"-focused as the outside truths, structures and constraints are internalised within a person.

"Double Helix" refers to the interaction between the existence problems in the environment and the adaptive systems in people, organisations and societies. The Helix One conditions include the following:

- What were the atmospheric conditions? The temperature ranges? The barometric pressure? The weather patterns? Lunar, cosmic and electromagnetic flux?

- What was the habitat? Was there ice, desert or rain forest? Was there urban sprawl, mountain tops, barren wasteland or fertile farmland?

- Were food and water readily available? Of what kind and of what quality? How much energy was required to meet biologica needs? What minerals were present? What chemicals, proteins or sugars?

- What was the human factor? How many people were there? How crowded were they? What were the cultural traits, the languages, the values and norms? What were temperaments, peaceful or aggressive?
- What level of complexity and technology emerged? What were the levels of thinking and conception? What were the power structures? What were the reward systems? What were the tolerance ranges?

- What were the rhythms and cycles in the culture? What excesses were developing in resource use, materials production, energy consumption and information? What were the unresolved historic issues? What were the traditions and social memories? What were the icons and relics from the past?

- What were the environmental challenges? Was there too much crowding or over-use? What were the "wild cards" in the form of episodic catastrophe or natural disaster?

- How many and what kinds of niches were available? What portion of the population had access to those niches? How competitive was life? Were there deep fissures or conflicts beneath the social surface?

- What views of the future dominated? To what extent were the scenarios congruent or mutually exclusive? Were goals clear or ambiguous? Who stood to gain or lose from the scenarios?

Michael Crasford and David Marsh argue in *The Driving Force* (London: Heinemann, 1989) that change is propelled by specific chemical and environmental factors but especially the availability of food. Henry Hobhouse in *Forces of Change: An Unorthodox View of History* (New York: Little, Brown and Company, 1989) lists food along with population growth and distribution as the primary change factors. Paul Colinvaux in *The Fates of Nations: A Biological Theory of History* (New York: Simon & Schuster, 1980) makes a strong case for the impact of the struggle for niches on breeding habits, technological development and the competitive advantages from the interaction of these factors.

By "biopsychosocial systems" Graves implied the unitary nature of biology, psychology, sociology, anthropology and other social and behavioural sciences. Obviously this view disturbs those in academic settings who have vested interests in protecting territory and defending the uniqueness of the respective "fields of study", or who have been schooled in narrow, self-serving academic disciplines.

For a popular example of how New Paradigm thinkers engaged in negotiation activities, see Len Leritz - *No-Fault Negotiating* (New York: Warner, 1990), especially his description of the kinds of personality behind the "no-fault" style.

Chapter 3
Spirals of Change

See Watzlawick, Weakland and Fisch - *Change: Principles of Problem Formation and Problem Resolution* (New York: W.W. Norton, 1974).

In *The Futurist*, a publication of the World Future Society in Washington of April 1974, Graves warned:

"The present moment finds our society attempting to negotiate the most difficult, but at the same time the most exciting, transition the human race has faced to date. It is not merely a transition to a new level of existence, but the start of a new movement in the symphony of human history. The future offers us, basically, three possibilities: (1) Most gruesome is the chance that we might fail to stabilize our world and, through successive catastrophes, regress as far back as the Ik tribe has. (2) Only slightly less frightening is the vision of fixation in the DQ/ER/FS societal complex. This might resemble George Orwell's 1984 with its tyrannic, manipulative government glossed over by a veneer of humanitarian sounding doublethink and moralistic rationalizations, and it is a very real possibility in the next decade. (3) The last possibility is that we could emerge into the GT level and proceed toward stabilizing our world so that all life can continue."

The National Values Centre has developed a research instrument around the Stages of Change entitled *The Change State Indicator*. Profiles of American and South African managers have been striking. South African populations have much higher scores in GAMMA, DELTA and NEW ALPHA, while their American counterparts are higher in ALPHA and BETA. South Africans also lean much more heavily toward Second Order rather than First Order Change and seem to tolerate much more chaos than Americans.

Chapter 4
Boers, Britons and Blacks

For an excellent history of South Africa see Allister Sparks - *The Mind of South Africa* (London: Heinemann, 1990)

Chapter 5
The Place Called South Africa

A wealth of material analysing the current political, economic and social positions in South Africa is available, both in book form (for example N. Nattrass and E. Ardington - *The Political Economy of South Africa* (Cape Town, Oxford University Press, 1990), in academic journals and in the quality magazines such as *Leadership, Die Suid-Afrikaan* (in Afrikaans) and *Frontline*. A 1991 *Leadership* special issue entitled "The Watershed Years" is especially recommended.

Chapter 6
Currents of Conflict and Change

There is a tendency for present generations to read into past generations a complexity of thinking that might not have existed. Dudley Kidd - *The Essential Kafir* (London: A.I. & C. Black, 1925) is useful. Modern-day versions of the same type of analysis of the Purple tribal order are to be found in two other publications: Heinz Kuckertz - *Creating Order* (Johannesburg: Witwatersrand University Press, 1990) and Axel-Ivar Berglund - *Zulu Thought-Patterns and Symbolism* (London, Hurst & Co, 1976).

Quite clearly, indigenous African populations had not reached the level of complexity (in social organisation and technology) as had the Europeans who encountered them. There are a number of obvious reasons for this disparity. Cheikh Diop, until recently director of the Carbon Dating Centre at the University of Dakar, Senegal, claimed:

"In the precolonial period the entire continent was indeed covered by monarchies and empires. No spot where man lived, even in the virgin forest, escaped monarchic authority. What happened then? The Africans gradually lost their ability to decide their own fates. The local federating authority dissolved, or was at any rate diminished and rendered powerless. Internal evolution was consequently thrown off balance. In the cities where detribalization had already taken place, a return to the past was out of the question: individuals would continue to be united by social bonds. But where clanic organizations still predominated, where social limits were still determined by the territory of the clan or tribe, there would be a sort of turning inward, an evolution in reverse, a retribalization reinforced by the new climate of insecurity." See his book *Precolonial Black Africa,* translated from the French by Harold Salemson (Trenton, New Jersey: Africa World Press Edition, 1987).

South Africa's *Financial Mail* (August 16, 1991) reviewed British historian Paul Johnson's latest book, *The Birth of the Modern*

(London: Weidenfeld & Nicolson, 1991), and included this extract:

"In the first two decades of the 19th century a kind of political revolution took place in black society, leading to much bigger and better organised states, run by warrior chieftains who operated a system of military clientage, rather like the bastard feudalism of the 14th and 15th centuries in Western Europe. The Zulu, Swazi and Sotho kingdoms, which still keep their identity, emerged at this time. The most successful of the warrior-kings was a fearsome man called Dingiswayo."

The African societies had moved into the CP-Red Third Level range and were functioning in empires of various designs. The societies had not yet emerged via the rigours, discipline and sacrifice-now-to-obtain-later thinking which would be indicative of a move into the DQ-Blue Fourth Level ring on the Spiral. As we document in Chapter 17, Africa as a whole had yet to experience that transformation, making it difficult if not impossible for the ER-Orange Fifth Level system of free market, multiparty democracy to take hold.

Afrikaners are hardly a monolith. The volk on volk violence between police and the Afrikaner Weerstandsbeweging is evidence enough of that. The "Battle of Ventersdorp", in which three members of the AWB were killed, could be only the first physical clash between the right wing and F.W. de Klerk's government. Consider the following types:

Homo Afrikaner Prometheus (power empire) - typified by the modern-day Boer in the AWB and some elements in the police and the defence force. The images are of power, conquest, domination and fierce independence.

Homo Afrikaner Puritanus ("right way" ideology) - expressed in the rural Dutch Reformed Church elder, many of the cultural purists and keepers of the historic Boer orthodoxy and history.

Homo Afrikaner Bureaucratus (transition between Blue and Orange) - found in the civil servant and others who maintain the system but use measurement and technology in keeping control.

Homo Afrikaner Pragmatus (pragmatic enterprise) - the emerging Afrikaner Yuppie, business executive, professional or media-sensitive politician.

Homo Afrikaner Humanus (egalitarian harmony) - seen in those who are socially aware and who, because they believe in the equality of all, regardless of race or ethnicity, are active as writers, church leaders, politicians and businessmen with a social conscience.

Homo Afrikaner Integratus (integrative, evolutionary) - the new thinking system which is emerging in many as the reform process unfolds and the natural differences in people begin to surface. One encounters this pattern in think tanks, in a number of high-level executives and within certain academic environments.

Homo Afrikaner Globalus (global renewal) - the planetary visionaries and functional thinkers who are only now becoming apparent. One finds this new paradigm within certain functions of organisations such as the Council for Scientific and Industrial Research, especially among individuals who are sensitive to environmental issues.

Chapter 7
Political Spectrums and Psychological Spirals

F.W. de Klerk today represents the middle in South African politics. His good friend Margaret Thatcher once remarked that it was dangerous to stay in the middle of the road because that is where you get run over by traffic from both directions. The extreme right sees de Klerk as a traitor to the Volk, having sold out to the communists in the ANC. (Absurdly, it even detects subliminal messages extolling the New World Order on SABC television).

The Left sees de Klerk as part of the apartheid system and believes he deliberately staged the right-wing violence at Ventersdorp to gain sympathy from the West. It is extremely difficult, at a time of intense political conflict, for the mid-range to stand its ground against the assault of both wings.

In 1987 Wynand Malan, MP for Randburg, leader of the National Democratic Movement and later to become co-leader of the Democratic Party, launched a personal initiative to close the widening gap between the two wings in South African politics. He sought to build personal bridges between the grass roots and the leaderships across most of the spectrum. In private meetings with various groups, he sought to soften some of their hardline stances and asked them to entertain the idea of being South Africans one and all. He often used the metaphor of two fish bowls. The government and the extra-parliamentary forces could see each other but there was no real communication or interaction. Malan was, in our view, very effective. He had the right credentials and the tone and manner which invited response. In any explosive conflict, such as faces South Africa at present, facilitation has a most important role to play. Malan has no doubt burned several bridges in the process of counteracting the dangerous polarisation at play - especially among those of the mindset which declares: "Either you are for me or against me." But he continues, at time of writing, to play a crucial facilitating role.

During the entire decade of the 1980s the National Values Centre sought contact with those it considered would be the major role players in the 1990s. A systematic attempt was made to introduce the concept of the Spiral to men and women across all racial, ethnic and political groupings with the hope that when real crisis was encountered they would have the potential to act from a more powerful paradigm. This included a number of ministers and deputy ministers in both P.W. Botha's and F.W. de Klerk's cabinets. In 1986 the opportunity presented itself to begin interacting with Dr Denis Worrall, as ambassador in London and when he returned to challenge cabinet minister Chris Heunis in the parliamentary election of 1987. Dr Worrall had a keen and perceptive mind and clearly had the capacity to discern the big picture being described.

The National Values Centre had no involvement in, or prior knowledge of, the decisions by Malan and Worrall to leave the National Party, but neither decision was found surprising. Their action was clearly in response to P.W. Botha's style and substance. In a real sense, Botha was the first-stage rocket of the reform movement and he deserves due credit for that. He took the process as far as he could but, unhappily, almost stayed affixed to the second stage as the process was attempting to enter orbit.

Chapter 8
Misfits and Mayhem

Various publications have dealt dispassionately and objectively with the communal violence which has convulsed South Africa over recent years. They include A. de V. Minnaar - *Conflict and Violence in Natal/KwaZulu* (Pretoria: Human Sciences Research Council, 1990) and various issues of *Indicator S A* (University of Natal).

The violence had led, at time of writing, to the formation of a Peace Commission, convened to write a code of conduct for law enforcement officers as well as political parties. The initiative was facilitated by people accepted to be neutral actors - the churches and the business commnity. Dr Louw Alberts, Dr Johan Heyns, Rev Frank Chikane, John Hall (of the South African Chamber of Business) and Barlow Rand played a major role in moving the opposing groups through the delicate negotiation process. It was too early to tell, at time of writing, whether the initiative would succeed in curtailing political violence and whether the same process could be used to deal with other issues that divide and threaten the country.

Chapter 9
The Pigmentation of Politics

The issue of race continues to plague countries, societies and communities about the world. We reject definitions of people based on types or traits. A small example from South Africa: A senior defence force officer remarked that "white" recruits no longer seemed to have the lower leg strength necessary in parachute troops, while "black" recruits did. He hastened, in the resulting furore, to explain that whites who went through the training course ended with exactly the same qualities as blacks. What he probably meant was that they entered at a disadvantage, having not experienced the same physical rigours as blacks. Young white men are exhibiting no more than an effect of the ER-Orange materialistic value system. Young blacks given the same opportunity to drive cars and remain at home watching television as "couch potatoes" would be exactly the same. The characteristic is not "white" - it is a manifestation of the Orange value system. Stereotypes of black and white are deadly because they fail to reflect the reality of differences.

Much of this chapter draws on Michael Banton - *Racial Theories* (Cambridge, 1987).

Janice Hale-Benson, an African-American educationist, has constructed in *Black Children* a major educational theory and programme around basic differences between the learning styles of black (African) and white (European) children.

African and Afro-American cultures, in contrast with European-based societies, are circular (relational) instead of linear (analytic). In language the African strives for circumlocution rather than exact definition, while Western thinking drives toward clarity, precision, climax, closure and detail. The Euro-American cognitive style is stimulus-centred, parts-specific, linear-progressive, with long concentration and attention spans.

Professor Hale-Benson's analysis can be seen in another perspective. What she identifies as African or African-American reflects, in our theoretical framework, differences in the value systems profile and the extent to which the mind's processing systems have been impacted on by language structures. Much of what she describes as "relational" indicates a higher degree of BO-Purple Animistic thinking in the black children she has studied. (Millions of other African-Americans will show a preference for the linear processing; millions of other Euro-centred children will fall into the relational preference).

Her comparative lists of differences in fact perfectly fit the so-called "left" and "right" brain differentiations in learning styles. The experience of the National Values Centre with black high schools in South Chicago confirms this finding. The differences are neither genetic nor are they permanent types or traits. Instead they represent different responses to the conditions of existence described in Chapter 2.

Walter Williams, the black Professor of Economics at George Mason University in Fairfax, Virginia, has been vocal in his attacks on types or classifications based on race or ethnicity. "Black education is in shambles," he claims. "All standardized methods of academic achievement show a significant gap between the performance of black students and the nation as a whole." He strongly criticises the current trend to inject an Afrocentric curriculum into education - one which asserts that Africa was the centre of world culture and learning; that Greece derived its culture from blacks; that Africa has a rich history of mathematical, scientific and literary accomplishment which was either stolen or suppressed by the whites. These and other "findings" are taught by racists who reason that whites - "ice people" - are warlike because of their lack of melanin, which in turn gives blacks an intellectual advantage. Williams finds in the Afrocentric agenda a generalised, elitist attack on Western values and "a subtle support of barbarism, so much a part of the 'multiculturalism' movement."

"What are the essentials of Western values?" he asks. "They include: the supremacy of the individual and his possession of inalienable rights such as life, liberty, property and the pursuit of happiness; freedom from arbitrary control by the state; self-responsibility based on his ability to determine good and evil; and the competence of the individual. You don't have to be European to subscribe to these values."

Professor Williams describes the healthy aspects of the Fourth and Fifth Levels of thinking within the Gravesian framework of levels of psychological existence. Once again, the Spiral rejects racial and ethnic categories as being historical artefacts, not rigid types or traits. They are inventions of the mind, not permanent states of nature.

Lawrence Schlemmer, Director of the Centre for Policy Studies at the University of the Witwatersrand, warns in an article in the *Sunday Star* (July 21, 1991) of the dangers of ignoring the power of ethnicity. He cites Donald Horowitz's publication, *A Democratic South Africa: Constitutional Engineering in a Divided Society* (Cape Town: Oxford University Press, 1991). If ethnic groupings are "ranked", in that one is afforded privileges over the other, the result will be disaster. While the topic is regarded in many circles in South Africa as taboo, Horowitz and Schlemmer insist that the nettle of ethnicity must be recognised and grasped. Schlemmer concludes: "Domination by contrived 'patriotic majorities' in a diverse society may do as much damage as apartheid."

Bobby Godsell, an Anglo-American executive, voices the same concern in an article entitled "The Austro-Marxists ride again", published in *Frontline* (May, 1991). He reports in a conference he and Peter Berger attended, on the issue of national identity versus group identity. He concludes: "Perhaps it is the perversity of human desire that clans, tribes, groups will always want their own piece of real estate - flag, anthem, postage and yes, even gallows. Yet the world now - as before, but even more so - often does not permit this."

Mind-generated groupings become filters through which complex issues are simplified and distorted. James N. Rosenau noted in *Turbulence in World Politics* (Princeton University Press, 1990), Page 420:

"The world today can be viewed as fragmented into a number of mutually exclusive cultures that tend to faster divergent interpretations of the meaning of events. The norms of each culture nourish varying conceptions of their interests, thus opening gulfs between them and making it difficult to see the world through the eyes of adversaries or, indeed, from the perspective of any culture other than one's own."

Ethnicity appears in the Second and Fourth Levels of biopsychosocial systems development and is the natural response to conditions in the milieu. These explosive yet necessary human systems can be dealt with only through the shaping of the first Helix - addressing the exact conditions that give them birth or reactivate them, even though the more complex systems have formed on the Spiral. The Graves technology provides a precise formula for managing these ethnically-based value systems.

Chapter 10
Bushmen of the 21st Century

The best book on multiple intelligences is Howard Gardner's *Frames of Mind: Theories of Multiple Intelligences*. The Harvard professor and director of Project Zero identified seven different intelligences that exist within the mind's processing systems.

For a good discussion of the technique of paradox resolution see Charles Hampden-Turner - *Charting the Corporate Mind* (New York: The Free Press, 1990).

Chapter 11
Common Ground, Common Purpose

Since South Africans are spread all the way up and down the Spiral, the only realistic "common ground" is the Spiral itself. Managing the Spiral in a healthy fashion ought to be the "common purpose".

For example, because of the damage done by both apartheid and sanctions, millions of "Young Lions" have been trapped in the Third Level-Red-Egocentric system with little hope of a better tomorrow. We recommend the establishment of DQ-Blue-Authoritarian conduits - such as military-style camps - to facilitate this passage. In addition, the dishonesty and greed factors are rampant in South Africa, which calls for a more stringent control system all the way along the developmental Spiral - whether the crime is "blue collar" or "white collar" in origin.

In dealing with anti-social behaviour from any quarter, the following system should be utilised, with application in families, communities, schools and certainly in the entire legal, law enforcement and criminal justice operations. This list is to be found in George Edgin Pugh - *The Biological Origin of Human Values* (New York: Basic Books, 1977):

1. Increase the probability that such behaviour will be detected.

2. Increase the psychological and legal penalties associated with being detected.

3. Decrease the potential rewards or benefits that can be obtained from such behaviour.

4. Ensure that legal sanctions are more swiftly and reliably applied.

5. Provide better moral and ethical education so that individuals will understand the social norms and the social ideal and be more aware of the social risks and penalties involved.

6. Provide better education concerning the personal social and psychological benefits that are to be derived from a lifestyle that contributes positively to society.

7. Modify the social or physical structure of the society so that innate altruistic motivations can operate more effectively.

8. Provide better social conditioning experience in early childhood so that such anti-social behaviour will be foreign to the normal pattern of behaviour.

9. Use jails (and perhaps in extreme cases capital punishment) to remove chronic offenders from society.

Chapter 12
Flatlanders and Flowstaters

The question of development and its basic causes continues to be debated around the world, especially at the World Bank, the International Monetary Fund, the Development Bank of Southern Africa and the African Development Bank.

Edward Osborn, head of the Nedbank Economic Unit, raised this issue in an article in *Business Day* (August 16, 1991) entitled: "SA must be wary of carpetbaggers bearing foreign aid." The article included a picture of US Congressman Stephen Solarz - inferring that he might bear such a carpetbagging label. Other Americans would qualify as well. Osborn warns against a dependency on foreign aid because it brings with it the social and psychological virus of the donor country. A vast percentage of United States foreign aid and defence spending is actually spent inside the US in buying products and services which are then sent to - if not dumped on - the receiving country, which is expected to be grateful.

Congress is notorious for using foreign aid and development grants as an excuse to fund what are called the "beltway bandit" consultancy groups and think tanks located around Washington. Are South Africans certain that they want the involvement of such groups - whether white-owned or black-owned - if they lack an understanding of the unique South African situation? Osborn observes:
"SA is in a far better position to determine its own developmental needs and structures. It must not be hassled into undertaking foreign assistance projects to suit the donor simply because aid is being pushed at the country."

We recommend the establishment of a clearing house to monitor the use of foreign resources and a think tank to provide information to the donor countries as to the specific needs in creating a Seventh World society rather than clone the social, political, educational and health care systems of another culture - especially of a closed First World system.

Chapter 13
'n Boer Maak 'n Plan

The strongest opposition to the recommendations of this chapter will come from elites within the CP-Red-Exploitative range, whether black or white, which demand power, position, privileges and patronage without demonstrating the competencies necessary to manage the Spiral. Red thinking is highly sensitive to criticism, refuses to acknowledge any weakness and is incapable of learning from the environment. A Red system is easily detected by suggesting that it is not yet ready to manage complexity. The resulting anger is usually a manifestation of fear, and this thinking pattern will use intimidation and threat to achieve its goals. Africa has been cursed by such developments, as Chapter 17 describes.

A negative response can also be expected from various forms of closed DQ-Blue Fourth Level thinking - whether from the left or the right wings - since this system believes it alone has the truth. "One right way" rigid thinkers will reject any form of compromise, pragmatism or synthesis.

Finally, beware the low side of the Orange Fifth Level system that is always "on the take", looking for the angle, manoeuvring for the inside track and the shady deal.

At the end of his book, *The Essential Kafir* (written in 1925), Dudley Kidd asked: "The Kafir - what is to become of him?" His reply is interesting and timely, if somewhat paternalistic and patronising.

"I know one missionary - needless to say he is American - who wished to keep his Kafirs away from beer-drinks, and thought the most practical method to adopt was to keep them busily employed. So he asked one man what work he could do. He said he could only make baskets. The American missionary instantly said he would undertake to buy every basket he made. The next native could only make mats: the missionary undertook to take all he could make. And so on. He then gave the seed of new vegetables, which would need attending to just when the beer-drinks were most frequent, and thus began to raise his natives. Could not this be done on a large scale? It would be easy to teach the natives how to make their baskets and mats a little better. They would soon pick up new ideas, and thus natural industries might be fostered and a normal growth of personality be obtained. It may be possible to give him some degree of self management in his own internal matters by-and-by."

What Kidd is describing is the process that works in the Law of the Spiral - only it is not confined to "natives" but applies to all human beings who are ratcheting up the existential staircase.

Chapter 14
How Should Who Manage Whom ...?

The National Values Centre has been monitoring South African managers for an entire decade, using the Values Test. Shifts in the profiles have been revealing as the CP/DQ system gives way to elevated scores in ER, with a split between the FS and GT systems. The Graves technology has been introduced through a series of multi-media workshops, conferences and informal meetings, catering to the largest scientific, research-based and business-oriented institutions in the country - participants coming from executive suites as well as hostels for migrant mineworkers.

The testing process has now been upgraded from a pencil and paper format to a software programme named the *Values Monitor*. The *Monitor* includes a new approach to identifying corporate cultures and readiness for change, as well as the location and intensity of the Purple, Red, Blue, Orange, Green, Yellow and Turquoise value systems.

The National Productivity Institute (with offices in Pretoria, Durban and Cape Town), reflects the changes which are occurring in South African industry. Under the leadership of Dr Jan Visser, NPI is considered world class in productivity improvement and measurement - essentially within the DQ and early ER systems of values. Its 6M programme, that introduces BO-Purple, CP-Red and even DQ-Blue value systems to the nature of ER-Orange thinking with regard to free enterprise, has been used all over South Africa and in other societies as well.

In the past couple of years Visser and his team have realised that significant productivity improvement can occur only through a holistic, systemic and big picture strategy. Unless there are better education, new organisational structures and a healthy economy, large-scale improvements in productivity are not possible. John Parsons and several others on the NPI board, and within its functions, are now seeing the potential for a new initiative based on this kind of understanding, certainly assisted by New Paradigm thinking. NPI is now looking at an expanded role in Africa as issues regarding stability, economic wellbeing and worker competency are being revisited in the entire continent.

Other public entities, recently privatised parastatals as well as the private sector itself, are now searching for new models of management that are congruent with the unique Seventh World conditions of South Africa. The National African Federated Chamber of Commerce and Industry (Nafcoc) has launched such a developmental project to identify and train black business leaders to take their place on the boards of listed companies.

Mofaso Lekota, executive director of Nafcoc, says: "Black and white South Africans have more in common than we have differences". The worst aspect of apartheid is our inheritance of real inequality, unequal access to economic opportunity; unequal access to income and wealth and unequal ownership patterns.

Nafcoc has set a 10-year target to increase black representation on the boards of listed companies to 30 percent and to increase to 60 percent the number of blacks in low, middle and top-management levels of listed and unlisted companies.

Mr Lekota has called on South Africans to "rally their support around principles that we have identified as common. It is important to find the future South Africa on the basis of national consensus," he says.

Such consensus should be built about the Code and Law of the Spiral, otherwise quotas, tokenism, class action and lawsuits alleging racial discrimination will plague government, business and industry for the next 50 years. We strongly suggest that South Africans avoid the American experience and carefully build their own developmental tracks based on competency, not racial quotas.

Chapter 15
At the Coalface

The Middelburg Forum continues to evolve. It has facilitated a mass meeting of the people of Mhluzi at which the chairman of the Conservative Party town council addressed the community, along with the white township administrator and officials from the Transvaal Provincial Administration and the local Regional Services Council. Close to 10 000 people were in the football stadium, with not a policeman in sight.

The Forum has not been able to instantly resolve all Middelburg's problems. The community still has bulk services crises, boycotts, a lack of housing etc, but the Forum makes a difference.

After the initial euphoria of finding they could talk like civilised people around a conference table, Middelburg-style experiments and processes have to come to grips with the reality of their historic problems. At this point major structural changes have to be considered. Payments for lights and water should not be used to pay the salaries of the township councillors instead of going direct to the utility. The "white" town should not be in the position of selling such services to the "black" township. The fee card system should be used so that each resident is credited for payment instead of punished in a group cut-off. In other words, the initial stages of the community forum process tend to be focused on immediate problems and interpersonal relationships. The next stage of development requires an approach that deals with basic structural problems that keep in place the great divides between town and township. Many of these issues obviously will not be resolved until some kind of national accord is achieved. Otherwise squatter camps will be fiercely rejected by ratepayers who are unwilling or unable to pay sudden rate increases because squatters happen to descend on their municipality instead of the next one.

Chapter 16
Quo Vadimus - Where Do We Go?

The Eight Big Stabilisers should be seen as a single process, not eight different operations. We suggest that the entire process be removed as far as possible from the party political arena and placed in the hands of competent technocrats who are concerned only with achieving results.

While the transitional political structure should seek inclusiveness, consensus and coalition, the stabilisation process itself should be removed as far as possible from this area of even potential disagreement. A technocratic agency of exceptional technical and scientific skills needs to be established to plan and implement stabilisation measures, ultimately answerable to some body such as our suggested "Council of the Wise", but immune to political pressures. It would have to be provided with budgets but essentially left to operate on its own and be judged on results. South Africa is fortunately richly endowed with apolitical figures of intelligence, integrity and technical skill. Dr Brian Clarke, President of the Council for Scientific and Industrial Research, is one who comes to mind.

We realise that such a technocracy would usurp some of the functions normally associated with civil government, but point out that conditions in South Africa are so far from normal that civil government has broken down in many areas and will not be easily restored. The technocracy would be an emergency and temporary arrangement operating in areas of critical need. It would also be in constant liaison with the organs of elected government at all levels.

Such a technocracy would operate out of the GT-Yellow Seventh Level value system and would be run mainly by New Paradigm thinkers. Everybody along the Spiral would be invited to add value to the specific ring where he has competency, and this includes politicians of all hues and levels of professionalism. We believe the adversarial political system - admirable is it is in Britain or America - is not appropriate to South Africa at its current level of development, nor to Africa as a whole.

Note the inherent interdependence of all eight stabilisers. Without calm and safe townships, houses cannot be built. Unless the health issues are addressed, the job creation process will flounder. Unless AIDS is arrested, it may become as much a barrier to external investment as apartheid and violence. Without quality education of the workforce, the complexity of thinking necessary to work in high technology industry will not appear. If there is no proper nutrition, quality education is impossible. Without safe and proper housing, the standard of living will not be high enough to develop stable neighbourhoods. Without a creative and realistic squatter policy, First World environments will be impaired, causing massive emigration of talent. Everything connects to everything else, making New Paradigm thinking a vital necessity if all these matters are to be addressed in a powerful and positive manner.

Our point is that there is no single and universal system of government that will work for all societies and all cultures in perpetuity. It could even turn out that democracy, as we know it in the Western tradition, is only a blip on the radar scope of the human species; that other systems are only now appearing on the horizon. South Africa could well be the first country - forced by circumstance - to recognise that something new has to be created to deal with the complexity of a World to the Power of Seven.

Chapter 17
Beyond the Limpopo

From 1985 to 1989 Blaine Harden was bureau chief of the Washington Post in sub-Saharan Africa. His book, *Africa: Dispatches from a Fragile Continent* (New York: Norton, 1990) is frightening and real, and should be read with an open mind.

Harden has a long section on Liberia, America's experiment in colonialism in Africa. Master Sergeant Doe, one of the more corrupt in a long line of African dictators, was carefully courted by the American Department of State. According to Harden, the courtship was conducted by none other than Ambassador William L. Swing, currently assigned to Pretoria. Harden writes (Page 243): "Then American ambassador William L. Swing tutored Doe in the art of statecraft. Swing told colleagues the young head of state was a good student and an 'endearing boy'." We mention this merely to show that even the American State Department can be terribly wrong in its assessments.

In a chapter under the title "The good, the bad and the greedy", Harden provides a composite portrait of what he calls "The Big Man". Readers will recognise a description of the CP-Red-Egocentric leader - who for centuries has reeked over the entire planet of rapine, pillage and plunder. Harden writes about the African continent, but what he is describing is not specifically black or African - it is merely something human at the Third Level on the evolving Spiral.

On the New Paradigm

Barrow, John D. *Theories of Everything: The Quest for Ultimate Explanation* (Oxford: Clarendon Press, 1991).

Bertalanffy, Ludwig von. *Perspectives on General System Theory* (New York: George Braziller, 1975).

Bishop, Jerry E. and Michael Waldholz. *Genome* (New York: Touchstone, 1990).

Capra, Fritjof. *The Turning Point* (New York: Simon and Schuster, 1982).

Corning, Peter A. *The Synergism Hypothesis* (New York: McGraw Hill, 1983).

Ferguson, Marilyn. *The Aquarian Conspiracy* (Los Angeles: Tarcher, 1980).

Fuller, R. Buckminster. *Critical Path* (New York: St. Martin's Press, 1981).

Gleick, J. *Chaos: Making A New Science* (New York: Viking, 1987).

Harrison, Edward. *Masks of the Universe* (New York: Macmillan, 1985.)

Hawkins, Gerald S. *Mindsteps to the Cosmos* (New York: Harper & Row, 1983).

Leonard, George B. *The Transformation: A Guide to the Inevitable Changes in Humankind* (Los Angeles: Tarcher, 1972).

Mayr, Ernst. *Toward a New Philosophy of Biology* (Cambridge: Harvard, 1988).

Pagels, Heinz R. *The Cosmic Code: Quantum Physics as the Language of Nature* (New York: Simon and Schuster, 1982).

Popper, Karl R. *The Open Universe* (New Jersey: Rowman and Littlefied, 1956).

Miller, James Grier. *Living Systems* (New York: McGraw-Hill, 1987).

Munitz, J. K. *Theories of the Universe: From Babylonian Myth to Modern Science* (New York: Free Press, 1957).

Prigogine, L. and Stengers, L. *Order Out of Chaos* (London: Heinemann, 1984).

Salk, Jonas. *The Survival of the Wisest* (New York: Harper & Row, 1973).

Wilber, Ken. *The Holographic Paradigm* (Boulder & London: Shambhala, 1982).

Wilber, Ken. *Eye to Eye: The Quest for the New Paradigm* (Boulder & London, 1990).

Wolf, Fred Alan. *The Body Quantum* (New York: Macmillan, 1986).

On Evolutionary and Developmental Thinking

Adler, Mortimer J. *Haves Without Have-Nots* (New York: Macmillan, 1991).

Augros, Robert and George Stanciu. *The New Biology: Discovering the Wisdom in Nature* (Boston & London: Shambhala, 1988).

Bauer, P. T. *Equality, the Third World, and Economic Delusion* (Cambridge: Harvard University Press, 1981).

Berger, Peter L. *The Capitalist Revolution* (New York: Basic Books, New York, 1986).

Binford, Lewis R. *In Pursuit of the Past* (New York: Thames and Hudson, 1983).

Black, Jan Knippers. *Development in Theory & Practice: Bridging the Gap* (Boulder: Westview, 1991).

Brown, Michael H. *The Search for Eve* (New York: Harper & Row, 1990).

Calvin, William H. *The Ascent of Mind: Ice Age Climates and the Evolution of Intelligence* (New York: Bantam, 1990).

Chilton, Stephen. *Grounding Political Development* (Boulder: Rienner, 1991).

Crawford, Michael & David Marsh. *The Driving Force: Food, Evolution and the Future* (London: Heinemann, 1989).

Colinvaux, Paul. *The Fates of Nations: A Biological Theory of History* (New York: Simon and Schuster, 1980).

Corballis, Michael S. *Human Laterality* (New York: Academic Press, 1983).

De Soto, Hernando. *The Other Path: The Invisible Revolution in the Third World* (New York: Harper & Row, 1989).

Fagan, Brian M. *The Journey from Eden: The Peopling of Our World* (London: Thames and Hudson, 1990).

Habermas, Jurgen. *The Theory of Communicative Action* (Boston: Beacon Press, 1987).

Graves, Claire W. *The Graves Technology* (Denton, Texas: National Values Center, 1991).

Harris, Marvin. *Cultural Materialism: The Struggle for a Science of Culture* (New York: Random House, 1979).

Harris, Marvin. *Cannibals and Kings: The Origins of Cultures* (New York: Random House, 1977).

Harth, Eric. *Dawn of a Millennium: Beyond Evolution and Culture* (New York: Penguin Books, 1990).

Harth, Erich. *Windows on the Mind* (New York: Morrow, 1982).

Hobhouse, Henry. *Forces of Change* (New York: Arcade, 1989).

Hoffer, Eric. *The Ordeal of Change* (New York: Harper & Row, 1963).

Hofstadler, Douglas R. Godel, Escher, Back: *An Eternal Golden Braid* (New York: Vintage Books, 1980).

Hoogvelt, Nkie M. *The Sociology of Developing Societies* (London: Macmillan, 1982).

Imbrie, John and Katherine Palmer Imbrie. *Ice Ages: Solving the Mystery* (Cambridge: Harvard University Press, 1986).

Jaynes, Julian. *The Origin of Consciousness in the Breakdown of the Bicameral Mind* (Boston: Houghton Mifflin, 1976).

Keen, Sam. *Faces of the Enemy: Reflections of the Hostile Imagination* (San Francisco: Harper & Row, 1986).

Korzybski, Alfred. *Science and Sanity: An Introduction to Non-Aristotelian Systems and General Semantics* (Lakeville, Connecticut: The Institute of General Semantics, 1950).

Kuhn, Thomas S. *The Structure of Scientific Resolutions* (Chicago: University of Chicago Press, 1970).

Logan, Robert K. *The Alphabet Effect* (New York: Morrow, 1986).

Laszlo, Ervin. *Evolution: The Grand Synthesis* (Boston & London: Shambhala, 1987).

Naroll, Raoul. *The Moral Order: An Introduction to the Human Situation* (London: Sage Publications, 1983).

Ornstein, Robert and Paul Ehrlich. *New World, New Mind: Moving Toward Conscious Evolution* (New York: Doubleday, 1989).

Parsons, Talcott. *The Social System* (London: Routledge & Kegan Paul, Ltd., 1951).

Prentky, Robert A. *Creative and Psychopathology: A Neurocognitive Perspective* (New York: Praeger, 1980).

Pugh, George Edgin. *The Biological Origin of Human Values* (New York: Basic Books, 1977).

Reader, John. *Man on Earth* (Austin: University of Texas, 1988).

Restak, Richard M. *The Infant Mind* (New York: Doubleday, 1986)

Rivlin, Robert and Karen Gravelle. *Deciphering the Senses: The Expanding world of Human Perception* (New York: Simon and Schuster, 1984.)

Robbins, Lawrence H. *Stones, Bones, and Ancient Cities* (New York: St. Martin's Press, 1990).

Roxborough, Ian. *Theories of Underdevelopment* (London: MacMillan, 1981).

Sale, Kirkpatrick. *Dwellers in the Land* (San Francisco: Sierra Club Books, 1985).

Sanderson, Stephen K. *Social Evolutionism* (Oxford: Blackwell, 1990).

Schmookler, Andrew Bard. *The Parable of the Tribes: The Problem of Power in Social Evolution* (Berkeley: University of California Press, 1984).

Schmookler, Andrew Bard. *Out of Weakness* (New York: Bantam, 1988).

Sklair, Leslie. *Sociology of the Global System* (New York: Harvester, 1991).

Tanner, Nancy Makepeace. *On Becoming Human* (New York: Cambridge, 1981).

Taylor, Gordon Rattray. *The Great Evolution Mystery* (London: Secker and Warburg, 1983).

Tucker, Robert W. *The Inequality of Nations* (New York: Basic Books, 1977).

Wilber, Ken. *Up from Eden: A Transpersonal View of Human Evolution* (New York: Anchor Press, 1981).

Wills, Christopher. *The Wisdom of the Genes: New Pathways in Evolution* (Oxford: Oxford University Press, 1991).

On Mind, Intelligences, and Learning

Ackerman, Diane. *The Natural History of the Senses* (New York: Random House, 1990).

Andreasen, Nancy C. *The Broken Brain: The Biological Revolution in Psychiatry* (New York: Harper & Row, 1984).

Banton, Michael. *Racial Theories* (Cambridge: Longon, 1987).

Becker, Robert O. and Gary Selden. *The Body Electric: Electromagnetism and the Foundation of Life* (New York: Morrow, 1985).

Bergland, Richard. *The Fabric of Mind* (New York: Viking, 1985).

Cetrob, Marvin and Owen Davies. Crystal Globe: *The Haves and Have-Nots of the New World Order* (New York: St. Martin's Press, 1991).

Corballis, Michael C. *The Lopsided Ape: Evolution of the Generative Mind* (Oxford: Oxford University Press, 1991).

Diamond, Marian Cleeves. *Enriching Heredity: The Impact of the Environment on the Anatomy of the Brain* (New York: The Free Press, 1988).

Erdmann, Erika and David Stover. *Beyond a World Divided* (Boston: Shambhala, 1991).

Gardner, Howard. *Frames of Mind: Theories of Multiple Intelligences* (New York: Basic Books, 1983).

Halberstam, David. *The Next Century* (New York: Morrow, 1991).

Hale-Benson, Janice E. *Black Children: Their Roots, Culture, and Learning Styles* (Baltimore: John Hopkins, 1986).

Hart, Leslie A. *How the Brain Works* (New York: Basic Books, 1975).

Healy, Jane M. *Endangered Minds: Why Our Children Don't Think* (New York: Simon and Schuster, 1990).

Hobson, J. Allan. *The Dreaming Brain* (New York: Basic Books, 1988).

Hooper, Judith and Dick Teresi. *The 3-Pound Universe* (New York: Macmillan, 1986).

Liebenberg, Louis. *Art of Tracking: The Origin of Science* (Cape Town: David Philip, 1990).

Lumsden, Charles J. & Edward O. Wilson. *Promethean Fire: Reflections on the Origin of Mind* (Cambridge: Harvard, 1983).

Paulos, John Allen. *Innumeracy: Mathematical Illiteracy and its*

Consequences (New York: Hill and Wang, 1988).

Rosenau, James N. *Turbulence in World Politics* (Princeton: Princeton University Press, 1990).

Sakaiya, Taichi. *The Knowledge-Value Revolution,* translated by George Fields and William Marsh (Tokyo: Kodansha International, 1991).

Sowell, Thomas. *A Conflict of Visions* (New York: Morrow, 1987).

Satzlawick, Paul, John Weakland, and Richard Fisch. *Change* (New York: W. W. Norton, 1974).

Williams, Linda Verlee. *Teaching for the Two-Sided Mind: A Guide to Right Brain/Left Brain Education* (New York: Simon & Schuster, 1983).

On Innovations in Management and Organisational Design

Ackoff, Russell. *Redesigning the Future* (New York: Wiley & Sons, 1974).

Adizes, Ichak. *Corporate Life Cycles* (Englewood Cliffs, New Jersey: Prentice Hall, 1991).

Boyett, Joseph H. and Henry P. Conn. *Workplace 2000* (New York Dutton, 1991).

Davis, Stanly M. *Future Perfect* (Reading, Massachusetts: Addison-Wesley, 1987).

de Pree, Max. *Leadership is an Art* (New York: Doubleday, 1989).

Emery, F. (ed) *Systems Thinking* (New York: Penguin Books, 1969)

Hampden-Turner, Charles. *Charting the Corporate Mind* (New York: Free Press, 1990).

Kelley, Robert E. *The Gold Collar Workers: Harnessing the Brainpower of the New Workforce* (Reading, Massachusetts: Addison-Wesley, 1985).

Keppel-Jones, Arthur. *When Smuts Goes: A History of South Africa from 1952-2010* (Pietermaritzburg: Shuter & Shooter, 1949).

Koopman, Albert. *Transcultural Management* (Oxford: Basil Blackwell, 1991).

Leritz, Len. *No-Fault Negotiating* (New York: Warner, 1990).

Lynch, Dudley and Paul Kortes. *Strategy of the Dolphin* (Morrow, 1989).

Potter, Beverly. *The Way of the Ronin: Riding the Waves of Change at Work* (Berkeley, California: Ronin Publishing, 1984).

Putnam, Howard D. *The Winds of Turbulence* (New York: Harper Business, 1991).

Senge, Peter. *The Fifth Discipline: The Art & Practice of the Learning Organization* (New York: Doubleday, 1990).

Schrage, Michael. *Shared Minds: The New Technologies of Collaboration* (New York: Random House, 1990).

Sproull, Lee and Sara Kiesler. *Connections: New Ways of Working in the Networked Organization* (Cambridge: The MIT Press, 1991).

Toffler, Alvin. *PowerShift* (New York: Bantam, 1991).

Vail, Peter B. *Managing as a Performance Art* (San Francisco: Jossey-Bass Publishers, 1991).

On African and South African Experiences

Adam, Heribert and Hermann Giliomee. *The Rise and Crisis of Afrikaner Power* (Cape Town: David Philip, 1979).

Adam, Heribert, and Kogila Moodley. *South Africa Without Apartheid* (Los Angeles: University of California Press, 1986).

Berger, Peter L. *A Future South Africa: Visions, Strategies and Realities* (Cape Town: Human & Rosseau Tafelberg, 1988).

Berglund, Axel-Ivar. *Zulu Thought-Patterns and Symbolism* (London, Hurst & Company, London, 1976).

Carter, Gwendolen. *The Politics of Inequality* (New York: Praeger, 1958).

Cruse, Harold. *Plural but Equal: Blacks and Minorities in America's Plural Society* (New York: Morrow, 1987).

de Klerk, Willem. *(R)evolution: Afrikanerdom and the Crisis of Identity* (Johannesburg: Jonathan Ball, 1984).

de Villiers, Marq. *White Tribe Dreaming* (New York: Viking, 1987).

Diop, Cheikh. *Precolonial Black Africa,* translated from the French by Harold Salemson (Trenton, New Jersey: Africa World Press Edition, 1987).

Doyle, A. Conan. *The Great Boer War* (London: Smith, Elder, & Co., 1900).

du Toit, Pierre. *Power Plays: Bargaining tactics for transforming South Africa* (Johannesburg: Southern, 1991)

Elphick, R. and H. Giliomee (eds). *The Shaping of South African Society 1652-1820* (Cape Town: Longman-Penguin, 1979).

Frederikse, Julie. *The Unbreakable Thread: Non-Racialism in South Africa* (Johannesburg: Ravan Press, 1990).

Giliomee, H. and L. Schlemmer. *Up Against the Fences: Poverty, Passes and Privilege in South Africa* (Cape Town: David Philip, 1985).

Green, Nick and Reg Lascaris. *Third World Destiny* (Cape Town: Human & Rouseeau Tafelberg, 1988).

Harden, Blaine. Africa: *Dispatches from a Fragile Continent* (New York: W. W. Norton & Company, 1990).

Horowitz, Donald. *A Democratic South Africa: Constitutional Engineering in a Divided Society* (London: Oxford University Press, 1991).

Huntley, Brian, Roy Siegfried & Clem Sunter. *South African Environments into the 21st Century* (Cape Town: Human & Rousseau Tafelberg, 1989).

Johnson, Paul. *The Birth of the Modern* (London: Weidenfeld & Nicolson, 1991).

Kidd, Dudley. *The Essential Kafir* (London: A. I & C. Black, 1925).

Kodjo, Edem. *Africa Tomorrow* (New York: Continuum, 1987).

Kuckertz, Heinz. *Creating Order* (Johannesburg: Witwatersrand University Press, 1990).

Lamb, David. *The Africans* (New York: Random House, 1982).

Leach, Graham. *The Afrikaners: Their Last Great Trek* (Johannesburg: Southern, 1989).

Lelyveld, Joseph. *Move Your Shadow: South Africa, Black and White* (New York: Times Books, 1985).

Lodge, Tom. *Black Politics in South Africa since 1945* (Johannesburg: Raven, 1983).

Louw, Leon and Frances Kendall. *South Africa* (Bishop, Ciskei: Amagi, 1986).

Marais, H. C. (ed) South Africa: *Perspectives on the Future* (Pretoria: Owen Burgess Publishers, 1988).

Meintjes, Stephen & Michael Jacques. *The Trial of Chaka Dlamini* (Johannesburg: Amagi Books, 1990).

Meredith, Martin. *The First Dance of Freedom: Black Africa in the Postwar Era* (London: Hamish Hamilton, 1984).

Mutwa, Credo. *Let No My Country Die* (Pretoria: United Publishers International, 1986).

Neuhaus, Richard John. *Dispensations: The Future of South Africa as South Africans see it* (Grand Rapids, Michigan: William B. Eerdmans Publishing Company, 1986).

Pheko, Motsoko. *Apartheid: The Story of a Dispossessed People* (London: Marram Books, 1984).

Saayman, Graham (ed). *Modern South Africa in Search of a Soul* (Boston: Sigo Press, 1990).

Sparks, Allister. *The Mind of South Africa* (London: Heinemann, 1990).

Stultz, Newell M. *The Nationalists in Opposition - 1934-1948* (Cape Town: Human & Rousseau, 1975).

Van der Post, Laurens. *The Dark Eye in Africa* (London: The Hogarth Press, 1955).

Walker, E. A. *A History of Southern Africa* (London: Longmans, 1964).

Wilson, F. and M. Ramphele. *Uprooting Poverty* (Cape Town: David Philip, 1989).

Wilson, Monica and Leonard Thompson. *The Oxford History of South Africa. 2 vols.* (London: Oxford University Press, 1971).